International City/County ICMA Management Association

Accountability for Performance: Measurement and Monitoring in Local Government

The International City/County Management Association is the professional and educational organization for appointed administrators and assistant administrators in local government. The purposes of ICMA are to enhance the quality of local government and to nurture and assist professional local government administrators in the United States and other countries. To further its mission, ICMA develops and disseminates new approaches to management through training programs, information services, and publications.

Local government managers—carrying a wide range of titles—serve cities, towns, counties, councils of governments, and state/provincial associations of local governments. They serve at the direction of elected councils and governing boards. ICMA serves these managers and local governments through many programs that aim at improving the manager's professional competence and strengthening the quality of all local governments.

The International City/County Management Association was founded in 1914; adopted its City Management Code of Ethics in 1924; and established its Institute for Training in Municipal Administration in 1934. The institute, in turn, provided the basis for the Municipal Management Series, generally termed the "ICMA Green Books."

ICMA's interests and activities include public management education; standards of ethics for members; the *Municipal Year Book* and other data services; urban research; and newsletters, a monthly magazine, *Public Management,* and other publications. ICMA's efforts toward the improvement of local government management—as represented by this book—are offered for all local governments and educational institutions.

Accountability for Performance

Measurement and Monitoring in Local Government

Edited by
David N. Ammons

International
City/County
ICMA
Management
Association

PRACTICAL MANAGEMENT SERIES
Barbara H. Moore, Editor

Accountability for Performance
Balanced Growth
Capital Financing Strategies for Local Governments
Capital Projects
Current Issues in Leisure Services
The Entrepreneur in Local Government
Ethical Insight, Ethical Action
Hazardous Materials, Hazardous Waste
Local Economic Development
Long-Term Financial Planning
Managing for Tomorrow
Pay and Benefits
Performance Evaluation
Personnel Practices for the '90s
Police Practice in the '90s
Practical Financial Management
Productivity Improvement Techniques
Quality Management Today
Resolving Conflict
Shaping the Local Economy
Strategic Planning for Local Government
Successful Negotiating in Local Government

The Practical Management Series is devoted to the presentation of information and ideas from diverse sources. The views expressed in this book are those of the contributors and are not necessarily those of ICMA.

Library of Congress Cataloging-in-Publication Data

Accountability for performance : measurement and monitoring in local
    government / edited by David N. Ammons.
        p.   cm. — (Practical management series)
    Includes bibliographical references.
    ISBN 0-87326-105-4 (pbk.)
    1. Local government.   2. Government productivity.   3. Total
quality management in government.   4. County services—Evaluation.
5. Municipal services—Evaluation.   I. Ammons, David N.
II. International City/County Management Association.   III. Series.
JS145.A23   1995
352--dc20   95-40999
                                                                  CIP

Printed in the United States of America.
99 98 97 96 95
5 4 3 2 1

Foreword

Local government managers are committed to improving services in their communities, and more and more of them are finding performance assessment an essential tool in that effort.

Systematic measurement of performance is not a new idea, but a number of factors have strengthened interest in the topic. First, a number of management innovations—including total quality management and customer-based service provision—depend on the type of information yielded by performance assessment systems. Second, local governments are faced with continued budget constraints and increasing public pressure for accountability. Third, a number of national organizations—including the American Society for Public Administration, the National Academy of Public Administration, and the Governmental Accounting Standards Board—have adopted resolutions supporting regular assessment of service quality. In 1994, ICMA launched the Comparative Performance Measurement Consortium, a project designed to facilitate the development of benchmarks for local government services.

A well-designed performance assessment system has a wealth of applications: it can be used to determine accountability, to improve service quality, to allocate resources, to formulate and justify budgets, and to evaluate departmental and individual performance. Such a system goes far beyond tracking expenditures: in its analysis of resource use, a performance assessment system does not simply ask "How much?" but "How wisely?"

Through twelve carefully selected articles, *Accountability for Performance: Measurement and Monitoring in Local Government* covers the full range of techniques for developing performance measures, incorporating them into a performance monitoring system, and—most important—ensuring that the results are used. In addition, the volume offers a number of rich case examples showing performance assessment systems in action.

This book is part of ICMA's Practical Management Series, which is devoted to serving local officials' needs for timely information on current issues and problems.

We wish to thank David N. Ammons, who compiled the volume, and the individuals and organizations that granted ICMA permission to use their material. We also wish to thank Sandy Chizinsky and Barbara H. Moore for their editorial guidance.

William H. Hansell, Jr.
Executive Director
International City/County Management Association

About the Editor

David N. Ammons is a senior associate at the Carl Vinson Institute of Government at the University of Georgia. He has served in various administrative capacities in four municipalities—Fort Worth, Texas; Hurst, Texas; Phoenix, Arizona; and Oak Ridge, Tennessee—and has taught in the public administration programs of the University of Georgia and the University of North Texas.

Dr. Ammons is the author or coauthor of four books on local government: *Municipal Productivity, City Executives* (with Charldean Newell), *Recruiting Local Government Executives* (with James J. Glass), and *Administrative Analysis for Local Government*. He consults with city and county governments on organizational and management issues, including performance measurement and productivity improvement.

Dr. Ammons has degrees from Texas Tech University (B.A.), Texas Christian University (M.P.A.), and the University of Oklahoma (Ph.D.).

About the Authors

Unless otherwise noted, contributors are listed with their affiliations at the time of writing:

Allan E. Alter, special projects editor, *CIO* magazine.

Ted Gaebler, president, the Gaebler Group, a division of MRC, a public-sector management consulting firm in San Rafael, California.

Craig Gerhart, director, Office of Management and Budget, Prince William County, Virginia.

James R. Griesemer, vice chancellor, University of Denver.

Ellen P. Jean, senior management auditor, City of Portland, Oregon.

David Osborne, consultant to state and local governments.

Theodore H. Poister, professor, School of Public Administration and Urban Studies, Georgia State University.

Ellen Doree Rosen, professor emerita, John Jay College of Criminal Justice, City University of New York.

Stanley Y. Siu, industrial engineer, Works and Operations Division, Operations Department, City of Winnepeg.

James E. Swiss, associate professor of political science and public administration, North Carolina State University.

Pamela Syfert, Deputy City Manager, Charlotte, North Carolina.

Richard C. Tracy, director of audits, City of Portland, Oregon.

Contents

Appendix

Introduction

Trying to judge the adequacy of local government operations solely on the strength of a financial balance sheet and a few positive or negative service anecdotes is ill advised. Yet many local governments rely on little more than that.

There is a better way. In recent years, as concern for accountability has taken center stage, dozens of local governments have responded by bolstering their ability to assess the services they provide. In these communities, customary financial reporting is coupled with meaningful information about the services being provided—including, for example, information about efficiency, quality, and the results achieved.

Greater accountability is only one of the rewards that come with systematic performance monitoring. A measurement system that tracks important performance dimensions of local government operations can also document performance strengths, alert officials to performance deficiencies, and validate the effectiveness of performance improvement initiatives.

Support for expanded use

Prominent endorsements of the use of performance measures in the public sector have intensified interest in that endeavor; however, the recent wave of encouragement is hardly the first. More than half a century ago, Clarence Ridley, then ICMA's executive director, teamed with Nobel-laureate-to-be Herbert Simon to write a book urging local governments to measure their performance and offering guidelines for doing just that.[1] A few years later, the federal government's Hoover Commission recommended "performance budgeting," using much the same rationale. Writing in *Governing* magazine, Alan Ehrenhalt recently drew attention to the resilience of performance measurement as a management strategy, noting that a common strand of management thought links the planning-programming-budgeting system (PPBS) of the 1960s, zero-based budgeting (ZBB) of the 1970s, and management by objectives (MBO) of the 1980s to the current enthusiasm for benchmarking. As noted by Ehrenhalt, "It is a good idea. It was a good idea in 1943. But it is basically the same idea it was in 1943. It just keeps getting renamed."[2]

This time, momentum seems to be building. Respected professional groups, including the American Society for Public Administration (ASPA), the Governmental Accounting Standards Board (GASB), the Government Finance Officers Association (GFOA), the International City/County Management Association (ICMA),

---

Performance monitoring and reporting by public organizations

1. The National Academy of Public Administration strongly recommends that units of government at all levels make a concerted effort to encourage agency heads and program managers to monitor program quality and outcomes as part of an overall system aimed at improving the performance and credibility of major public programs. Performance monitoring should be an essential part of program administration and the budget process. The National Academy of Public Administration strongly recommends that public officials and program managers implement performance monitoring systems that can usefully be implemented within the present state of the art. Legislators, chief executives, and relevant professional groups should encourage agency heads and key program managers to:

a. Obtain agreement between policymaking and operating levels (and, where appropriate, between levels of government) on appropriate indicators of program cost, quantity and quality of services, and important program outcomes;

b. When feasible, involve citizens or their representatives in setting goals for progress/outcomes and monitoring results;

c. Regularly collect information on program performance in terms of the agreed-on performance indicators;

d. Develop procedures for establishing realistic performance expectations that take into account the influence of client characteristics, local conditions, and other factors beyond the control of program staff;

and the National Academy of Public Administration (NAPA), have all promoted improved performance measurement and monitoring. A 1991 NAPA resolution shown in the accompanying sidebar is representative of the stance taken by those organizations. In addition, several associations have offered encouragement and guidance through the publication of books, pamphlets, and articles on the subject. Publications of the Urban Institute and ICMA have been landmark documents in that effort.[3]

Since the mid-1980s, GASB has taken an especially prominent role in encouraging the development and reporting of improved performance measures. By 1990, that organization had declared that "the time had come" for what it labeled service efforts and accomplishments (SEA) reporting.[4] SEA information

---

e. Use information on program performance, changes in program performance, and differences between actual and expected performance to improve program performance; and

f. Regularly report to elected officials and the public on program performance, changes in program performance, results achieved in different geographic areas, and differences between actual and expected performance.

2. At the same time, the public, the media, and elected officials should be reminded that program results can be influenced both by program activities and by client characteristics, local conditions, and other factors beyond the control of program staff. Performance reports, therefore, should include explanatory information on key factors likely to have affected program performance.

3. As experience is gained with performance monitoring and reporting and as performance trends become clear, chief executives, agency heads, and program managers should propose realistic performance targets in terms of program goals and agreed-on program quality and outcome indicators—and subsequently monitor and report on progress in achieving those performance targets.

4. The National Academy of Public Administration strongly encourages further broad experimentation, research, and development of even more effective performance monitoring techniques for an increasingly complex public service. As more experience is gained and the necessary resources and procedures become available, performance monitoring and regular reporting should be extended to major programs at all levels of government.

Resolution adopted by the National Academy of Public Administration November 8, 1991.

would include measures of input (service efforts), but would "focus primarily on measures of service accomplishments (outputs and outcomes) and measures of the relationships between service efforts and service accomplishments (efficiency)."[5]

What is performance monitoring?

Performance monitoring in local government can and does take many different forms. The common denominator in all forms is the accumulation of evidence on the adequacy of local government operations. Although casual observation of operations, supplemented by anecdotes of positive or negative service experiences, might be construed to be performance monitoring in the broadest sense, most progressive local governments and staunch advocates of performance monitoring have more rigorous and systematic approaches in mind. In systematic performance monitoring, key dimensions of performance—and the effects of that performance— are carefully measured, recorded, and compared with previous results or relevant norms.

How does performance monitoring differ from performance measurement?

Performance measures are the ingredients of a performance monitoring system. They are *raw* ingredients when collected in the form of workload measures—calls received, applications processed, arrests made, or other counts of activity or demand. They are *refined* ingredients when they report performance efficiency or effectiveness.

A good performance monitoring system depends on good performance measures. Developing a good set of performance measures, however, is not a simple matter. Fortunately, help is available in the form of recommended sets of measures for many of the most common local government services. For example, a set of recommended effectiveness measures for police services is shown in Figure 1. These measures go well beyond the simple counting of emergency calls received, suspects arrested, and crimes solved. They delve more deeply into the question of police effectiveness—that is, the extent to which crime control objectives are being achieved.

The set of service efforts and accomplishments (SEA) indicators recommended by GASB for the fire suppression function calls for input indicators along with measures of output, outcome, and efficiency (Figure 2). Including more refined measures substantially increases the value of a performance monitoring system.

How does performance monitoring differ from performance auditing?

While *monitoring* implies tracking and checking performance against relevant norms, *auditing* implies studying operations in depth. Although the routine collection of operating data and the detailed study of some aspect of operations are both forms of performance monitoring in a general sense, the term *performance auditing* is normally reserved for the latter. In contrast to more routine forms of performance monitoring, performance audits—sometimes called management studies, effectiveness audits, operational audits, performance evaluations, performance reviews, program audits, program evaluations, or program results audits—probe for details, often attempting to document the link between program elements and results.[6]

Performance audits differ from compliance audits, which focus primarily on judging whether operations conform to approved procedures or laws. They also differ from financial audits, which typically ignore matters of economy, efficiency, and program effectiveness—chief concerns of performance audits. A local government practitioner, reflecting on the differences between performance auditing and other forms, noted that in performance auditing the principal focus is not on whether money is spent legally but on whether it is spent wisely.[7]

Although a good set of performance measures will reveal operational status, even an outstanding set cannot be expected to reveal the *cause* of any performance deficiencies. This does not mean that routine monitoring systems have little value. Business profit-and-loss statements do not explain *why* a company experiences success or failure.[8] For that matter, a local government's financial statement does not provide answers of that type either. In both the public and the private sector, knowing the current condition often is a step that leads either to immediate corrective action (if the source of the problem is obvious upon quick examination) or to more detailed analysis to discover relationships and causes.

The time and expense typically required to complete a thorough performance audit tend to constrain the use of that tool, making it unrealistic for most local governments to expect more than a few audits to be completed in a given year. Routine performance monitoring, therefore, is generally a more practical administrative tool for most managers.[9] Even without the level of detail possible in performance audits, timely performance information can alert managers to operating problems and help them assess the effectiveness of corrective actions.

Unlike some performance audits, a good monitoring system rarely requires sophisticated analytic techniques. Despite its

Figure 1. Measures of effectiveness for crime control services.

Overall objective: To promote the safety of the community and a feeling of security among the citizens, primarily through the deterrence / prevention of crime and the apprehension of offenders, providing service in a fair, honest, prompt, cooperative, helpful, sensitive, and courteous manner, to the satisfaction of the citizens.

Objective	Quality characteristic	Specific measure	Data collection procedure
Prevention of crime	Reported crime rates	1. Number of reported crimes per 1,000 population, total and by type of crime	Incident reports
	Victimization rates	2. Number of reported plus unreported crimes per 1,000 households (or residents or businesses), by type of crime	Household survey
	Different households and businesses victimized	3. Percentage of (a) households, (b) businesses victimized	Household survey, business survey
	Physical casualties	4. Number and rate of persons (a) physically injured, (b) killed in course of crimes or nontraffic, crime-related police work—including victims and police	Incident reports
	Peacekeeping in domestic quarrels	5. Percentage of domestic quarrels and other disturbance calls with no arrest and no second call within x hours	Dispatch records, incident reports
		6. Number of injuries to (a) citizens (after police arrival), (b) police per 100 domestic quarrel calls	Incident reports
Apprehension of offenders	Crimes "solved" at least in part	7. Percentage of reported crimes cleared, by type of crime and whether cleared by arrest or by "exception"	Incident reports
	Completeness of apprehension	8. Percentage of "person-crimes" cleared, by type of crime[1]	Incident reports, arrest reports
	Quality/effectiveness of arrest	9. Percentage of adult arrests that survive preliminary court hearing (or state attorney's investigation) and percentage dropped for police-related reasons, by type of crime	Arrest and court records
		10. Percentage of adult arrests resulting in conviction or treatment (a) on at least one charge, (b) on highest initial charge, by type of crime	Arrest and court records

Category	Measure	No.	Description	Data source
	Stolen property recovery	11.	Percentage of stolen property that is subsequently recovered: (a) vehicles, (b) other property	Incident reports, arrest or special property records
Responsiveness of police	Response time	12.	Percentage of emergency or high-priority calls responded to within x minutes and percentage of nonemergency calls responded to within y minutes	Dispatch records
	Perceived responsiveness	13.	Percentage of (a) citizens, (b) businesses that feel police respond fast enough when called	Household survey, business survey, complainant survey
Feeling of security	Perceived safety	14.	Percentage of (a) citizens, (b) businesspersons who feel safe (or unsafe) walking in their neighborhoods at night	Household survey, business survey
Fairness, courtesy, helpfulness/ cooperativeness, honesty[2]	Fairness	15.	Percentage of (a) citizens, (b) businesses that feel police are generally fair in dealing with them	Household survey, business survey, complainant survey
	Courtesy	16.	Percentage of (a) citizens, (b) businesses that feel police are generally courteous in dealing with them	Household survey, business survey, complainant survey
	Helpfulness/ cooperativeness	17.	Percentage of (a) citizens, (b) businesses that feel police are generally helpful, cooperative, and sensitive to their concerns	Household survey, complainant survey
	Honesty	18.	Number of reported incidents or complaints of police misbehavior, and the number resulting in judgment against the local government or employee, by type of complaint (civil charge, criminal charge, or other service complaints), per 100 police	Police and mayor's office records
		19.	Percentage of citizens who feel police are in general honest and can be trusted[2]	Household survey, complainant survey
Citizen satisfaction with police handling of miscellaneous incidents		20.	Percentage of persons requesting assistance for other than serious crimes who are satisfied (or dissatisfied) with police handling of their problems, categorized by reason for dissatisfaction and by type of call	Complainant survey
Citizen satisfaction with overall performance		21.	Percentage of (a) citizens, (b) businesses that rate police performance as excellent or good (or fair or poor), by reason for satisfaction (or dissatisfaction)	Household survey, business survey, complainant survey

Figure 1. concluded

Objectives	Quality characteristic	Specific measure	Data collection procedure
	Police safety	22. Number of injuries to police officers (a) per 100 officers, (b) per 100 calls	Police injury reports
Vice and drug offenses[3]			
Apprehension	Level and focus of arrest activity	23. Number of arrests for vice- and drug-related crimes, by type of crime and by "big fish" or "little fish"	Booking records
	Quality of arrests	— Measures 10 and 11	Arrest and court records
	Illegal materials seized	24. Quantity and street value of illicit drugs seized	Police property records
	Drug usage	25. Percentage of arrestees who test positive for illegal drugs	Arrest records
		26. Street price of illegal drugs	Special data collection effort
Citizen satisfaction	Citizen perception of seriousness of problem	27. Percentage of citizens who feel that (a) pornography, (b) prostitution, (c) gambling, (d) "soft" illegal drug usage, (e) "hard" illegal drug usage, (f) sale of illegal drugs is a major problem in their neighborhood or community	Household survey

Source: Harry P. Hatry, Louis H. Blair, Donald M. Fisk, John M. Greiner, John R. Hall, Jr., and Philip S. Schaenman, *How Effective Are Your Community Services? Procedures for Measuring Their Quality* (Washington, DC: Urban Institute and ICMA, 1992), 72–73. Reprinted by permission.

[1] One person committing four crimes or four persons committing one crime would be four "person-crimes." When the number of offenders involved in a crime is unknown, as may frequently happen with such crimes as burglary, "one" criminal can be assumed for this statistic (or the historical average number of offenders for that type of crime could be used).

[2] A satisfactory approach to measuring the degree of corruption, malfeasance, or negligence is lacking. Data on the number of complaints received by the city on these problems should be examined, particularly when their number increases substantially.

[3] These offenses have special measurement difficulties, so measures for them have been grouped separately. Deaths from drug overdoses per 1,000 population might also be considered as part of this family of measures that indicate the magnitude of the local drug problem—only in part a reflection of police work.

methodological simplicity relative to audit techniques, however, the presence of a monitoring system—and the history it provides—can nevertheless be extremely helpful when undertaking a more rigorous study of a selected program. The availability of good indicators of performance quality and outcomes can make intermittent program evaluations easier and far less expensive than they would be otherwise.[10]

Arrangement of chapters

This volume is divided into three parts. Part 1, "Performance Measurement," includes three articles focusing on that key ingredient of performance monitoring. Among the topics addressed are the various types of performance measures, characteristics of good measures and good sets of measures, and tips for developing and applying performance measures. Part 2, "Performance Monitoring," consists of a pair of articles describing how local governments can monitor their operations. These selections emphasize the incorporation of performance measures into a monitoring system that can be used for management and policy decisions and for accountability. Part 3, "Performance Monitoring in Action," includes seven articles that feature the performance monitoring experiences of individual local governments.

Principal lessons

Each of the articles included in this volume offers a unique perspective and special insight into the topic of performance monitoring. Although the pages that follow defy simple summary, there are a few recurring points. Here are three such points—or principal lessons—though readers who examine the material that follows are sure to discover others for themselves.

Foundation for progressive management   Most recent management initiatives rely on an ability to assess current conditions and to measure improvement. Local governments that wish to establish customer-oriented or results-oriented management or to undertake strategic planning, total quality management, or benchmarking cannot proceed far without a reasonably sound performance monitoring system.

Success factors   The success of a performance monitoring system depends on many factors, including

- Careful development of suitable performance measures
- Use of appropriate data collection techniques
- Timely reporting of performance information
- Relevant context for performance assessment

Figure 2. Recommended SEA indicators for fire departments: Fire suppression.

Indicator	Rationale for selecting indicator
Inputs	
Personnel	
Full-time personnel	
Part-time and volunteer personnel	Provides information on labor resources used
Total man-hours worked	
Total operating expenditures	Provides information on resources committed to suppression
Total capital expenditures	activity
Man-hours in training programs	
Percentage of fire fighters reaching an	Provides information on preparedness
NFPA-recommended certification level	
Outputs	
Number of fire calls answered	A measure of suppression workload; readily available
Outcomes	
Water supply	
Minimum water volume available	Measures availability of water needed to suppress fires—
Minimum water flow available	a measure of fire fighting readiness
Population with access to adequate water supply	
Response time	
Average response time	Measures success in delivering timely service; currently
Percentage of responses in under x minutes	measured by fire departments

Average time to control fires
 Single-alarm, residential
 Single-alarm, industry
 Two-alarm, industry
Percentage of fires spread limited to $x\%$
 Square feet on arrival
 Single-alarm, residential
 Single-alarm, industry
 Two-alarm, industry

} Measures success in minimizing fire damage

Efficiency

Operating expenditures per capita — Provides per capita cost of service information for operations

Capital expenditures per capita — Provides per capita cost of capital investment

Operating expenditures per $100,000 of property protected — Relates operating cost information to value of property protected

Capital expenditures per $100,000 of property protected — Relates capital investment to value of property protected

Source: GASB Research Report, Service Efforts and Accomplishments Reporting: Its Time Has Come, *Fire Department Programs*, is copyrighted by the Governmental Accounting Standards Board, 401 Merritt 7, P.O. Box 5116, Norwalk, Connecticut 06856-5116, U.S.A. Portions are reprinted with permission. Copies of the complete document are available from the GASB.

Note: The recommended indicators presented in this exhibit are illustrative. They are intended to serve as a starting point for use in the development of a comprehensive set of SEA indicators for external reporting of an entity's results of operation. This exhibit does not provide illustrations of indicator disaggregation or of comparison data such as trends, targets, or other comparable entities. Both disaggregation and comparison data are important aspects of SEA reporting.

- Suitable opportunities for operating officials to explain especially favorable or unfavorable results (i.e., the use of explanatory notes)
- Timely feedback to reporting units
- A demonstrated linkage between the performance monitoring system and important decision-making processes.

Key element of accountability   In a democratic society, governments are expected to be accountable not only to members of the elected and appointed leadership but also to the public as a whole. Financial accountability is part of that obligation, but so is performance accountability. Recognition of that fact led GASB to quote a former U.S. Comptroller General to support its own call for SEA reporting:

Governments and agencies entrusted with public resources and the authority for applying them have a responsibility to render a full accounting of their activities. . . . Thus governmental accountability should identify not only the objects for which the public resources have been devoted but also the manner and effect of their application.[11]

1. Clarence E. Ridley and Herbert A. Simon, *Measuring Municipal Activities: A Survey of Suggested Criteria for Appraising Administration* (Chicago: International City Managers' Association, 1943).
2. Alan Ehrenhalt, "Performance Budgeting, Thy Name Is . . ." *Governing* 8 (November 1994): 9.
3. See, for example, the successor to a popular volume first published in 1977: Harry P. Hatry, Louis H. Blair, Donald M. Fisk, John M. Greiner, John R. Hall, Jr., and Philip S. Schaenman, *How Effective Are Your Community Services? Procedures for Measuring Their Quality,* 2d ed. (Washington, DC: The Urban Institute and ICMA, 1992).
4. Harry P. Hatry, James R. Fountain, Jr., Jonathan M. Sullivan, and Lorraine Kremer, *Service Efforts and Accomplishments Reporting—Its Time Has Come: An Overview* (Norwalk, CT: GASB, 1990).
5. GASB, *Concepts Statement No. 2 of the Governmental Accounting Standards Board on Concepts Related to Service Efforts and Accomplishments Reporting* (Norwalk, CT: GASB, April 1994), 25.
6. Harry P. Hatry, "Determining the Effectiveness of Government Services," in *Handbook of Public Administration,* ed. James L. Perry (San Francisco: Jossey-Bass, 1989); and Jolene Ann Lauria, "Performance Auditing for Local Government," *Management Information Services Report* 21, no. 1 (January 1989).
7. Mark Funkhouser, "Why Is Performance Auditing Such a Well-Kept Secret?" *Tennessee Town and City* (25 April 1988): 8.
8. Joseph S. Wholey and Harry P. Hatry, "The Case for Performance Monitoring," *Public Administration Review* 52 (November/December 1992): 608.
9. Hatry, "Effectiveness of Government Services," 480.
10. Wholey and Hatry, "Case for Performance Monitoring," 605.
11. Comptroller General of the United States, *Standards for Audit of Governmental Organizations, Programs, Activities, and Functions* (Washington, DC: U.S. General Accounting Office, 1972), 1–2; cited in GASB, *Concepts Statement No. 2,* 13.

PART 1

Performance Measurement

Performance measures are basic building blocks for performance monitoring and core diagnostic and evaluative tools for performance improvement. Ideally, a good set of performance measures can answer four key questions:

- How many?
- How efficiently?
- Of what quality?
- To what effect?

Armed with such information, local officials can identify operational strengths and weaknesses and can assess the effectiveness of steps taken to correct deficiencies.

Proponents argue that performance measurement is an indispensable element of accountability in a democratic society.[1] Full accountability should mean more than simply producing a balance sheet showing how much revenue the local government collected and spent. It should also entail a reporting of what the taxpayers received in services—both quantitatively and qualitatively.

The articles in Part 1 address the essentials of performance measurement. Just as successful corporations focus on their objectives and track key indicators of performance, so, too, should local governments. To be most useful for managerial and policy decisions, performance measures must go beyond the simple workload counts characteristic of most local government measurement systems: measures of efficiency and effectiveness are needed as well.

The authors in Part 1 offer a variety of suggestions for developing performance measures, but all three articles share an emphasis on making the measurement system useful. In addition to offering tips on developing measurement and monitoring systems, the articles stress the importance of focusing on outputs, outcomes, and efficiency—rather than on inputs or compliance with customary processes.

Along with offering valuable guidelines for organizations initiating or improving a performance monitoring system, Part 1 examines two closely related concepts: benchmarking and productivity measurement. Organizations that engage in benchmarking in its fullest sense identify the performance level of best-in-class performers or establish other suitable targets, compare their own performance to those benchmarks, and devise means of reducing any performance gap.

In public sector applications, some units of government have defined benchmarking more broadly, to include efforts to achieve performance targets or "benchmarks" set arbitrarily without the benefit of best-in-class comparisons. Either way, a fundamental element in the process is the development and maintenance of a set of measures that can be used to track progress on important dimensions of performance. A broad-based benchmarking project entitled the Comparative Performance Measurement Consortium was initiated by ICMA in 1994.[2]

For many, if not all, local government officials, the purpose of improving performance measurement is ultimately to increase the productivity of their operations. But measuring efforts and accomplishments is not quite the same as measuring productivity. Governmental productivity has been defined as "the efficiency with which resources are consumed in the effective delivery of public services."[3] That definition emphasizes the importance not only of efficiency, which encompasses the quantitative relationship between inputs and outputs, but also of effectiveness, which includes service quality. Identifying and measuring inputs, outputs, and service quality is often rather complicated. Ellen Doree Rosen's article helps sort out and simplify some of the key factors.

1. See, for example, GASB, *Concepts Statement No. 2 of the Governmental Accounting Standards Board on Concepts Related to Service Efforts and Accomplishments Reporting* (Norwalk, CT: GASB, April 1994), 13; and Comptroller General of the United States, *Standards for Audit of Governmental Organizations, Programs, Activities, and Functions* (Washington, DC: U.S. General Accounting Office, 1972), 1–2.

2. "Why Let Other Organizations Judge Your Performance on Standards of Measurement That You Did Not Create?" *ICMA Newsletter* 75 (16 May 1994), supplement no. 3.

3. Nancy S. Hayward, "The Productivity Challenge," *Public Administrative Review* 36 (September/October 1976): 544.

Performance Measurement in Local Government

Aggressive businesses and industries measure performance meticulously. In their popular book on excellence in corporate America, Tom Peters and Bob Waterman characterized top companies as "measurement-happy and performance-oriented."[1] They found that the *very best of the best* complemented their measurement systems with an action orientation that separated them from the pack. Outstanding companies carefully monitor and record the relevant dimensions of performance— they know the important facts and figures—and they act on that knowledge.

Cities, counties, and other public sector agencies confront a far different circumstance. Without the pressure of competition or the unforgiving bottom line of profit or loss, governmental units are apt to neglect performance measurement as they focus on more pressing matters. Carefully conceived systems of performance measurement are more than a little complex; often they are more than a little threatening to the status quo; and they do impose expenses on the organization in terms of development and ongoing administration. Consequently, performance measurement is often allowed to slip in priority, except among local governments that have an extraordinary commitment to management information.

Why measure performance?

Properly developed and administered, a performance measurement and monitoring system can offer important support to a host of management functions.[2] Each function has important ramifications for local governments that aspire to be excellent.

- *Accountability* Managers in top-performing organizations insist on accountability from their subordinates and, in turn, expect to be held accountable by their organization superiors. Performance measures document what was done by various governmental departments or units, and, ideally, how well it was done and what difference it made. Through such docu-

---

Benchmarking

In order to determine whether a local government's performance is favorable or unfavorable, it is necessary to compare that jurisdiction's performance marks against some relevant peg. Among local governments that monitor their own performance, many compare current performance to figures for the same measures in previous reporting periods. Some compare the performance measures of different units in the same jurisdiction providing similar services or compare performance records with predetermined targets. Until recently, relatively few used national or state standards, private sector performance, or the performance records of other jurisdictions as "benchmarks" for gauging their own jurisdiction's performance.[1]

In the private sector, benchmarking has been widely acclaimed as a technique that contributes to performance improvement. By identifying best-in-class performers and the practices that make them so, industries may refine their own processes in a quest to meet or exceed the benchmarks set by outstanding performers.

Public sector application of the term *benchmarking* has been a bit broader. In some cases, objectives or targets set arbitrarily by a state or local government itself have been labeled benchmarks. In other cases, the term has been used in a manner more consistent with private sector application. Following the corporate pattern, the term *benchmark* might be reserved for anticipated or desired performance results anchored either in professional standards or in the experience of respected local governments.

Local governments desiring to identify suitable benchmarks for their operations confront two major issues. One is data availability. Information is needed on standards and on the experience of several other communities for a range of local government func-

mentation, outstanding departments and entire organizations earn the trust of their clients and citizens as they demonstrate a good return in services provided for tax dollars received.

- *Planning/budgeting* Local governments with an objective inventory of the condition of public services and facilities, a clear sense of service preferences among their citizens, and knowledge of the cost of providing a unit of service at a given level are better equipped to plan their community's future and to budget for that future. Again, performance measurement—incorporating unit costs and indicators of citizen demand or preference—is key.

---

tions. In most cases, that information is not easily secured. The second issue is comparability. In assembling suitable benchmarks, each jurisdiction must be vigilant in identifying factors that make some jurisdictions suitable for comparison and others unsuitable. Cost comparisons are especially vulnerable: differences in reporting periods, accounting practices, and cost of living may confound simple comparison. Social and economic factors that may influence the difficulty of a given jurisdiction's incoming workload may similarly set it apart from its counterparts and limit the value of comparisons. Care is therefore in order as communities select their benchmarks.

Cautionary notes are appropriate for jurisdictions embarking on benchmarking, but so are words of encouragement. The principle of accountability demands that department heads and managers be able to tell elected officials how their operations are doing and that elected officials, in turn, be able similarly to inform the public. How a local government is doing in comparison to last year is interesting, but not as interesting as how it is doing in comparison to national standards or to the performance of others in the same line of work. Such comparisons are sometimes difficult and often require explanations. The willingness to grapple with that difficulty and to provide those explanations may well distinguish public officials truly committed to the principle of accountability from those who are not.

1. Harry Hatry, "Performance Measurement Principles and Techniques: An Overview for Local Government," *Public Productivity Review* 4 (December 1980), 312–39.

Source: Adapted from David N. Ammons, "Performance Measurement and Benchmarking," in *Municipal Benchmarks*, 1996. Copyright © 1996 by Sage Publications, Inc. Reprinted by permission of Sage Publications, Inc.

- *Operational improvement*   Local governments that measure performance are more likely to detect operational deficiencies at an early stage. Furthermore, performance records enhance their ability to confirm the effectiveness of corrective actions.
- *Program evaluation / MBO / performance appraisal*   Carefully developed performance measures often provide valuable information for the systematic evaluation of program effectiveness. Management-by-objectives (MBO) programs and pay-for-performance systems for managerial employees, where they exist, typically are tied to performance measures. In some cases, employee performance appraisals or other forms of systematic performance feedback have been based, at least in part, on individual performance relative to established measures.
- *Reallocation of resources*   A clear indication of program effectiveness and unit costs—in essence, a scorecard on tax dollar investments and returns in various service functions— can aid decision makers in reallocation deliberations, especially in times of financial duress.
- *Directing operations / contract monitoring*   Managers equipped with a good set of performance measures are better able to detect operational strengths and weaknesses, to provide feedback to employees and work units, and to deploy close supervision where it is needed most. Performance measures also provide evidence useful in determining whether the service quality specified in contractual arrangements is, in fact, being achieved.

Stated simply, performance measurement provides local governments with a means of keeping score on how their various operations are doing. As noted by Harry Hatry, that scorekeeping function is vital:

Unless you are keeping score, it is difficult to know whether you are winning or losing. This applies to ball games, card games, and no less to government productivity. . . . Productivity measurements permit governments to identify problem areas and, as corrective actions are taken, to detect the extent to which improvements have occurred.[3]

Types of performance measures

Efforts to identify different types of performance measures have sometimes yielded lengthy lists.[4] Most measures, however, may be categorized as one of four types: workload measures, efficiency measures, effectiveness measures, or productivity measures.

Workload measures indicate the amount of work performed or the amount of services received. By comparing workload measures reporting, say, the number of applications processed by the personnel department, the number of sets of city council minutes prepared by the city clerk, the number of arrests by the patrol division of the police department, and the number of trees planted by parks crews with the corresponding records from a previous year, a local government official or citizen can see whether workload volume is up or down. Although that information can be of some value, it reveals only how much work was done—not how well it was done or how efficiently.

Efficiency measures reflect the relationship between work performed and the resources required to perform it. Typically, efficiency measures are presented as unit costs, but they can take other forms as well.

Unit costs are calculated by dividing total costs of a service or function by the number of units provided. For example, if 2,000 feet of 8-inch sewer line are installed by municipal crews at a total cost of $80,000, then the unit cost of sewer line installation is $40 per foot. A reversal of the ratio—dividing the number of units by the resources consumed—reveals the number of units produced per dollar and is also an efficiency measure (e.g., three-tenths of an inch of sewer line per dollar.) Other forms of efficiency measures reflect alternative types of resource input (for example, units produced per labor-hour) or production relative to an efficiency standard. If meter readers complete only one-half of their assigned rounds, if repairs by county auto mechanics take twice as long as private garage manuals say they should, or if expensive maintenance equipment is operated only 10 percent of the time it is available, questions of efficiency relative to a prescribed or assumed standard may be raised.

Effectiveness measures depict the degree to which performance objectives are being achieved or otherwise reflect the quality of local government performance. Meter reading error rates of less than 0.5 percent, a consistent record of fire suppression with only minimal spread, and low return rates on auto repairs reflect effective operations. Response times and other measures of service quality are only indirectly related to effectiveness, but are typically included among effectiveness measures for their presumed linkage.

Productivity measures combine the dimensions of efficiency and effectiveness in a single indicator. For example, where "meters repaired per labor hour" would reflect efficiency and "percentage of meters repaired properly" (e.g., not returned for further repair within six months) would reflect effectiveness, "unit costs (or labor-hours) per *effective* meter repair" would reflect productivity. The costs (or labor-hours) of faulty meter repairs as well as the costs of effective repairs would be included in the numerator of such a calculation, but only good repairs would be counted in the denominator—thereby encouraging efficiency *and* effectiveness by meter repair personnel.

Examples of each of the four types of performance measures for several common local government functions are provided in Figure 1. The value of workload measures is limited. Much greater insight into the performance of local government operations may be gained from efficiency, effectiveness, and productivity measures.

Figure 1. Examples of the four principal types of performance measures.

Function	Workload measure	Efficiency measure	Effectiveness measure	Productivity measure
City clerk	Number of sets of city council meeting minutes prepared	Employee-hours per set of city council minutes prepared	Percentage of city council minutes approved without amendment	Percentage of city council minutes prepared within seven days of the meeting and approved without amendment
Library	Total circulation	Circulation per library employee	Circulation per capita	Ratio of circulation per capita to library costs per capita
Meter repair	Number of meters repaired	Cost per meter repair	Percentage of repaired meters still functioning properly six months later	Cost per properly repaired meter (i.e., total cost of all meter repairs divided by number of meters needing no further repairs within six months)
Personnel	Job applications received	Cost per job application processed; cost per vacancy filled	Percentage of new hires/promotions successfully completing probation and performing satisfactorily six months later	Cost per vacancy filled successfully (i.e., employee performing satisfactorily six months later)

Criteria for a good set of performance measures

Properly developed sets of performance measures possess several distinctive characteristics.[5] Good sets include measures that are

- *Valid*   They measure what they purport to measure—that is, a high score on a given measure does, in fact, reflect possession of the underlying dimension or quality.
- *Reliable*   The measure is accurate and exhibits little variation due to subjectivity or use by different raters (for example, a measuring tape is a reliable instrument in that it is highly objective, and two different persons using the same instrument are likely to get very similar measurements).
- *Understandable*   Each measure has an unmistakably clear meaning.
- *Timely*   The measures can be compiled and distributed promptly enough to be of value to operating managers or policy makers.
- *Resistant to perverse behavior*   The development of a performance measure raises the profile of the performance dimension being examined. That higher profile sometimes brings unintended consequences or even strategies designed to "beat the system"—for instance, if police department performance is measured solely by the number of tickets written, police officers may become overzealous in issuing tickets; if garbage collection workers are rated solely by the number of tons collected, a few enterprising crews may decide to water down the garbage before having it weighed. The best sets of performance measures have little vulnerability to such actions because they have been devised carefully and also because they typically include multiple measures that address performance from several dimensions and thereby hold potentially perverse behavior in check.
- *Comprehensive*   The most important performance dimensions are captured by the set of measures. Some minor facets of performance may be overlooked, but the major elements are addressed.
- *Nonredundant*   By favoring unique measures over duplicative measures, the best sets of performance measures limit information overload for managers, other decision makers, and consumers of local government reports. Each measure contributes something distinctive.
- *Sensitive to data collection cost*   Most dimensions of local government performance can be measured either directly or through proxies. In some cases, however, measurement costs may exceed their value. Good sets of performance measures include the best choices among *practical* measurement options.

- *Focused on controllable facets of performance*   Without necessarily excluding important, overarching, and perhaps relatively uncontrollable characteristics relevant to a particular function, good sets of performance measures emphasize outcomes or facets of performance that are controllable by policy initiatives or management action. For example, while a police department's set of performance measures might include the rate of domestic homicides in the jurisdiction, a good set of measures would also include indicators of public safety more widely considered controllable by police efforts.

Sources of performance data

Typically, performance data are secured from various combinations of the following sources: existing records, time logs, citi-

---

Benchmarking: Applying the *"Consumer Reports* concept" to the public sector

Consumers understand the concept of benchmarking. Mass-market magazines provide detailed performance information about everything from computer disk drives to cars. Newspaper and magazine articles frequently identify the best buy in terms of price and performance. Many consumers will not make a major purchase without first consulting *Consumer Reports* or some other magazine that provides solid analysis of product features, quality, performance, and price.

Given the public's constant exposure to product and service comparisons in the mass media, it is only natural that citizens are beginning to expect similar kinds of performance information from government.

Benchmarking is the application of the *Consumer Reports* concept to the public sector. It gives elected officials as well as citizen/consumers comprehensive, accurate, and reliable information about services. They can judge performance and make choices about how that service can be improved. Benchmarking results in a report card.

A sample "report card" benchmarking the performance costs and service levels of eleven fire departments is shown at right.

Source: Excerpted from William G. Gay, "Benchmarking: Achieving Superior Performance in Fire and Emergency Medical Services," *Management Information Services Report* 25, no. 2 (February 1993): 1, 12.

zen/client surveys, trained observer ratings, and specially designed data collection processes.

The simplest and most desirable source of performance measurement data is the set of records already being maintained by
a local government. Workload counts, complaint records, and response times for various services are common, even among local
governments with modest performance reporting practices. Such
information can serve as the foundation of a performance measurement system and sometimes can be converted to higher-level
measures. Depending on its level of precision, for example, workload data might be combined with expenditure information to
yield efficiency measures.

Time logs completed on either a comprehensive or a random
basis provide resource-input information for labor-related efficiency measures (e.g., work units per employee-hour) or for

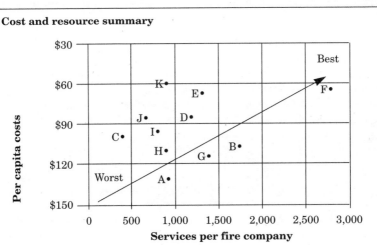

Cost and resource summary

Data analysis
The number of activities per company ranged from a low of 464 to a high of
2,677.

- The 11-department average was 1,098 activities annually, or 3 daily.
- The least busy department conducted 1.3 activities daily, while the
  busiest department conducted 7.3 activities daily.

Performance objective
Performance in the top 20 percent for the provision of suppression company services.

- Suppression companies should provide no fewer than 1,800 services
  annually or approximately five to six activities daily.
- This could be accomplished by increasing service levels or right-sizing
  the organization to better match service needs.

measures comparing actual work completed in a given amount of time to the amount of work expected on the basis of engineered work standards. Apart from vehicle maintenance and perhaps a handful of other services, however, engineered work standards are rarely available for common local government functions.

The surveying of users of particular services or citizens in general is a feedback mechanism used by a number of local governments. That practice may get an additional boost from the customer focus and current popularity of the total quality management (TQM) movement.

Surveys typically tap respondent perceptions regarding the adequacy of selected services, the nature of any perceived deficiencies, and the extent to which respondents avail themselves of various services and facilities. In order for a survey of citizens in general or of users of a particular service to contribute meaningfully to a local government's performance measurement system, the survey must be conducted with sufficient scientific rigor to produce reliable results. Such rigor typically introduces costs that exceed those of tempting, low-cost alternatives, but surveys conducted "on the cheap" are frequently misleading and can be easily discredited. Carefully designed and properly randomized telephone surveys have been found to be a widely accepted, moderately priced alternative to highly desirable but more expensive face-to-face interviews and low-cost, low-response-rate mail surveys.

Trained observer ratings have been used successfully in several cities for evaluating the condition of facilities and infrastructure. Typically, persons employed in clerical or other positions outside the department responsible for facility maintenance are trained to serve on an intermittent basis as raters of street cleanliness or parks maintenance, for example. Instructed on the finer points of distinguishing between various grades of facility condition and customarily armed with photographic depictions of those grades, trained observers can provide a more systematic evaluation of condition than can usually be drawn from records of citizens' compliments or complaints or even from citizen surveys. The effective administration of trained observer programs requires careful attention to training and issues of reliability. Supervisors often spot-check facilities to corroborate ratings and, where two or more raters assess the same facility within a short period of time, supervisors usually re-inspect if the grades of raters are more than one unit apart.

Unfortunately, information already on hand or readily available through customary means does not always meet current performance measurement needs. Analysts may discover, for example, that existing workload counts and random time logs have been based on estimates rather than on precise figures. The citizen survey everyone in town likes to quote may turn out to be suspect because it was conducted using questionable methods— relying on a tear-out questionnaire in the local newspaper. Even federal figures, presumed to be rock solid, may be less comprehensive and conclusive than originally thought; FBI crime statistics, for example, include only *reported* crimes—not all crimes actually committed. Typically, at least a few new data collection procedures must be introduced to support the development of a good set of performance measures.

Status of performance measurement in local government

A little more than a half-century ago, a pair of esteemed observers noted the availability of a number of "rough and ready measurement devices," but nevertheless conceded the limited development of performance measurement among city governments.

It is probably true that in the present state of our knowledge the citizen can often better judge the *efficiency* of his local government by the political odor, be it sweet or foul, which emanates from the city hall than by any attempt at measurement of services.[6]

Over the years, various movements to improve management practices, rationalize decision making, or enhance accountability often have encouraged improved performance measurement. Respected professional associations, including the American Society for Public Administration, the Governmental Accounting Standards Board, the Government Finance Officers Association, and the International City/County Management Association, have promoted the practice. Some local governments have responded to that encouragement. Many of the writings on performance measurement in local government repeat familiar names as exemplars: Sunnyvale, California; Phoenix, Arizona; Charlotte, North Carolina; Dayton, Ohio; Palo Alto, California; Savannah, Georgia; Randolph Township, New Jersey; Dallas, Texas; Aurora, Colorado; New York City; Alexandria, Virginia; Charlottesville, Virginia; and Portland, Oregon.[7] These communities, however, are far from typical in the advanced status of their performance measurement systems. Despite survey responses suggesting widespread and fairly sophisticated performance measurement in local government, more exacting research involving the examination of actual performance reporting documents reveals far more limited development.[8] Not all cities and counties even engage in performance measurement. Among those that do, most rely heavily on workload measures. Some report a few efficiency or effectiveness measures for various functions. Rarely are productivity measures reported.

Although performance measurement is well developed and still improving in some local governments, most have a long way to go. Speaking of his own city in the not-too-distant past, one Philadelphia official remarked, "If you were to ask how much it cost to pick up a ton of trash, I hope you weren't waiting for an answer the same year."[9] The situation, he noted, had improved greatly in recent years. Perhaps the remarks of an Indianapolis official put the development of performance measurement and program evaluation systems in proper perspective: "We're coming from an era of cleaning our clothes on rocks, and now we have come up with a hand-cranked washing machine. It's a much better life, but of course we'd rather have an automated washing machine, eventually."[10]

Overcoming resistance to performance measurement

The likelihood is great that some form of resistance will be encountered in efforts to develop or enhance performance measurement systems. Although the precise source often is not predictable, *some* resistance almost inevitably will come from *somewhere*. The proper starting point for developing a coping strategy is to try to understand the reasons for that resistance.

Typically, performance measurement is seen by various groups or individuals in the organization as a threat to their status. Some employees may fear that it is the first step in a process that will lead to tougher work standards and a forced speed-up of work processes, perhaps to be followed by the layoff of workers who are no longer needed or who cannot keep up.

Supervisors and managers may feel threatened by what they perceive to be the insinuations of a performance measurement drive. Believing that executive and legislative satisfaction with their performance would generate no such movement, they may sense an accusation of poor performance. They fear loss of status or even loss of employment if performance measures confirm those accusations, and they feel certain of a loss of discretion as the upper echelons gain yet another means of looking closely over their shoulders.

Even some top local government officials, who would seem to have so much to gain from improved performance measures, may resist their development. Especially prone to do so are those who believe that, by virtue of their own political adeptness or membership in the dominant political coalition, their preferences are more likely to prevail in political negotiations without the influence of performance facts and figures.

Seven essential steps in public sector benchmarking

Simply put, benchmarking is a rigorous yet practical process for measuring your organization's performance and processes against those of best-in-class organizations, both public and private, and then using this analysis to improve services, operations, and cost position dramatically. The great news is that the process of benchmarking is neither complex nor scientific. Benchmarking, in fact, consists of seven common-sense steps.

Step 1. *Determine which functional areas within your organization will benefit most from benchmarking.* Give priority to functions that make up a high percentage of the organization's cost, that are especially influential in shaping customer assessment of services, that appear to show room for improvement, or that are capable of being improved.

Step 2. *Identify the key performance variables to measure cost, quality, and efficiency for the functions you have selected.*

Step 3. *Pick the best-in-class organizations for each benchmark item.* Best-in-class organizations are those that perform each function at the *lowest cost* or with the *highest degree of quality or efficiency.* Best-in-class organizations can be comparable directly to yours in size, structure, and organization, but this is not required for every study candidate.

Step 4. *Measure the performance of the best-in-class organizations for each benchmarked function.*

Step 5. *Measure your own performance for each benchmarked item, and identify the gaps between you and the best-in-class.*

Step 6. *Specify actions and programs to close the gaps in your favor.*

Step 7. *Implement and monitor your benchmarking results.*

Source: Excerpted from Kenneth A. Bruder, Jr., and Edward M. Gray, "Public-Sector Benchmarking: A Practical Approach," *Public Management* 76 (September 1994): S9–S14. *Public Management* is published by ICMA.

Usually, such fears are overblown. Rarely are performance measurement efforts inspired by sinister or mean-spirited motives. Although detractors often fear worker exploitation or loss of supervisory discretion, the most commonly prescribed blueprints for measurement system development call for the involvement of those parties rather than for their exclusion. Measurement initiatives typically are most successful when they secure the input and support of frontline employees and supervisors. When that happens, a new measurement and reporting system—and the clarification of work unit objectives and priorities that accompanies the system's development—is likely to earn accolades from those parties rather than charges of exploitation.

Persons who fear that politics will be displaced in local decision making through the rationalizing influence of objective performance measures need not be overly concerned. Advances in management practices may, at most, supplement political considerations in decision making. In a democratic setting, politics can never be displaced—nor should it be.

Resistance in advances in performance measurement may emanate from a variety of concerns and may be manifested in different forms. A few things in this regard, however, are fairly predictable. Proponents of improved performance measures should expect three common declarations from opponents.

"You can't measure what I do!" If the performance of a department or office has not been measured in the past, it should not be surprising that incumbents might reason that their activities must be unmeasurable. If their performance could have been measured, it already would have been. Offices or departments making this declaration are often characterized by non-routine work and the absence of an existing data collection system. Both factors can make measurement difficult. Rarely is it impossible.

Sometimes a bit of creativity is necessary to devise either a suitable direct measure or a proxy that measures performance indirectly. Often, interviewing skills are even more important. "If your office closed shop for a few weeks, I know you would be missed," the interviewer might suggest. "But who would suffer the greatest impact, and what aspect of your work would they miss the most?" Gradually, with cooperation from employees and relevant officials, a widely accepted set of performance measures can emerge.

"You're measuring the wrong thing!" Once again, the involvement of service providers is key to resolving their complaints or calming their fears. It could be that relatively insignificant performance dimensions *are* being measured and that more impor-

tant dimensions are being ignored. If so, the remedy is to replace the former with the latter. The involvement of service providers can assure corrective action.

On the other hand, it is possible that the debate over appropriate performance measures may have uncovered a fundamental problem. A difference of opinion may exist between upper management and the service delivery unit over desired elements of service, or the unit may simply have labored under a long-standing misconception about what management wants. Such disagreements or misunderstandings should be resolved.

Yet another group of stakeholders in measuring the right thing are citizen-customers. Their involvement, typically through strategic planning processes, focus groups, and citizen commissions, can enhance the likelihood that the right things are being measured.

"It costs too much and we don't have the resources!" Understandably, departmental officials who already feel that their resources are stretched too thin may be reluctant to tackle new, time-consuming measurement and reporting tasks that may syphon program resources. Those officials are a little like the overburdened logger who, facing a stack of uncut logs, felt he could not spare the time to sharpen his dull saw. Well-meaning but reluctant officials must be persuaded of the value of performance measurement as a tool for improving services and making better use of scarce resources.

There is no reason to embark on performance measurement improvements unless better measures are expected to lead to improved services, to make services more efficient, or to make them more equitable. Service providers must be assured of management's commitment to those ends and convinced of management's resolve to use performance measurement to improve, rather than to drain resources from, services to the public. It may be helpful to point out to skeptics that most local government officials in jurisdictions that have performance measurement systems report that their systems have been worth the expense.[11]

Developing a performance measurement and monitoring system

Performance measures will not lead inevitably to improved performance. Although the act of measuring an operation for its results draws attention to that function and may thereby inspire greater efforts and improved performance, such results cannot be guaranteed. Performance measurement is merely a tool. If wielded properly, it can identify areas of performance adequacy and areas of performance deficiency; however, it can neither explain the former nor prescribe remedies for the latter. Reliable explanations and appropriate prescriptions require subsequent analysis of targeted operations.

Performance measurement and monitoring systems may be developed in a variety of ways. The steps outlined in the accom-

---

Steps in the development and administration of a performance measurement and monitoring system

1. Secure managerial commitment.
2. Assign responsibility (individual or team) for spearheading/coordinating departmental efforts to develop sets of performance measures.
3. Select departments/activities/functions for the development of performance measures.
4. Identify goals and objectives.
5. Design measures that reflect performance relevant to objectives:

   - Emphasize service quality and outcomes rather than input or workload.
   - Include neither too few nor too many measures.
   - Solicit rank-and-file as well as management input/endorsement.
   - Identify the work unit's customers and emphasize delivery of services to them.
   - Consider periodic surveys of citizens, service recipients, or users of selected facilities.
   - Include effectiveness and efficiency measures.

6. Determine desired frequency of performance reporting.
7. Assign departmental responsibility for data collection and reporting.
8. Assign centralized responsibility for data receipt, monitoring, and feedback.
9. Audit performance data periodically.
10. Ensure that analysis of performance measures incorporates a suitable basis of comparison.
11. Ensure a meaningful connection between the performance measurement system and important decision processes (e.g., goal setting, policy development, resource allocation, employee development and compensation, program evaluation).
12. Continually refine performance measures, balancing the need for refinement with the need for constancy in examining trends.
13. Incorporate selected measures into public information reporting.

panying sidebar have been gleaned from the experience of several local governments and distilled from the writings on this topic, but many variations on this pattern are possible and, indeed, perhaps desirable in a given setting.

1. Thomas J. Peters and Robert H. Waterman, Jr., *In Search of Excellence: Lessons from America's Best-Run Companies* (New York: Harper & Row, 1982), 240.

2. Mark Glover, "Performance Measurement: Local Government Efforts and Successes," SECOPA 1993 Conference, Cocoa Beach, FL, 7 October 1993; David Osborne and Ted Gaebler, *Reinventing Government: How the Entrepreneurial Spirit Is Transforming the Public Sector* (Reading, MA: Addison-Wesley, 1992), 156; Lawrence H. Thompson, "Service to the Public: How Effective and Responsive Is the Government?" Statement before the U.S. House of Representatives Committee on Ways and Means, 8 May 1991, U.S. General Accounting Office, GAO/T-HRD-91-26, 14; U.S. General Accounting Office, *Performance Budgeting: State Experiences and Implications for the Federal Government* (Washington, DC: U.S. GAO, February 1993), GAO/AFMD-93-41, 1; Lance L. Decker and Patrick Manion, "Performance Measurement in Phoenix: Trends and a New Direction," *National Civic Review* 76 (March-April 1987), 119–129; Harry P. Hatry, "Local Government Uses for Performance Measurement," *Intergovernmental Personnel Notes* (May-June 1980).

3. Harry P. Hatry, "The Status of Productivity Measurement in the Public Sector," *Public Administration Review* 38 (January/February 1978), 28.

4. Harry P. Hatry, "Performance Measurement Principles and Techniques: An Overview for Local Government," *Public Productivity Review* 4 (December 1980): 312–39.

5. Hatry, "Performance Measurement Principles and Techniques"; Charles K. Bens, "Strategies for Implementing Performance Measurement," *Management Information Services Report* 18 (November 1986); Harry P. Hatry, Louis H. Blair, Donald M. Fisk, John M. Greiner, John R. Hall, Jr., and Philip S. Schaenman, *How Effective Are Your Community Services? Procedures for Measuring Their Quality*, 2d ed. (Washington, DC: The Urban Institute and ICMA, 1992), 2–3.

6. Clarence E. Ridley and Herbert A. Simon, *Measuring Municipal Activities: A Survey of Suggested Criteria for Appraising Administration* (Chicago: International City Managers' Association, 1943), ix.

7. See, for example, Hatry et al., *How Effective Are Your Community Services?* 1; Bens, "Strategies for Implementing Performance Measurement," 1; Osborne and Gaebler, *Reinventing Government*, 349; and Geoffrey N. Smith, "Mayoral Measures," *Financial World* 161 (18 February 1992): 8.

8. Harry P. Hatry and Donald M. Fisk, *Improving Productivity and Productivity Measurement in Local Governments* (Washington, DC: Urban Institute, 1971); Hatry, "Status of Productivity Measurement"; Charles L. Usher and Gary C. Cornia, "Goal Setting and Performance Assessment in Municipal Budgeting," *Public Administration Review* 41 (March/April 1981), 229–35; Susan A. MacManus, "Coping with Retrenchment: Why Local Governments Need to Restructure Their Budget Document Formats," *Public Budgeting and Finance* 4 (autumn 1984): 58–66; Rosemary B. LeGrotte, "Performance Measure-

ment in Major U.S. Cities" (Ph.D. diss., North Texas State University, 1987); Gloria A. Grizzle, "Linking Performance to Funding Decisions: What Is The Budgeter's Role?" *Public Productivity Review* 11 (spring 1987): 33–44; David N. Ammons, "Overcoming the Inadequacies of Performance Measurement in Local Government: The Case of Libraries and Leisure Services," *Public Administration Review* 55 (January/ February 1995): 37–47.

9. Katherine Barrett and Richard Greene, "The State of the Cities: Managing for Results," *Financial World* 163 (1 February 1994): 44.

10. Ibid.

11. Robert P. McGowan and Theodore H. Poister, "Impact of Productivity Measurement Systems on Municipal Performance," *Policy Studies Review* 4 (February 1985): 532–40.

The Art of Performance Measurement

David Osborne
and Ted Gaebler

Government is famous for its endless figures and forms. To an outsider, it seems like an industry that pays an enormous amount of attention to numbers. People in government are always counting something or churning out some statistical report. But most of this counting is focused on inputs: how much is spent, how many people are served, what service each person received. Very seldom does it focus on outcomes, on results.

This is true in part because measuring results is so difficult. Measuring profit in business is fairly straightforward. Measuring results in government is not. Normally it takes several years to develop adequate measures: an agency's first attempt often falls woefully short. It may measure only outputs, not outcomes. It may define outcomes too narrowly, driving employees to concentrate on only a few of the results the organization actually wants to achieve. It may develop so many measures that employees can't tell what to concentrate on.

Even Sunnyvale, California, perhaps the most sophisticated government we know when it comes to performance measures, still has some measures that cry out for refinement. As Sunnyvale, Phoenix, and hundreds of other government organizations have developed their measurement systems, however, they have learned a number of basic lessons:

REINVENTING GOVERNMENT: HOW THE ENTREPRENEURIAL SPIRIT IS TRANSFORMING THE PUBLIC SECTOR (pp. 349–359), © 1992 by David Osborne and Ted Gaebler. Reprinted by permission of Addison-Wesley Publishing Company, Inc.

1. There is a vast difference between measuring process and measuring results When public organizations set out to measure performance, their managers usually draw up lists that measure how well they carry out some administrative process: how many people they serve; how fast they serve them; what percentage of requests are fulfilled within a set period of time. In essence, they measure their volume of output. But outputs do not guarantee outcomes. A vocational school might pump out more and more graduates of a welding program, for instance. But if those graduates cannot find jobs as welders, what good is the program? It may be generating impressive outputs without generating any positive outcomes.

The tendency to focus on process is natural: managers measure what their agencies do, and in rule-driven organizations, people think of their jobs as following certain processes laid down by the rules. If they follow those processes faithfully and produce the expected volume of output, they are doing their jobs. They rarely think of the outcomes: what impact the activity has on those the agency is designed to serve. Yet a perfectly executed process is a waste of time and money if it fails to achieve the outcomes desired.

The National Center for State Courts provides a good example. With the U.S. Department of Justice, it set out to create performance standards for trial courts. The purpose, stated explicitly, was to focus not on "the structures and machinery of the courts," but on "their performance (*what courts actually accomplish with the means at their disposal*)" (emphasis added). Yet the group found itself struggling constantly with what Dr. Ingo Keilitz, who staffed the project, calls "process creep." Some members assumed that "good management is an outcome," Keilitz remembers. "And we would say, 'But good management is not an end in itself.' We argued until we were blue in the face."

Process measures can be useful, of course. Good management is important, and process measures can help organizations get a handle on how they can improve their management. Organizations that use Deming's Total Quality Management, for instance, constantly measure their internal processes so they can see where problems lie and correct them. In addition, the outcomes desired by any given organization are often very difficult to measure, or will not become evident for a long time. In such cases, organizations often choose process measures that appear to be reliable proxies for the ultimate outcome. For example, Pennsylvania's Ben Franklin Partnership measures things like the amount of private investment attracted to match each of its grants—on the assumption that projects which attract significant private investment have a better chance of contributing to economic growth than projects that have difficulty attracting private investment.

The problem comes when organizations measure only process—as too many do. Fox Valley Technical College measures many process issues: the number of courses scheduled but later dropped; the use of evaluation techniques that stress skill competency rather than the ability to take written exams; the amount of computer-based instruction offered; and so on. If it did not also measure how many graduates got jobs in the fields for which they trained, their satisfaction, and the satisfaction of employers, however, it might create ever better courses that resulted in ever fewer job placements. Once robots have replaced welders, it makes no sense to keep working to improve one's welding courses.

2. There is a vast difference between measuring efficiency and measuring effectiveness.   Efficiency is a measure of how much each unit of output costs. Effectiveness is a measure of the quality of that output: how well did it achieve the desired outcome? When we measure efficiency, we know how much it is costing us to achieve a specified output. When we measure effectiveness, we know whether our investment is worthwhile. There is nothing so foolish as to do more efficiently something that should no longer be done.

Both efficiency and effectiveness are important. But when public organizations begin to measure their performance, they often measure only their efficiency. Typically, a traditional Defense Department might measure how much it costs to house and feed its troops—and strive constantly to drive that number down. Yet as Bob Stone put it in his four-page "Department of Defense Construction Criteria": "The goal is not to minimize the life-cycle cost of the facilities, but to maximize the performance of the people who use the facilities."

The public certainly wants efficient government, but it wants effective government even more. Citizens may be pleased that they spend less per student on education than other states, but if their schools are the worst in the country, they are not likely to be pleased for long. They may enjoy a low tax rate, but if that means they spend an hour getting to work on clogged highways, they usually vote to invest in a more effective transportation system.

Focusing on efficiency more than effectiveness also tends to alienate public employees. When governments stress the cost of each unit of work, they often develop a green-eyeshade mentality that belittles the intelligence and skill of their workers. Most employees want to be effective. Most will gladly do what is necessary to increase their organization's impact. But if their superiors concentrate solely on their efficiency—on how quickly they do each unit of work—they will begin to feel as if they are on an assembly line.

George Britton, a deputy city manager in Phoenix, notes that his city got heavily into efficiency measurement during the 1970s. "We thought every street sweeper ought to do 65 lane-miles a day," he says:

But that collapsed, because it got caught up in a green-eyeshade philosophy. And it lost track of asking the question: Why are we doing this service? Governments do a lot of services very efficiently, without asking why they do them. We lost the relationship between efficiency and effectiveness. You're only being effective if you're doing something that needs to be done.

Improving the usefulness of performance information

1. *Address service quality and outcomes explicitly when reviewing services and programs.*
2. *Ask program managers to set a target for each performance indicator. Assess progress regularly against these targets.* Actual performance against the targets should be reported, and managers should review with their staff the program's performance after each report has been issued.
3. *Provide performance data in a timely manner.* Performance reports probably should be prepared at least quarterly, if not monthly. With most governments' current computer capability, such reports usually should be available within two to four weeks after the end of each reporting period.
4. *Calculate key breakouts of the data for each indicator.* Breaking out the aggregate data for outcome and service quality indicators will be much more useful to program staff in assessing where the service has been successful and where it has failed. It will help staffers direct their attention to where improvements are most needed.
5. *Include indicators of both "intermediate" outcomes and "end" outcomes in the performance measurement process, but clearly identify both types of indicators.* A community policing program might track the number of households participating in various neighborhood-based activities, such as neighborhood watch programs, as an intermediate outcome, but it also should attempt to track declines in crime rates and increases in feelings of security, the intended end outcomes.
6. *Ask programs to provide explanatory information with each performance report.*

3. There is an important difference between "program outcomes" and broader "policy outcomes"   When the National Center for State Courts developed its performance standards, it came up with outcome standards that measure public satisfaction with a court's accessibility, fairness, reliability, speed, political independence, and accountability. To measure these things, courts use public surveys, focus groups, and the like. But none of these measures deals with the broader outcomes most important to the public: crime rates, public safety, conviction rates, recidivism rates, justice for victims of crime, or satisfaction with the way in which disputes are resolved. Judges would argue, of course, that the courts are not the only institutions responsible for things like crime rates, conviction rates, and

---

7. *In agency training programs, routinely provide information on performance measurement and its uses to supervisors and managers.* This training should include information on the performance measurement process and on ways to use the information, such as for allocating resources, performance contracting, formulating budgets, helping with budget justifications, and making performance appraisals.

8. *Incorporate outcome-related performance requirements into contracts wherever feasible.* In writing contracts, pay more attention to what is to be accomplished and less to how the contractors are to accomplish it. Requests for proposals and even, in some cases, requests for bids should specify the results expected in quantitative terms to the extent possible.

9. *Consider including service quality and outcome progress information as part of the performance appraisal process for internal employees, especially supervisors and managers.*

10. *Use information on service quality outcomes in formulating and justifying budgets.* Agency managers should discuss at least qualitatively what they believe the outcome and quality implications will be.

11. *Finally, avoid expectations that outcome information will indicate the causes of the outcomes.* Outcome information provides only a score.

Source: Excerpted and adapted from Harry Hatry, Craig Gerhart, and Martha Marshall, "Eleven Ways to Make Performance Measurement More Useful to Public Managers," *Public Management* 76 (September 1994): S15–S18. *Public Management* is published by ICMA.

---

public perceptions of safety. They would be correct. Yet these are the outcomes people care most about.

This dilemma confronts many public organizations. They can measure the outcomes of their specific program or activity, but those numbers are not as important as certain broader measures. A jobs program for welfare recipients might measure its job placement rate and the wages of those placed, for example. But what about the number of people coming onto the welfare rolls, the length of time they stay on, and the size of the overall caseload? Managers of the jobs program would argue that they should be held responsible for their job placement numbers, but not for the total caseload or the number of people signing up for welfare.

Again, they would be correct. The latter numbers are affected by broader policy questions: who is eligible; how attractive welfare is compared to low-skill, low-wage work; and how much low-wage work is available. Yet if the welfare department does not measure both sets of numbers, it may think it is doing a terrific job of getting people off welfare, while its rolls are actually growing! This is precisely what has happened to many states over the past decade. Massachusetts' Employment and Training (E.T.) Choices program is justifiably considered one of the best in the nation. Yet, although it placed roughly 10,000 people a year in jobs between 1983 and 1990, the department's AFDC caseload started at 90,000, never got below about 84,000, and headed past 100,000 when a recession began.

Statistics like these underscore the importance of measuring both *program outcomes* and *policy outcomes*. Programs like E.T. Choices need information on how well they are achieving their goals. Indeed, E.T. Choices' managers collected that information religiously and continually used it to refine and improve their efforts. But they also need information on broader trends, such as the percentage of the population on welfare and in poverty. With this information, it becomes clear that E.T. Choices is innovating within a broader welfare system that contains powerful incentives for people to get on and stay on welfare. At some point, one can hope, such information will trigger efforts to change the broader system, rather than simply triggering more efforts to train and place people in jobs.

Figure 1 outlines the difference between outputs (process) and outcomes (results), between program outcomes and policy outcomes, and between efficiency and effectiveness. It then illustrates those differences for several different public services. To use street sweeping as an example, it illustrates that one would measure the *output,* or process, by measuring the number of miles swept. But if one wanted to measure the *outcome,* or result,

Figure 1. What to measure.

	General definition	Street sweeping	Welfare: Job training
Output (or process)	Volume of units produced	Miles swept	Numbers of people trained
Outcome (or result)	Quality/effectiveness of production: degree to which it creates desired outcomes	Cleanliness rating of streets	Numbers of people placed in jobs, working, and off welfare after six months, one year, and beyond. Impact on their lives.
Program outcome	Effectiveness of specific program in achieving desired outcomes	Cleanliness rating of streets as a result of sweeping	Numbers placed in jobs, working, and off welfare after six months, one year, and beyond. Impact on their lives.
Policy outcome	Effectiveness of broader policies in achieving fundamental goals	Measures indicating how much litter citizens leave on streets	Percentage of potential work force unemployed, on welfare, and in poverty; percent of welfare population on welfare more than one year, five years, etc.
Program efficiency	Cost per unit of output	Costs per mile of streets swept	Cost per job trainee; placement; retained job; etc.
Policy efficiency	Cost to achieve fundamental goals	Cost for X level of street cleanliness	Cost to achieve desired decrease in unemployment, poverty rate, welfare caseload, etc.
Program effectiveness	Degree to which program yields desired outcomes	Level of citizen satisfaction with cleanliness of streets	Numbers placed in jobs, working, and off welfare after six months, one year, and beyond. Impact on their lives.
Policy effectiveness	Degree to which fundamental goals and citizens' needs are met	Do citizens want to use their money this way, e.g., would they rather spend it on repaving streets?	Effect on larger society: e.g., poverty rate, welfare caseload, crime rate, later spending to remediate poverty, etc.

one would have to measure the cleanliness of the streets—as rated, perhaps, by objective, trained observers. This latter measure would be the *program outcome.* A *policy outcome* would look at a broader question: how much litter do citizens leave on the streets, and how effective is public policy at minimizing this amount?

To determine *program efficiency,* an organization would simply measure the cost per mile swept. But to determine *policy efficiency,* it would have to measure the cost to achieve a desired level of street cleanliness, by whatever method—street sweeping, prevention, community self-help. Finally, to measure *program effectiveness,* a city might measure citizen satisfaction with the level of street cleanliness. But to measure *policy effectiveness,* it might ask citizens whether they wanted their money spent keeping the streets clean, or whether alternative uses, such as construction or repaving, would be preferable.

For those interested in learning more about performance measurement, a number of experts have written widely on the subject. Harry Hatry at the Urban Institute has published a series of books, particularly for local governments. Jack Brizius, Michael Campbell, and Roger Vaughan have written about performance measurement in state government, for the Council of Governors Policy Advisers and the Corporation for Enterprise Development. In 1990, the Governmental Accounting Standards Board (GASB) released a research report on performance measurement, called *Service Efforts and Accomplishments Reporting: Its Time Has Come,* which provides a useful overview. GASB is also developing detailed research reports on a variety of specific fields, such as education, economic development, hospitals, mass transit, police, and water treatment.

The experts tend to agree on a series of further lessons:

Do both quantitative and qualitative analysis   Some valuable results are impossible to quantify. Others require so much paperwork and expense that they are not worth quantifying. Still others are quantifiable, but no one can say for sure whether the program in question was responsible for producing them. For all these reasons, it is important to combine quantitative measurement with qualitative evaluation. Good managers can get enormous insight into performance by looking at relevant numbers, but they can get equally valuable insight by spending time observing the program, agency, or provider; talking with workers; and listening to customers.

If all performance evaluation is done through numbers, service providers may also learn to "game" the numbers. "We watch the [enrollment and job placement] numbers, but we don't want our centers obsessed with them," explains Suzanne Teegarden, director of Massachusetts' Industrial Services Program.

Our worst centers are those that are numbers-driven. One of them—if the goal is 250 people enrolled, you can be sure they'll enroll 252. They aren't very energetic, and they don't take risks. Our best centers are the ones that really care, that get creative, that do it first and ask questions later. We know the centers well, so we know what the numbers mean.

Watch out for creaming   Service providers will usually deliver the numbers they're asked to deliver, even if they have to cut corners to do it. If they have to place 1,000 people in jobs in a year, they will find the 1,000 most employable people they can and give them training—a practice known as creaming. This is precisely what happened during the early years of the Job Training Partnership Act (JTPA). One solution is to set goals for each of several different target populations: 250 placements from among people who have been out of work for at least two years; 250 from those who do not have high school degrees; and so on. Another is to set different reimbursement rates for different populations. The job training industry has learned to use such mechanisms without any great difficulty.

Anticipate powerful resistance   Hard information about efficiency and effectiveness can be extremely threatening to service providers who doubt their ability to compete. Florida repealed a program that rewarded individual schools for improved performance. Arizona defunded a program that publicized the job placement rates of graduates from all postsecondary education and training institutions. The community colleges and technical schools found the information extremely threatening, because it revealed how effective they were at preparing people for real jobs. "You had big winners and big losers," says George Britton, who helped devise the system while serving under Governor Bruce Babbitt. "Whenever you single out people at the top and at the bottom, in a governmental function, it's very threatening." (Publication of such data is not impossible, however. Florida now does it successfully.)

Involve providers and employees in developing the correct measures   The best way to deal with resistance is to bring providers and employees into the process of defining the appropriate measures. To use data effectively, after all, people have to buy into its value. They need to "own" the specific measures used—to feel that they provide useful, relevant information that will improve the service they deliver. Those who oppose the idea, or oppose particular measures, need a fair hearing. Saddling people with inappropriate measures in whose development they have had no input is a sure way to create resistance, destroy morale, and encourage cheating.

Subject measures to annual review and modification   No measures are perfect. Since governance is not a science, it is impossible to isolate measures that perfectly reflect the outcomes of government activity. All we can do is hope for a close approximation, often using the best proxies available. Therefore it makes sense to modify and refine performance measures often, particularly as their flaws are revealed in practice. It also makes sense to commission an independent audit of the measures periodically, to see if they in fact measure what one thinks they measure. (Once the measures are refined, however, it is best to keep some measures steady over time, so as to be able to compare performance from one year to the next.)

Don't use too many or too few measures   If an organization sets too few measures, they may not reflect all of its goals. Hence its service providers may be driven to emphasize some goals at the expense of others. If it sets too many, it will dilute the power of all measures. Providers may become confused about priorities and burdened with paperwork, and managers may be overwhelmed by detail. If employees and service providers participate in the development of measures, and if they are allowed to correct the measures periodically, they will usually be able to find the right balance.

Watch out for perverse incentives   The funding formula used to finance nursing home care in Illinois during the 1970s created an incentive to keep people bedridden. The performance measures originally used by JTPA encouraged job training providers to cream. Perverse incentives like these can undermine the entire effort to measure performance. To avoid them, organizations should "game" new measures—anticipating how clever providers might respond—before imposing them.

Keep the measurement function in a politically independent, impartial office   If people are to rely on data, they must trust its objectivity. Hence it is a good idea to use an independent office, like the Phoenix City Auditor's Office, to do the measuring. In Florida, two private organizations, Florida TaxWatch and the Florida Council of 100 (a business group), have created a nongovernmental organization, Partners in Productivity, to develop performance measures for state government. In Great Britain, the national Audit Commission audits the performance not only of national government agencies but also of local governments. Because it publishes comparative information about efficiency and effectiveness, local governments pay close attention to its studies.

Focus on maximizing the use of performance data   Just developing measures does not guarantee that managers will use them to change what they do or that legislatures will use them to change what they fund. The Fund for the City of New York discovered, according to Greg Farrell, that "good measures and management information turned out to be much easier to conceive than to integrate into the conduct of government business. . . . Government managers are not, for the most part, *used* to having or using management information, especially for forward-looking purposes. And on many issues, political pressures are often so great that data seem to be beside the point when decisions are made." Hence while developing performance measures, organizations should try to develop budgets, management systems, and reward systems built around performance data.

Measuring Productivity

Ellen Doree Rosen

The unit of analysis

This is the description of one way "how to" measure the productivity of any public sector work unit. The first task is to decide on the unit.

In the public sector the output is always some kind of service that is produced by an organization and delivered across its borders to clients outside. If the organization is a teaching hospital, it delivers treatment to patients and training to doctors. If the organization is the hospital's purchasing unit, it delivers purchasing services across its boundaries to its clientele, which consists of other departments in the hospital.

In the first example, the unit of analysis is the hospital; in the second, it is the purchasing unit. The first step in measuring productivity is to choose: to decide clearly just *whose* productivity is to be measured. If, for example, it is the purchasing department, then purchasing services constitute the output, and only those resources that are used in producing purchasing services constitute the relevant input. The quantity of purchasing service and the quality of purchasing service are of significance. No other part of the hospital counts.

Productivity is measured indirectly by measuring outputs and inputs and then calculating the ratio. Let us start with inputs.

Adapted from Ellen Doree Rosen, *Improving Public Sector Productivity*, pp. 85–106, copyright © 1993 by Ellen Doree Rosen. Reprinted by permission of Sage Publications, Inc.

Measuring inputs

Inputs are resources—the resources consumed in producing outputs. Resources include labor, equipment, supplies, space, and utilities. Of these, labor is the major public sector resource, the biggest budget item for most agencies. Measuring and improving the productivity of labor is of primary importance in the public sector, because it is such a major resource and also because it represents so much potential that is untapped by traditional management systems.

The first point to note is that the input measure should include only those units of resource that are associated with the relevant output. For example, if a quality assurance officer in a state social services agency performs both investigative and auditing work, only the portion of the officer's work that is devoted to investigation would be counted in measuring the productivity of the investigative services; conversely, only the contribution to auditing would be counted in measuring the productivity of the auditing service. If the relevant output is "quality assurance," including both investigation and auditing, then the officer's full time would be counted as the relevant input. The same principle of matching input to output also pertains to any other kind of resource.

The usual practice in public sector productivity measurement is to deal with only one kind of resource at a time. This makes it possible to focus on the productivity of one factor, and it also simplifies the measurement process. For example, looking at the relationship between the output (services produced) and only the labor input used to produce it gives a clear measure of the productivity of labor. It can provide an uncluttered picture of the impact of a labor-specific innovation (such as a new training program) on productivity. On the other hand, if the point is to determine how new technology (such as a new type of sanitation truck) affects productivity, then only equipment (and not labor) would be the single type of resource considered. Thus it is possible to take the same output (such as tons of garbage collected) and, by measuring one resource or another, make specific findings about management options.

Sometimes, however, it is necessary to aggregate different inputs. For example, new word processing equipment may save labor resources but increase equipment resources consumed to do the same amount of work. How to calculate the net effect on productivity? Because labor is measured one way (usually, worker time) and equipment another (perhaps, number of machines), the only way to aggregate them is to convert both to estimated dollar values. The dollar is the lingua franca, the universal medium that turns apples and oranges into fruit salad.

However, it has its limitations for measuring public sector productivity, as we shall see.

Measuring labor inputs   To return to the more usual situation of considering one type of resource at a time, the most important and most commonly measured public sector input is labor. The dollar is not usually used for measuring labor in the public sector, because managers do not control labor costs—civil service categories and rules do. The dollar measure does not meet the measurement criterion of controllability. It gives misleading results: A new agency with many young people at the bottom of the civil service ladder would appear more productive than a unit with more old-timers.

Starting with the 1960s productivity measurement initiative by the Bureau of the Budget, the tradition has been established that public sector labor is measured in terms of worker time.[1] The amount of "worker-time" is calculated very simply:

Worker-time = Number of workers × Time per worker

Thus,

$$6 \text{ worker-hours} = 2 \text{ people working 3 hours each}$$
$$= 6 \text{ people working 1 hour each}$$
$$= 24 \text{ people working 1/4 hour each}$$
$$= 1 \text{ person working 6 hours}$$

The one stipulation for calculating and presenting these figures is that the units must be carefully labeled: "6 worker-hours," "5 worker-years," etc. It is also important to specify how a "worker-year" or "worker-day" is determined. There are choices, which is acceptable. That is how measures are developed. But the method for stipulating must be made clear to those who will use or borrow the figures. For example, what does 1 worker-year include? All calendar days? Only official working days? Vacation days? Leave days? Sick days?

A useful way to approach this decision is to consider the measurement criterion of "controllability." As a manager, I cannot hope to make better use of my workers by requiring them to come in on Sundays or on holidays. I can influence when a vacation takes place, not whether; it is generally an entitlement. Those days can be left out of the count; they contribute nothing to the productivity picture. Leave days and sick days are different; they may be taken or not. They may lie within the influence, if not the absolute control, of management. A productivity innovation, such as paying a cash bonus for unused leave days, might result in being able to produce more with the same work force. If leave days are included in the count of worker-days, the improvement will show up in the productivity figure because the same input (number of work days, including leave days) can be compared with the output before and after the innovation. For this reason, it is recommended that the "number of worker-days" should exclude weekends, holidays, and paid vacations but include sick and personal leave days.

Worker-time is a simple and rough count. It counts an entire day whether the worker is late or not (which is good, because cutting down on lateness or overextended lunch hours will show up as improved productivity: same number of days, more work done). It disregards the nature of the "worker": salary, education, skill level, type of work, and so on. This may also be a virtue. If the same number of worker-days can result in more or better service or both because, for example, skills have been upgraded through a training program or a better employee recruitment and screening process, then the productivity figure, if measured this way, will appropriately show an increase: same input (that is, same number of worker-days), but more and better output.

Data on the amount of worker-time should be available from existing personnel records. The labor of each worker who is on payroll, but not on vacation, during any working day counts as one worker-day, as long as the individual is assigned 100% to the relevant output. If not, the time must be prorated.

Measuring other inputs   Convenience is the guide to choosing counting units for nonlabor resources. Equipment input may be counted as "number of" something (copying machines, garbage trucks, railroad cars). The effect of an insulation or energy conservation program may be measured using as the input measure the number of kilowatt-hours or the energy costs (corrected for inflation for purposes of comparing over time). Space resources may be measured in footage or in rental costs, for example. Improved productivity of these resources will be reflected as more production per truck, per kilowatt-hour, or per square (or cubic) foot.

Measuring output quantity

As we will see, output quantity ("how much") and output quality ("how good") are measured by totally different strategies, but they are attributes of the same thing—some kind of output. How much of what? How good is what? The first step is to decide on the "what"—the output to be measured.

Step 1: Identify the outputs

List the major outputs   What is the mission of the unit? Some organizations produce only one or two kinds of service. Most complex organizations perform several or many functions. A state college registrar's office maintains student records, provides transcripts, registers students for courses, and certifies eligibility for graduation. A sanitation department removes garbage, maintains landfills, sweeps the streets, conducts inspections for sanitary code violations, and plows and sands the streets when it snows. Garbage removal services constitute one kind of output, street sweeping services another, and so on.

Our measurement team might start by brainstorming a list of the major functions. Representation from different parts of the organization and from clients is particularly important here. It is astonishing how, in practice, team members from one part of an organization are unaware of some of the services produced by other sections of the organization. Make a full list.

Prioritize and simplify   One or a few services will probably be of major importance—that is, they constitute a major part of the workload and consume most or a large part of the resources. Others may reasonably be grouped together as aspects of the same function; for example, conducting fire safety inspections and giving talks at schools can be grouped together as "fire prevention." Some services are patently trivial, candidates for the bottom of the list.

Select   One cannot, and should not, try to measure many kinds of output at the outset. Typically, one or two of the most important outputs are selected to start with. Later the system can be made more sophisticated by including more functions.

Step 2: Decide on output indicators
Select indicators   How will the selected output(s) be measured? The quantity of output is usually measured as "number of"units. (These are units of counting, not units of analysis.) What should the counting unit be? For example, will the output of "placement service" be measured by counting "number of interviews" or "number of placements"? Either is reasonable, each leaves something out, and each will have an effect on people's behavior. The decision of a team, rather than an individual, will decrease the likelihood of adopting egregiously partial or perverse indicators.

Adjust for workload difficulty   Some units of output may be significantly more difficult than others. Some investigations are brief background checks, others take a lot of digging; some job seekers are easily placed, others lack skills or personality; a fire in a one-family house is not the same as a fire in a 40-story office building. Differences in work difficulty can be dealt with several ways. If the "mix" of easy, moderate, and difficult work remains fairly constant over time or between agencies, then differences in difficulty can be disregarded: The difficulty of the "average" unit stays the same, and comparisons will be fair.

If workload differences are real and cannot be assumed to be consistently mixed in the same proportions, then different work can be grouped into two or three classes, with each class counted separately; for example, one figure can be derived for number of residential fires suppressed and another figure for number of commercial fires suppressed.

Finally, work of varying difficulty can be counted together by taking the least difficult unit of work (let us say, a one-family residential fire) and setting that as "one standard unit of work." The average apartment-house fire may be judged to be three times as much work to put out: Each apartment-house fire would be counted as three standard units. Each downtown office building may be counted as seven standard units. In this way, the total amount of fire-fighting service can be expressed in one figure. That has the virtue of simplicity, along with validity.

How can the relative weights be determined? An analysis of the fire department records may indicate the relative amount of time or effort each kind of fire demands. A group of individuals knowledgeable about the work might be called on to arrive at the figures, perhaps by use of the nominal group technique described below.

Attention to differences in work difficulty is important in enhancing the validity of the measurement system. More important, it serves as a very important way of controlling "creaming"— that is, the selection of easy cases and neglect of more difficult ones in order to pile up the output numbers. In the public sector, this practice is not only an unfair way of measuring, but also a denial of equity and a betrayal of the organizational mission when, for example, a state employment service neglects those who are most in need of help so that it can look good on the placement figures.

Measure the outputs

Collect the data   Like input data, output information is often already at hand. Agencies usually keep records of the number and type of units of service produced in any given time period: number of clients seen, applications processed, passengers carried. These records may have to be adapted or reclassified or augmented, but lack of this type of data is not a barrier to measurement of the output of most agencies.

Total the output   The total number of output units for the selected time period is the output figure. The measurement expert can provide guidance on selecting a time period that is long enough and representative enough. For comparison over time, similar seasons should be measured.

Aggregate outputs (optional)   If several different types of output have been selected for counting, it is possible to aggregate them using the same strategy as for aggregating work of varying difficulty.

Calculating efficiency

If the quality of outputs is put aside (disregarded, presumed to remain constant over time, or presented independently of the output quantity figures), then

$$\text{Output} \div \text{Input} = \text{Efficiency}$$

Because output (O) is expressed as "number of units of service" and input (I) is most usually expressed in terms of worker-time or equipment units, the most common public sector efficiency figure (and productivity figure, if quality is disregarded) reads something like "75 licenses issued per worker-week" or "1,200 passenger miles of transport per bus-day."

To summarize, output (rather than process or outcome) is generally measured and related to input to derive the productivity figure. There is no universal measure of output quantity; each kind of good or service is measured in units appropriate to it. Choices are made by measurers: which good or service to count, whether to differentiate levels of difficulty of work, how to aggregate different kinds of output. . . .

The typing pool produces thirty letters . . . per worker-day. Its productivity can now be compared with its own performance last year, or with that of another typing pool. But what if one pool produced clean, accurate, attractive copy, while the other produces messy, error-ridden work? Before these outputs can be compared usefully, the quality of the work must be considered.[2]

That is the subject of the next section.

Measuring output quality

Quantifying quality

Use of indicators   Ask several people, "How can you tell a high-quality train service from a poor one?" The answers are almost certain to take the form, "A good train service is reliable, fast, safe, comfortable, prompt, accessible." Some people may list a few attributes, some may list many. There may not be total agreement on whether every item belongs on the list. There would certainly be disagreement on the relative importance of each criterion. But the use of attributes or criteria as indicators, if not definers, of quality makes intuitive sense. It has face validity. If a panel of riders creates a weighted list of attributes, a list incorporating their different judgments, that list acquires content validity as well. That is, one can "demonstrate that the measure involved includes all the identified elements and assigns to each the proper weight."[3]

Can a list of attributes be developed? Clearly, yes. The nominal group technique, described below, is an excellent way to proceed—for compiling a list, narrowing the list down to a few key indicators, and deciding the relative importance of each so that they can be weighted. Theoretically, an individual "expert" could do the job, but having a representative group increases the validity. Getting such a group to identify and weight criteria is entirely feasible and not particularly costly in time or in effort. It also makes sense in terms of public relations: People understand and accept what they have had a hand in creating.

Nominal group technique   Sometimes it is necessary to make decisions where there is no objective way of knowing what is a "correct" or even a "good" answer. In such a situation, a practicable decision can be derived from the best judgments of a group of people. However, the usual group, especially if it contains people of differing ranks, presents the problem that some people will be inhibited and unduly influenced by the opinions of others.

The nominal group technique developed by Delbecq, Van de Ven, and Gustafson is a useful instrument for producing group consensus without the social dynamics.[4] "It has been found to be particularly effective in areas where there are many intangibles, little past history, large people involvement, and semistructured or unstructured processes."[5]

Here is how it works. Members of the group generate ideas by writing their judgments silently and privately. Then, in round-robin fashion, each member reads out one idea while a leader or facilitator lists the ideas (no criticisms allowed). People may volunteer to clarify ambiguous items. Next, everyone votes privately for a certain number of "most important" or "best" items. The results of the voting are made known to the group by the leader; everyone then votes again and again in a series of rounds. Unpopular ideas tend to be abandoned, and consensus builds over time.

Step 1: Choose quality indicators   What makes for a good mail service? Perhaps speed, accuracy, and courtesy.[6] For a good counseling service, garbage-collection service, tax-collection service, pothole-filling service, or park service? Alas for measurement, there is no one universal measure of the quality of everything.

Each kind of output, each service, is "qualified" by its own particular, customized set of indicators. What they all have in common is only the idea that quality implies "fit for use by the customer."[7]

Identify indicators   Measuring quality starts by developing a list of quality indicators for the particular output that is being measured. This involves "brainstorming" a list and then narrowing it down to perhaps two or three key attributes. Remember that trying to measure everything is a trap: As compared with the most important attribute(s), each additional item will probably take equally long to produce but yield only marginally more insight.

Which group might produce this list? One possibility is the measurement team itself, possibly with additional "customer" representation. Alternatively, the identification of quality criteria might be turned over to a special task force or even to an existing quality circle.

Decide on relative weights   If some quality criteria are significantly more important than others, they should be incorporated into the measurement system. The idea of weighting some elements as more important than others is well established in the productivity field.

As an example of weighting, consider a mail delivery service. Speed may be deemed twice as important as accuracy, and accuracy twice as important as courtesy. To reflect this, speed would be weighted at 4, accuracy at 2, and courtesy at 1, which means that speed would be counted four times, accuracy twice, and courtesy once in computing a weighted quality "average":

$$\text{Quality} = [4(\text{speed}) + 2(\text{accuracy}) + 1(\text{courtesy})] \div 7$$

Weights do not have to be expressed in round numbers, but round numbers are obviously simpler to use, as long as they do not create undue distortion. It is generally wiser to begin simply and then refine as time goes on.

Step 2: Measure the quality   How can each relevant attribute be scored? How can a number be assigned to show the level of performance with respect to any particular criterion? Alas, again, the type of score depends on the method used to collect the data. Each score is derived in its own way. Methodologically, this is all right, as long as the units are clearly labeled, but practically it makes for a more complicated procedure. The logic is straightforward, but the procedure has several steps.

Collect data on achieved quality   One way data on quality can be collected is through the process of observation. For example, trained observers, using a set of pictures as a guide, can rate the cleanliness of alleys. To take another example, one could mail test letters and observe how long it takes for them to arrive. If an adequate sample of mail is sent from several representative parts of the country to a representative set of destinations, then

---

Trained observers

The concept of trained observers involves simply training people to rate conditions in a city—its streets, sidewalks, parks, playgrounds, signs, and buildings. This is done by using scales that have been carefully chosen as meaningful to the public as well as to government employees and by training those observers in such a way that their results could be duplicated. The whole thing is nonsense if you cannot get interrater reliability—that is, the same results from two different raters or the same result from the same rater at another time. The training of the observers and the selection of the scale are key notions. To facilitate the training and to make the scale understandable, most of the scales hinge on photographs that illustrate the different levels of the scale in addition to verbal descriptions.

What are the main uses of trained observer ratings? Some may be obvious and others not. First of all, they are input to performance measures. If you want performance measures for the street-cleaning crews, then trained observer ratings of litter are one way to get reliable measures. If you want to measure park maintenance or examine the efficiency of road-repair crews, the use of trained observers is a good approach. Trained observers are also very useful in dealing with citizen equity issues, a political hot potato. Citizens are always complaining that the streets and sidewalks in their area are bad whereas those in the rest of the city are not. A systematic set of measures of the condition of the plant can show whether there is equity across areas or whether the citizen is actually right and some area is worse. Thus problems can be resolved objectively, not just as a response to squeaky wheels.

Source: Philip Schaenman, "Trained Observers," in *Managing for Results: Performance Measures in Government*, 1993 Conference Proceedings (Austin: The University of Texas, 1994).

a useful number could be derived: "average time for a letter to arrive." (Any subsequent comparisons should be based on the same
procedure.) The method just described has some loaded words:
adequate, representative, useful. The measuring expert should
know how to deal with these.

The same observational approach could be used to judge
speed of service by noting the travel time between set points. A
complication: "speed" or "rate" is calculated as the inverse of
time. It seems familiar when expressed as "miles per hour," but
less so when expressed as "average letter per number of days."
Just notice that the longer the letter takes, the smaller the score
will be: If it takes 1 day, then the score is $1 \div 1 = 1$; if it takes 4
days, then the speed score is 1/4.

Data on quality may also be obtainable from records. Quality
may be reflected in such figures as the number of complaints, the
number of reversals from above, or the number of units that have
to be redone because of error. These would usually be expressed
as percentages of units that are correct (error-free, unreversed,
or unprotested): for example, 99.7% of letters were delivered to
the right address; 82% of arrests survived a first screening; 60%
of the planted trees survived the first year. The fewer the flaws,
the higher the scores.

Quality data may be obtained from user surveys. For example, a survey might indicate how quietly the sanitation crew
worked, how courteously the unemployment office staff behaved,
how comfortable the bus seats were, how clear the instructions
were. Questionnaires often ask respondents to rate items on a
Likert scale (usually in five steps from "agree strongly" to "dis-
agree strongly"). The resulting score might be: "On a 1–5 scale,
with 5 being the most favorable opinion, seat comfort received an
average score of 4.3." The better the quality, the higher the score.

This phase of measurement has consisted of choosing the
means for collecting data and then measuring the actual performance level by the most appropriate means, even though the resulting scores for different criteria may take different forms.

Scores that remain expressed in different ways can be combined into one composite measure, but the resulting figure becomes prohibitively difficult to interpret and compare, as Hatry
and Fisk acknowledged in their early effort to incorporate quality
into the measurement of solid waste-collection service by calculating: tons of solid waste collected × average street cleanliness
rating on a 1–4 scale × percent of survey population expressing
satisfaction with collection.[8]

Compare achieved to desired levels   There is a way around
that situation. Each of those scores can be converted to a com-

mon system, permitting these various scores to be added together, averaged, and generally manipulated mathematically.
This is done by taking each actual, achieved score and comparing
it with an ideal, or desired score. For example, if 100% accuracy
is the desired level, and only 99.2% has been achieved, then:

$$\text{Actual} \div \text{Ideal} = 99.2\% \div 100\% = .99$$

If a two-day delivery time for the average letter is the goal desired, but it actually takes four days, then (hang on here, for the
division of fractions):

$$\text{Actual} \div \text{Ideal} = (1/4) \div (1/2) = (1/4) \times (2/1) = 1/2 = .50$$

If an average 4.5 courtesy rating on a Likert scale is the goal (set
in the knowledge that total satisfaction is not humanly possible),
but a rating of 4.3 has actually been attained, then:

$$\text{Actual} \div \text{Ideal} = 4.3 \div 4.5 = .96$$

The important thing to notice is that because, in each case,
the actual and the ideal are both expressed in the same units, the
units cancel out. What is left is a number somewhere between 0
and 1.

Exceptions are possible but unlikely. It is conceivable that
work can exceed the quality goal, which would produce a number
greater than 1. That would suggest that the standard has been
set too low or, as a less likely scenario, that too much effort is
being invested in perfection. Those responsible for the measurement system will need to explore the question of whether to
count or credit quality that exceeds standards.

At the other extreme, it is theoretically possible, but difficult
to imagine in practice, that the output would do more harm than
good and result in a negative number. As a general rule, neither
of these things should happen, and the score should lie between 0
(if everything is done wrong—for example, if every letter is mis-
directed) and 1 (if all the output meets the ideal set for it in every
dimension of quality).

Weight and aggregate scores   The use of the achieved-to-
ideal ratio has two great advantages. First, because all scores are
expressed the same way, the quality level is easy to read and
communicate, no matter what the criterion: A .99 on speed and a
.50 on durability tell the public works agency in a clear way just
how it is doing on each quality dimension of a pothole-filling service. It is easy to spot a drop or rise in performance with respect

to any single criterion and to track performance on each dimension from year to year.

Second, scores on several different attributes of quality can now be weighted and aggregated, thus producing a single overall quality score. For example:

$$\text{Quality} = [4(\text{speed}) + 2(\text{accuracy}) + 1(\text{courtesy})] \div 7$$
$$= [4(.50) + 2(.99) + 1(.96)] \div 7$$
$$= .71$$

As long as all of these variables are measured in a consistent way from year to year and as long as the ideal or desired scores remain unchanged, it is possible to track quality performance over time. If the assumptions (such as desired level) and the measurement procedure are clearly spelled out, other agencies or jurisdictions can compare their performance to this one by correcting for any differences between measurement systems. For example, if another jurisdiction also takes four days to deliver the average letter but has set three days as the desired delivery time, it will get a .75 reading, instead of a .50 reading for the same performance on the same aspect of quality.

The foregoing example points up the chief disadvantage of this measurement system. The score depends on the desired level; the lower the goal set, the better one looks on the score sheet. Unless the premises are clearly conveyed and clearly understood by potential users of these figures, there is the possibility that the system can be misused.

Using the quality measures

Applications of quality data   Individual or aggregate measures of service quality are of value and interest in their own right. They focus and reinforce organizational goals by specifying quality objectives, both qualitatively and quantitatively. Quality measures can be used in the control process: for example, as mentioned earlier, creaming (selecting only easy units of work) can be controlled by using "equitability" as a criterion of service quality.

Measures of quality can be used as formative feedback into the production process, pointing out areas in need of improvement and measuring the effect of improvement efforts. Quality measures, like other performance measures, may form the basis for a system of rewards. Conversely, if "public sector practitioners . . . contend that . . . how much they do is far less important than how well they do it,"[9] measures of quality can provide a reality check. Data on quality may be used in the budgeting or policy debates as evidence of high-quality performance. In the current emphasis on managing for quality, performance on the quality dimension becomes the lodestar by which to steer the organization.

However, for our purposes, the importance of quality measurement lies in its contribution to the measurement and improvement of productivity. Relating only the quantity of outputs to inputs gives an efficiency measure, which has been generally regarded as an incomplete picture of productivity. Quality must be considered.

Quality in the productivity formula   Just how to "consider" quality is a question as yet unsettled. There have been essentially four approaches.

1. *Disregard quality.* If quality is assumed to be unchanged, a constant, it can be disregarded in calculating productivity. For example, the federal government for many years simply made the assumption that quality did not vary and omitted it from the productivity picture. That was equivalent to not considering quality.

2. *Present quality information separately from efficiency measures.* Measures of the quality dimension of performance have been presented alongside, and independently of, measures of the efficiency dimension. Presumably, decision makers internalized both sets of information and somehow integrated both factors into their subsequent actions and policies.

3. *Use quality measures as a screening device.* One or more quality criteria may be established for a given kind of output. A minimum acceptable standard can then be set for each. When the output is measured, any unit of work that does not meet the standards can simply be excluded from the output count. This is the strategy adopted by Harry Hatry:

> Units of output are measures of the amount of workload accomplished. Unfortunately, the readily available workload counts often say little about the real product of the activity. For example, the number of park acres maintained says little about how they look; the number of gallons of water treated does not indicate the quality of that water. Whenever possible, defective outputs should be identified and should not be counted as output.[10]

However:

> The problem with eliminating defective units from the output count is that services can be inferior (slow, grudging, etc.) but not entirely useless. Such outputs should be counted, but not given the same value as activities that are fast, courteous, or otherwise satisfactory.[11]

4. *Use quality measures to discount output.* The fourth approach, the one adopted here, is not to eliminate, but rather to discount those units of output that fall below the desired standard.

We have seen that different quality indicators can be put into the same form (a number between 0 and 1). Several indicators can be aggregated into a weighted average, yielding one number between 0 and 1 that expresses the overall level of quality of an output. That overall number can be used as a coefficient of quality, K. If the output is multiplied by K, it is reduced in value according to the level of the quality. If the quality meets all desired standards, K will equal 1, and the output will be credited in full, undiminished. But as the quality level, the value of K, moves down, the output will be discounted—diminished proportionally. If $K = .9$, for example, the output will be counted as only 90% of the number of units.

Multiplying the output, O, by the coefficient, K, results in "*OK* work." Assuming that quantity of output times quality of output determines the effectiveness of implementation, then "*OK* work is effective work."[12] And *OK/I* equals productivity, with quality taken into account.

Despite disagreement over the term *effectiveness*, which we would have called *quality*, this formulation conforms to the conception that Walter Balk saw many years ago:

If the production process is defined in conventional systems terms, two fundamental control ratios appear. The first is that of output to input— or efficiency. The second is output to standards—or effectiveness. Frequently, improving productivity is a question of optimizing these ratios by keeping them in balance, one with the other.[13]

Summary: measuring productivity

The process of measuring public sector productivity is recapitulated below. Some services lend themselves easily to the complete process. Other services are difficult to specify. For example, it is no coincidence that sanitation work has been measured and analyzed so fully. The mission is unambiguous, resources are clearly identifiable, the output is readily measurable, and criteria can be derived for directly indicating quality. On the other hand, the mission of the Department of State is ambiguous; resources available to the Central Intelligence Agency are not clearly identifiable; the output of a university is difficult to measure; the quality of research and development work lacks obvious criteria. Not every kind of service can be readily measured, but many, if not most, can be—with a little imagination and confidence. The methodology exists.

1. Decide what work unit or organization is to be measured.
2. Make preliminary assessments. Is measurement expertise available? Is support available to impel the enterprise? Who will be involved? Is a measurement team feasible? Reporting to whom? Made up of whom?
3. Lay the groundwork by discussing it with everyone involved, and assemble the measurers.
4. Think about the mission and identify the major mission-related services produced by the work unit. Select one (or a few) of the most representative to start with.
5. Decide how to count the amount of output: in what units? for what time period?
6. Decide what type of input will be used. (The productivity of labor? of equipment? It is difficult to measure total factor productivity. Consider one resource at a time; labor is most usual.) Is it clear which input units go into producing the output?
7. Decide by what method data will be collected on quantity of input and quantity of output. (The measurement expert is important here.) Collect the data.
8. If only an efficiency measure is desired, stop here and calculate Output ÷ Input.
9. If quality matters, decide what criteria to use, what weight each criterion will carry, and what the ideal or standard level will be for each.
10. Decide how to collect data on each criterion and collect them.
11. For each criterion, calculate the achieved-to-desired score. If one overall quality rating is desired, aggregate the weighted scores.
12. To calculate productivity, quality considered, multiply the output figure, O, by the overall quality rating, K, and divide by the input figure.

1. Bureau of the Budget, *Measuring Productivity of Federal Government Organizations* (Washington, DC: GPO, 1964).
2. E. D. Rosen, "Productivity: Concepts and Measurement," in *Productivity and Public Policy,* ed. M. Holzer and S. S. Nagel (Beverly Hills: Sage, 1984), 34.
3. E. O'Sullivan and G. R. Rassel, *Research Methods for Public Administrators* (New York: Longman, 1989), 92.
4. A. L. Delbecq, A. H. Van de Ven, and D. H. Gustafson, *Group Techniques for Program Planning* (Glenview, IL: Scott, Foresman, 1975).
5. W. J. Presnick, "Measuring Managerial Productivity," *Administrative Management* (May 1980): 28.
6. E. D. Rosen, "OK Work: Incorporating Quality into the Productivity Equation," *Public Productivity Review* 5 (1981): 215.
7. R. G. Brinkerhoff and D. E. Dressler, *Productivity Measurement: A Guide*

for Managers and Evaluators (Newbury Park, CA: Sage, 1990), 48.

8. H. P. Hatry and D. M. Fish, *Improving Productivity and Productivity Measurement in Local Governments* (Washington, DC: Urban Institute, 1971), 19.

9. D. N. Ammons, "Common Barriers to Productivity Improvement in Local Government," *Public Productivity Review* 9 (1985): 301–2.

10. H. P. Hatry, "Performance Measurement Principles and Techniques," *Public Productivity Review* 4 (1980): 317.

11. Rosen, "OK Work," 211.

12. Ibid., 212.

13. W. L. Balk, "Toward a Government Productivity Ethic," *Public Administration Review* 38 (1978): 46.

PART 2

Performance Monitoring

Knowing what performance measures *are* is important. Incorporating such measures into an effective monitoring system—one that can influence management and policy decisions—is a significantly greater step.

To *monitor* performance implies, at the very least, periodic observation to assess the adequacy of services being delivered or work being performed. Under this most general definition, virtually every local government can claim to monitor its performance. The more rigorous definition used in this volume goes well beyond casual observation. True performance monitoring is focused on accountability, and it includes systematic observation, careful measurement, appropriate comparisons and analysis, and timely reporting. Five key characteristics are associated with a good accountability system. Such a system

- Focuses on outcomes
- Uses a few selected indicators to measure performance
- Provides information for both policy and program management decisions
- Generates data consistently over time
- Reports outcomes regularly and publicly.[1]

Local government performance may be monitored systematically on an intermittent, ad-hoc basis or on an ongoing basis. While detailed, ad-hoc analysis—commonly labeled performance auditing—is a valuable method of assessing performance or program effectiveness and is therefore addressed in this volume, performance monitoring *systems* usually connote an ongoing process.

Effective performance monitoring systems establish a vehicle for collecting, refining, and transporting performance data to the decision-making arena—whether at the work unit level, the department level, or the upper echelons of local government. Because they provide timely information on program outputs and accomplishments, such systems are pivotal to the success of such current managerial initiatives as customer-focused management, market-driven management, strategic planning, and total quality management.[2]

Performance monitoring systems track outputs, operating efficiency, product or service quality, and results. To be of value, they must reveal current performance in some meaningful context. Although the most common context is comparison with performance during an earlier period, other comparisons are also relevant. In some local governments, current performance is compared with that of other units or with performance targets. Ideally, a monitoring system will also provide comparisons of service quality or results among different population subgroups and different geographic areas within the jurisdiction. The most sophisticated systems will also compare performance with that of outside units matched for similar operating conditions (or, by statistical methods, control for differences in client characteristics, community conditions, or other factors that might otherwise give some units a performance advantage over others and make unadjusted comparisons unfair).[3]

Good performance monitoring systems are not idle exercises. They have clear operational significance. The much-heralded success of Phoenix's public works department in competing with and beating private collectors in bids for the city's sanitation routes has been attributed by local officials not only to a zeal for finding ways to improve operations and to a participatory management style, but also to a good system of cost accounting.[4] Phoenix's cost accounting system allows sanitation officials to track cost-per-mile figures for refuse trucks, costs per ton of garbage collected, costs per household, and other relevant statistics. That information, plus a management style that taps into the insights of drivers and other members of the sanitation team, allowed Phoenix officials to know where they were strong, where they needed improvement, and, as various improvement initiatives were tried, whether improvements were actually occurring.

Performance monitoring systems often rely on several sources of data. Ideally, existing records can be tapped for much of the needed information, but in most cases additional data collected by means of time logs, citizen or client surveys, trained observers, or other means will be required. Two of these data collection methods—citizen surveys and trained observer ratings—have received considerable attention in recent years.

At least one appropriate judge of the quality of services is the service recipient. That truism applies to local governments just as it does to any other service sector operation. In most cases, the recipient of local government services is the citizen. So, how can local governments discover how citizens judge their services? One good way of finding out is by asking them. In fact, many of the effectiveness measures recommended for local governments by the Urban Institute and others rely on carefully designed and properly administered citizen or client surveys.[5] (See Figure 1.)

Citizen surveys have been used in local government for many years. Sources of information on the do's and don'ts of questionnaire design, sample selection, and survey administration are fairly plentiful. Local governments that hire survey consultants to ensure that proper steps are taken or that carefully follow prescribed steps in conducting surveys themselves usually gain valuable information on citizens' perceptions. Unfortunately, local governments that try shortcuts or ignore prescribed steps often receive citizen input that lacks representativeness and may be extremely misleading. Some good sources of additional information on citizen and client surveys are included in the "For Further Reference" section found at the back of this volume.

Trained observers, used in a number of local governments to evaluate the condition of facilities and infrastructure, are another good source of information to supplement performance data collected by a department itself. The adequacy of parks maintenance, for example, can be rated by persons outside the parks maintenance operation who have been trained in the finer points of condition rating and who are typically furnished with a set of photographs depicting various grades of condition. Such ratings, as well as feedback from service recipients or citizens in general, can be a useful aspect of a performance monitoring system.

Moving from the collection of a handful of workload measures to the design and implementation of an effective performance monitoring system is not an easy or short trip. Although many local governments have faltered along the road, several others are making good progress, as noted in examples found in Part 3 of this volume. Insightful advice and the availability of good models can increase the odds of success.

In the first article in Part 2, James Swiss distinguishes performance monitoring systems from management-by-objectives (MBO) systems, describes "chains of output" and their relevance to performance monitoring, identifies principal methods of setting standards, and offers examples of performance monitoring reports for a children's services agency, a police department, and a recreation program. Theodore Poister's chapter provides further advice and uses a transit system example to demonstrate the value of performance monitoring.

Figure 1. Sample client survey for users of a recreation center.

To User of _____ Recreation Center

We need your help in evaluating and improving our programs. Please take a few minutes now to complete this questionnaire and return it to the person who gave it to you (or "return it in the enclosed self-addressed stamped envelope"). Your responses will be kept strictly confidential.

(Signed)
Director, Division of Recreation

1. About how often have you visited the _____ Recreation Center in the past three months?
   a. This is my first visit   _____
   b. More than 12 times   _____
   c. 6 to 12 times   _____
   d. 3 to 5 times   _____
   e. 1 or 2 times   _____

2. About how long did you stay on your most recent visit?
   a. Less than 1 hour   _____
   b. 1 hour or more, but less than 2 hours   _____
   c. 2 hours or more, but less than 4 hours   _____
   d. 4 hours or more   _____

3. How would you rate the following characteristics? Circle the appropriate number:
   1 = Excellent, 2 = Good, 3 = Fair, 4= Poor, 5 = Don't Know.

a. Variety of programs offered	1	2	3	4	5
b. Physical fitness programs offered	1	2	3	4	5
c. Crafts opportunities offered	1	2	3	4	5
d. Classes offered	1	2	3	4	5
e. Hours center is open	1	2	3	4	5
f. Condition of the equipment	1	2	3	4	5
g. Cleanliness of the center	1	2	3	4	5
h. Accessibility of the center from your home	1	2	3	4	5
i. Playground facilities	1	2	3	4	5
j. Safety conditions	1	2	3	4	5
k. Helpfulness of staff members	1	2	3	4	5
l. Courtesy of staff members	1	2	3	4	5
m. Knowledge and skills of staff members	1	2	3	4	5
n. Planning of activities	1	2	3	4	5
o. Publicity given to programs	1	2	3	4	5
p. Overall enjoyability of activities	1	2	3	4	5
q. New skills you acquired	1	2	3	4	5
r. Knowledge you acquired	1	2	3	4	5
s. Improvement in your physical well-being	1	2	3	4	5
t. Positive feeling about yourself	1	2	3	4	5

4. If you rated any of the above items as "Fair" or "Poor," please state why.
   _____
   _____
   _____
   _____

5. Overall, how would you rate the _____ Recreation Center and its programs?

Excellent   _____
Good   _____
Fair   _____
Poor   _____

6. Do you have any other comments or suggestions for improving this recreation center?

7. What is your age?

Less than 14   _____
14–18   _____
19–24   _____
25–34   _____
35–49   _____
50–64   _____
Over 65   _____

8. What is the zip code of your home?

9. How do you usually get to the _____ Recreation Center?

Walk   _____
Bike   _____
Drive   _____
Other (describe): _____

10. What is your sex?

Male   _____
Female   _____

11. Please indicate your race or ethnicity. (Check all that apply.)

White   _____
Black   _____
Hispanic   _____
Asian   _____
Other   _____

12. Which of the following comes closest to your total household income before taxes this year?

a. Under $9,999   _____
b. $10,000–$19,999   _____
c. $20,000–$29,999   _____
d. $30,000 or over   _____
e. Don't know   _____

Thank you very much for your help. Please return this to the staff member who gave it to you.

Source: Harry P. Hatry, John M. Greiner, and Maria Swanson, "Monitoring the Quality of Local Government Services," *Management Information Services Report* 19, no. 2 (February 1987): 13.

1. Jack A. Brizius and Michael D. Campbell, *Getting Results* (Washington, DC: Council of Governors' Policy Advisors, 1991), 17–21; cited in GASB, *Concepts Statement No. 2 of the Governmental Accounting Standards Board on Concepts Related to Service Efforts and Accomplishments Reporting* (Norwalk, CT: GASB, April 1994), 11.
2. Joseph S. Wholey and Harry P. Hatry, "The Case for Performance Monitoring," *Public Administration Review* 52 (November/December 1992): 605.
3. Ibid.
4. Wayne Hanson, "Phoenix: A Shining Example," *Government Technology* 5 (December 1992): 1, 74.
5. See, for example, Harry P. Hatry, Louis H. Blair, Donald M. Fisk, John M. Greiner, John R. Hall, Jr., and Philip S. Schaenman, *How Effective Are Your Community Services? Procedures for Measuring Their Quality,* 2d ed. (Washington, DC: The Urban Institute and ICMA, 1992).

Performance Monitoring Systems

James E. Swiss

There are many possible systems for monitoring the output of public organizations, but we will somewhat arbitrarily divide all output-oriented systems into two broad groups: management by objectives (MBO) systems and non-MBO systems that do not involve negotiated objectives and regular face-to-face management meetings. We will give the name of *performance monitoring systems* to this latter category, which includes all non-MBO output systems.

Many agencies use a performance monitoring system to track a number of important organizational outputs on a continuing basis, year after year. Reports on these output measures are circulated to top managers each month or quarter, often with a comparison to last year's figures. (Exhibit 1 is an example of several such reports.) Performance monitoring systems are widely used in government. For example, one national survey of city governments found that 67 percent employed such systems.[1]

Performance monitoring systems vs. MBO   As might be expected, pure MBO systems and pure performance monitoring systems are often combined to create various hybrids. But in their pure form, performance monitoring systems differ from MBO in five ways. We have already discussed two of these differences: Performance monitoring systems do not have negotiated goal setting, nor do they have follow-up face-to-face meetings. They also differ in three other ways.

Swiss, James, PUBLIC MANAGEMENT SYSTEMS, © 1991, pp. 128–166. Adapted by permission of Prentice-Hall, Upper Saddle River, New Jersey.

Performance monitoring systems usually focus on relatively routine tasks   Performance monitoring systems often cover the routine tasks performed by the operating level of an organization, such as processing forms, paving streets, reading meters, and collecting garbage. MBO, in contrast, is often used for one-time-only projects such as those handled by middle and upper managers.

Performance monitoring systems usually focus on organizations, not individuals   Performance monitoring systems can track the outputs of individuals (i.e., How many clients did Employee X place in jobs this month?), but much more often, they track agency-wide processes (How many clients did Division Y place in jobs this month?). Thus most of these systems lack the individual measures of MBO, which emphasize both the individual manager and the unit that he or she directs.

We often build the measures for each organizational unit by combining measures that have already been gathered for each individual worker. (This task can be done by hand or by computer if each similar job is given a code—an activity number—that allows the computer to add the individual job readings

---

Exhibit 1. Examples of performance monitoring system reports.

The following tables provide three examples of performance monitoring system reports, each from a different city.

The first table is taken from a New York City report on an agency that deals with children's services. The second table represents output measures and standards (no actual performance has yet been entered) for the police department in Dayton, Ohio. It is particularly good in showing how broader objectives (given in the first column) can be measured through several indicators (given in the second column). The last table represents a series of performance indicators for a recreation centers program for the city of Winston-Salem, North Carolina. The report is notable for the way it divides its indicators into measures of effectiveness, efficiency, and workload.

As noted, the Dayton objectives come from a report published before actual data had been gathered. But both the New York City and the Winston-Salem reports clearly show the standard for the time period covered, then show how well the city performed in meeting the standard. Such comparisons are the heart of all management systems; any variances between standards and actual performance can then be acted on by management.

Source: *The Mayor's Management Report* (New York: Citybooks, February 1988), 411–12; City of Dayton, *Annual Objectives, 1985*; City of Winston-Salem, *Annual Budget Program, 1986–87, Year-End Report,* 11 November 1987.

New York City human resources administration

Missions and indicators	FY 1987 annual actual	Annual plan	Fiscal year 1988 four-month plan	Four-month actual	FY 1989 preliminary plan
Agency-wide indicators					
Financial resources:					
Expenses (millions)	$ 4,801	$ 4,877	$ 695	$ 733	$ 5,152
Full-time employees	26,254	28,525	26,720	26,658	27,989
City-funded	24,360	26,534	24,785	24,801	26,166
Other	1,894	1,991	1,935	1,857	1,823
Full-time equivalent of part-time employees	41.0	41.0	DNA	12.5	DNA
Per diem employees	1,473	2,200	1,493	979	2,200
Total paid absence rate	4.52%	4.00%	4.00%	4.20%	4.00%
Sick leave	4.11%	3.63%	3.63%	3.75%	3.63%
Workers' compensation	0.41%	0.37%	0.37%	0.45%	0.37%
Cost of paid overtime (000)	$ 9,186	$ 8,354	$ 2,464	$ 2,561	$ 8,045
Major mission indicators					
Special services for children					
Full-time employees	4,205	4,618	4,284	4,148	4,582
Service complaints received	27	*	*	9	*
Complaints resolved	12	*	*	5	*
Resolved within 10 days (%)	0	100%	100%	0	100%
Abuse or neglect allegations:					
Cases	46,713	52,786	16,752	14,820	58,906
Children	76,536	86,486	27,863	24,865	96,617
Cases unfounded (%)	65%	60%	63%	64%	65%

continued

New York City human resources administration, cont.

Missions and indicators	FY 1987 annual actual	Annual plan	Fiscal year 1988 four-month plan	Four-month actual	FY 1989 preliminary plan
Cases acted on within one day following report to central register (%) (SCR)	94.0%	100.0%	100.0%	93.1%	100.0%
Cases acted on within one day following report to central register (%) (SSC Internal)	99.3%	100.0%	100.0%	99.2%	100.0%
New protective service cases opened (a)	16,817	21,114	6,366	5,335	20,617
Protective cases for which (recidivistic) reports of abuse and neglect are received	DNA	*	*	DNA	*
Percent for which reports are founded	DNA	*	*	DNA	*
New cases per worker per month	6.7	7.0	7.0	6.8	7.0
Article X petitions filed in family court	13,809	21,203	5,187	5,221	30,433
Average protective worker caseload	28.1	22.0	26.0	28.9	22.0
SSC field office preventive services cases (cumulative)	5,470	6,022	4,592	5,312	7,226
Contract preventive services cases (cumulative)	12,983	13,909	9,120	8,264	14,850
Contract preventive services cases referred by SSC (%)	29%	40%	32%	34%	40%
Children placed in foster care while receiving:					
Field office preventive services	329	*	*	36	*
Contract preventive services	572	*	*	40	*
Percent of preventive services caseload	4.9%	5.0%	*	0.4%	5.0%

CWRA requirements:					
Uniform case records completed on time (30-day, 90-day, and 6-month case reviews)	87%	100%	100%	76%	100%
Legal actions completed on time (%)	85%	100%	100%	88%	100%
Foster care:					
Children in foster care	18,245	21,130	18,918	18,998	by 3/88
Children discharged from foster care	DNA	DNA	DNA	DNA	DNA
Foster care bed gain (net)	1,942	5,280	1,629	1,210	by 3/88
Length of time to complete adoptions (years)	2.10	2.00	DNA	2.85	2.00
Children with goal of adoption adopted (%)	29.7%	31.1%	10.4%	6.8%	30.0%
Voluntary agency services:					
Adoptions	842	940	376	248	1,176
Adoptive placements completed within 27 months (%)	51%	65%	DNA	DNA	65%
Direct care services (by SSC):					
Adoptions	56	60	20	13	63
Adoptive placements completed within 27 months (%)	59%	65%	DNA	DNA	65%
Program assessment:					
Agency assessments completed	55	55	0	0	59
Agencies requiring administrative action	21	*	*	0	*
Contracts cancelled as a result of agency assessment	0	*	*	0	*

Note: DNA = Data not available.

1985 Departmental Objectives, Dayton, Ohio—Group: Community services　　　　　*Responsible agency: Department of Police*

Objectives	Performance criteria	Community objectives	Units	
			84 actual	85 estimated
* 1. To assist with overseeing the implementation phase of the communication dispatch system (CAD/MIS) for police and fire departments	1a. Date contract awarded	DH13		3/85
	b. Date renovation of signal building completed to house CAD system	DH14		12/85
	c. Date CADS is fully operational			6/86
* 2. To assist with the rewrite of CJIS	2a. Date specifications developed for CJIS rewrite	DH13		6/85
	b. Date CJIS system fully implemented			9/86
* 3. To develop a coordinated property matching system for the MIS that will result in increased recovery of stolen property in future years	3a. Date system designed	DH13		5/85
	b. Date records are entered into computer			7/86
	c. Date system fully implemented			9/86
4. To limit average response for priority 1 calls to 5–6 minutes and for all other calls to 11–12 minutes	4a. Average priority 1 call response time (minutes)	NV5		5 min.
	b. Average overall response time (minutes)			11 min.
* 5. To increase public awareness throughout the City of Dayton of the Abandoned Vehicle Program	5a. Date comprehensive news media release in 1985 explaining the Abandoned Vehicle Program	NV5		3/85
	b. Number of presentations made to neighborhoods on Abandoned Vehicle Program			14
* 6. To develop and implement a procedure policy with regard to pawn shops, junk yards, and second-hand dealers	6a. Date input solicited from pawn shops, junk yards, and second-hand dealers	NV5		3/85

Objective	Code	Value
b. Date draft for preliminary approval submitted to department director		6/85
c. Date new procedure fully implemented		10/85
*7. To implement a review model for criminal cases that are denied filing by the prosecutor's office	DH13	
7a. Date review panel established to determine if further investigation is needed		3/85
b. Dates quarterly reports of panel findings and recommendations submitted to department director		6/85 10/85 12/85
*8. To insure personal contact by investigation detectives on 90% of the complaints from Dayton citizens within 72 hours	NV5	
8a. Number of complaints received		0%
b. Percentage of complainants personally contacted within 72 hours		
c. Percentage of complainants personally contacted within 5 days		10%
9. To limit the number of residential burglaries to 1982 levels while decreasing the occurrence of residential burglaries by 4% in the highest residential burglary sector in each police district	NV5	
9a. Number of residential burglaries for 1982		5,759
b. Number of residential burglaries in 1985		
c. Percentage of reduction in each of the highest sectors		4%
10. To limit the number of commercial burglaries to 1980 levels while decreasing the occurrence of commercial burglaries by 4% in the highest commercial burglary sector in each police district	NV5	
10a. Number of commercial burglaries for 1982		
b. Number of commercial burglaries in 1985		
c. Percentage of reduction in each of the highest sectors		4%

*High-priority objectives.

Program Management Report, Winston-Salem, North Carolina—Program: Recreation centers

	Expected for year	Actual 1986–1987			Prior year		
		3rd qtr.	4th qtr.	Year-end total	3rd qtr.	4th qtr.	Year-end total
Effectiveness measures							
Percent of time cleanliness standards are maintained at all facilities	95%	96%	95%	96%	95%	95%	95%
Percent of program participants rating the cleanliness, safety, attractiveness, crowdedness, and accessibility as "satisfactory"	95%	92%	95%	94%	93%	94%	93%
Number of serious injuries (requiring medical attention) per 1,000 participants	.05	.02	.01	.03	.04	.01	.02
Percent of total attendance enrolled in supervised programs	65%	53%	47%	52%	50%	51%	49%
Percent of time service calls for minor maintenance of recreation centers are answered within 48 hours	95%	99%	96%	96%	91%	92%	91%
Attendance at structured programs	275,430	132,542	64,273	362,433			
Efficiency measure							
Cost per service call	$37.50	$39.50	$34.72	$35.08	$44.13	$36.48	$38.73
Workload indicators							
Number of service calls received	625	228	174	795	234	168	718

Highlights

- The program exceeded its goals for the percent of time all facilities meet cleanliness standards and the percent of time service calls are answered within 48 hours.
- Although the objective for the percent of total attendance enrolled in supervised programs was not achieved, there was a 3% increase over prior year, and actual attendance at structured programs exceeded expectation.
- The recreation centers program received a higher number of service calls during FY86–87. Many of the service calls were for minor maintenance-related tasks; therefore, the cost per service call was lower than expected.

together.) If we simply track what Bob Smith, a hard-working city street paver, does each day, we have useful *operational-level* information that will help first-level supervisors. But such information does not fit comfortably into a management system because the information is too detailed to be of any use to middle and higher managers; they have no need to know what a specific worker did on a specific day. It is only when we aggregate (combine) the information on the performance of the ten or twelve people working with Bob Smith, and total it for the month, that we now have information useful to middle management: "Unit C has paved two more miles than expected this month."

Performance monitoring systems use the same output categories year after year   Because they concentrate on continuing, routine, agency-wide processes, performance monitoring systems use the same measures year after year. This continuity is valuable because it allows year-to-year comparisons. MBO systems, on the other hand, often deal with the project-oriented tasks of middle and upper managers. Because a manager's priorities often shift, the outputs measured by MBO are likely to shift each year as well. For example, the director of a clinic may emphasize outreach measures in the first year's MBO goals that she negotiates with her subordinates. In the second year, after enough patients have been secured, she may emphasize cost control. And in the third year, under new pressures, she may emphasize measures of quality control. Meanwhile the performance monitoring system may continue, year after year, to measure routine items such as number of visits, number of return visits, and number of complaints.

MBO and performance monitoring systems are complementary, not competitive. Thus a transportation department may use a performance monitoring system to track the performance of its paving division. Each year the division's outputs will be tracked by the same continuous output measures, such as "miles paved" and "potholes filled." The same department may track the performance of an upper-level manager by a changing series of MBO output measures. One year these measures may emphasize repairing relations with the legislature, while the next year they may emphasize increasing organizational efficiency. Both systems measure organizational output; both are useful for their differing roles.

Choosing output indicators: Guidelines

Any complex government organization produces literally dozens of outputs. Out of all of these outputs, which should be tracked? This choice is more important for a performance monitoring system than for MBO. MBO is a project-oriented system, and therefore the objectives tend to be temporary; each year new projects or outputs are chosen as priorities shift. But a performance monitoring system's measures are used year after year to provide a long-range record of organizational performance, and so the initial choice of outputs to be measured commits the system for a number of years. Once the procedures for gathering, collating, and analyzing data are in place, any change in output indicators may involve great organizational disruption. Thus the choice must be made carefully.

When we speak of choosing outputs to track and measure, we are speaking of choosing particular performance indicators. A performance indicator is a numerical measure of some aspect of organizational performance. For a high school, "number of graduates" would be one possible performance indicator, as would "number of college scholarships earned." There are of course many others. Performance indicators are usually just called *indicators;* another synonym is *measures.*

Determining data needs before determining data availability   One of the most common mistakes made in designing an output monitoring system is to begin by surveying the data available and then using availability as the primary consideration in choosing which outputs to measure. This is the wrong order. Such a procedure is reminiscent of the anecdote about the pedestrian who late one night came across a man on his hands and knees, frantically searching for something under a lightpost. The pedestrian asked him what he was looking for. "My keys," replied the man, pointing. "I lost them over there in the bushes."

"If you lost them over there," asked the puzzled pedestrian, "then why are you looking for them way over here?"

"Because," said the man, "this is where the light is."

Data can be very illuminating, but an organization must make sure that they are in fact illuminating the area that the organization is most concerned about. An agency that tracks particular data primarily because they are available puts itself in the same position as the man who lost his keys. Agency decision makers should first sit down and determine what particular indicators would best measure what the organization accomplishes. In other words, what information would be most useful in making decisions? Only after deciding what data would be most useful should they consider whether such data are available. If the data on hand do not serve the purpose, new sources of data can be chosen by carefully balancing usefulness against the convenience of gathering. Beginning the choice of output indicators by surveying the available data subconsciously biases the process—

designers begin to think that the available data are the best, after all.

Avoiding too many (or too few) output measures   The more output measures that are used, the more likely the organization will be tracking a reasonable composite of its real activities, and the less tendency there will be for misreporting and goal displacement. But at the same time, the more measures that are tracked, the more unwieldy the management system becomes. Large numbers of indicators—some programs gather over 100—can obscure the handful of indicators that are really important for decision making and guiding behavior. Moreover, there are usually costs involved in gathering each new measure—costs in time, effort, and money. Therefore managers need to consider whether the value of an additional measure outweighs the costs of gathering and monitoring it.

In general, it is easier to track a large number of outputs for organizations whose work is highly routinized, highly unchanging, and very tangible. Thus far more outputs can be tracked for a sanitation department or a transportation department than for a police SWAT team or a planning department. For most programs, three indicators would be too few, twenty too many. But a more exact balance must be worked out for each agency on a case-by-case basis. During the last decade, administrators working in most types of government programs have helped develop a large and growing literature that suggests specific output indicators for each type of function.

Which outputs to monitor:
Analyzing through chains of outputs

Developing chains of output   The question of which outputs should be monitored can be analyzed through the concept of "chains" of organizational outputs. "Chains of outputs" is a simple concept.[2] All programs have a number of effects—some immediate and produced directly, others delayed and produced by ripple effects. A *chain of outputs* is simply a diagram of the expected outputs for one program; it begins with the most immediate, localized effects and proceeds, step by step, to the broader societal impacts.

The easiest way to develop an output chain is to begin with the most immediate and obvious output and to ask, "Why do we want this output?" then to take the resulting answer, and ask the question again. This process can be repeated until a natural stopping point is reached.

For example, for an antiflu program administered by a public clinic, the most immediate and obvious output may be "number of patients treated." Depending on the definition of "treatment," this indicator falls right on the edge between an output and a process measure. As we have discussed and will further discuss, it is always better to focus on outputs—effects on people outside the organization—rather than on internal processes or activities. However, sometimes the two blend along the edges. One of the advantages of the chain is that it is unaffected by these close calls between "activities" and "immediate outputs." If we accidentally begin with a process measure, building a chain will shortly bring us to true outputs.

The next link of the chain is produced by asking, "Why did we wish to treat a large number of patients?" and taking the most immediate answer: "To inoculate them." This reply establishes the next link, "number of patients inoculated."

But why inoculate them? "To produce fewer cases of flu." But why do we wish fewer cases of flu? "Fewer flu cases" is not a free-standing good; for example, it would be a useless measure if the treatment cured flu but caused a worse disease. The answer is "to improve life expectancy and reduce sick days." Why? The chain may go a bit longer, but eventually a final, "ultimate" output such as "greater happiness for all" is likely to be the ending point. Such final outputs can be left for philosophers, not managers; but the immediate and intermediate outputs that lead to them are very useful. Different observers will produce slightly different chains for the same programs—somewhat shorter or longer, a few different links—but the basic pattern will remain very similar. The chain for the health clinic is shown in Exhibit 2, with chains for other programs. For reasons of space, some plausible links have been omitted to shorten the chains.

A note here about terminology: We will use the terms *immediate outputs,* which produce *intermediate outputs,* which produce *ultimate outputs.* According to some dictionary definitions, the word *ultimate* indicates one single final point, but the term can also be used to mean "fundamental" (or sometimes, loosely, "near the end"). We'll employ the latter, broader definitions, so that we can have more than one "ultimate output." That is, the term will designate the last few outputs in the chain.

Some authors prefer different terminology. They define *outputs* much more narrowly, as only the immediate effects of a program. In their terminology, *outputs* lead to *impacts* (similar to our *intermediate outputs*). Impacts, in turn, lead to *outcomes* (our *ultimate outputs*). Either set of terms is serviceable, but of course *outputs, impacts,* and *outcomes* blend into each other, and therefore it is often impossible to be certain whether a particular effect is an impact or an outcome. One advantage of our terminology is that its terms (*immediate, intermediate,* and *ultimate*) emphasize

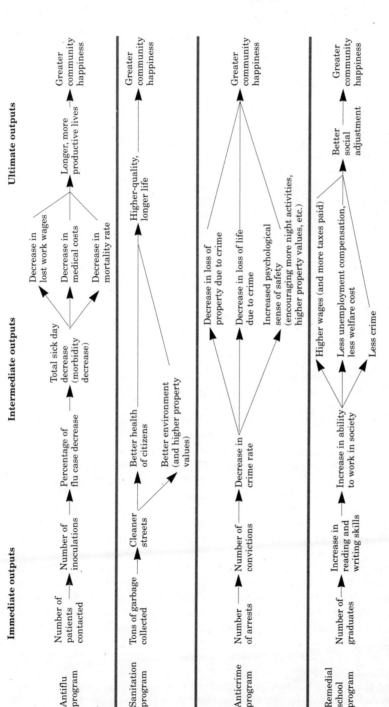

Exhibit 2. Illustrative chains of output.

the blend, indicating that there are no clear, sharp dividing lines between the categories.

Moving down the chain: Advantages and disadvantages

There are two truisms about the chain of outputs for any program. First, the initial outputs, the ones listed to the left of any chain, are the easiest to measure because they are the most tangible and most immediate results. Management systems require frequent, often month-to-month, measurements; accordingly, such systems often focus on the easy-to-measure outputs to the left. This is particularly true of performance monitoring systems, which have very frequent reporting periods.

Unfortunately, the second truism about chains is: The initial links are also the ones most susceptible to goal displacement. For example, it is relatively easy for workers in a school program to increase the "number of students graduated" if that is the output measured. However, this increase may not affect a link further down the chain, such as "increased student skills in reading and writing."

As we move further down the chain, to the right, we come closer to our "real" desired outputs. But these intermediate and ultimate outputs are harder to measure (especially routinely), and they are often affected by factors outside our program. Thus "higher wages" is further down the chain for the remedial school program in Exhibit 2, but it is difficult to measure, and many nonprogram factors (such as an improving economy) may have affected it.

Proxy (surrogate) measures   Where does this discussion leave us? Of course it is impossible to stop every month to determine increases in intermediate and ultimate outputs such as a school program's increase in reading and writing skills. However it is important for top managers to realize that their immediate output measures such as "number of patients inoculated" or "number of students graduated" are meaningless in themselves. They are simply *proxies* or *surrogates* for the desired intermediate and ultimate outputs. A proxy is a measure that acts as a stand-in for the actual output that we wish to measure. When we use such surrogate indicators, we are making the assumption that the links in the chain will not break and that increases in early measures will lead to increases in the desired ultimate outputs.

Most indicators used in management systems are to some extent surrogates or proxies because it is often so difficult to measure the desired ultimate outputs. In fact, because many ultimate outputs are long-range effects, they may not be clear for a decade

or more. Often, then, we use measures of immediate and intermediate outputs as proxies for the ultimate outputs that we cannot
currently measure. In and of themselves, proxies are necessary
and useful; but the manager must always remember that they are
in fact stand-ins.

Recap: Processes vs. outputs   Process (also called activity)
measures are sometimes confused with output measures, but
they are quite different. Process measures register what goes on
inside an organization. Thus they might include such categories
as number of students taught, forms processed, or miles traveled.

An output measure, on the other hand, reflects the *product* of
an organization. In other words, an output measure registers an
effect or change on people who do not work for the organization.
Diseases prevented, lives saved, skills learned, fires extinguished, and criminals arrested are all output categories. Because outputs represent the reason the organization exists, they
are far more important than process measures.

As with all distinctions, there are some grey areas in real life.
At the very edge, some process measures begin to blend into the
measures of very immediate outputs. But most often, the distinc-
tion between the two is easy to make. We simply need to ask of
any indicator, "Is this an indicator of something going on inside
the organization (a process measure); or is it an indicator of effects on outsiders (an output measure)?"

**An extreme example of proxy indicators: Workload indica-
tors**   Most managers would like to emphasize measures of ultimate output, but they often employ measures of immediate and
intermediate outputs as surrogates. Sometimes, however, managers push the use of proxy measurements one step further. They
abandon outputs altogether and begin using indicators of internal organizational processes as proxy measures. These process-
based proxies are often called *workload indicators*. For a police
department, for example, process indicators might include measures of witnesses interviewed, miles patrolled, and forms completed. None of these items shows the department's effect on
outsiders; therefore none of them clearly indicates whether the
department is doing a good job. For that, we need output indicators such as arrests made, convictions secured, and crime rates.

Workload indicators are an extreme example of proxies because process indicators are very far removed from the desired
output—so far removed that we should be suspicious of whether
they have much to do with increasing the output at all. For example, this year an agricultural extension agent may travel more
miles in visiting farmers and process more forms, and thus his

workload indicators have risen. Yet the agent may well not have helped the farmers one bit more. It is often necessary to keep track of processes for reasons of internal management, but treating such workload indicators as output surrogates is generally risky and undesirable.

One final example: Some school programs claim excellence because of a low student-teacher ratio. However, this is simply a workload indicator. School officials are assuming a chain of outputs that leads from a low ratio to more individual attention to pupils, which in turn leads to better learning. But do the links of this chain actually hold? Some educational research indicates that student-teacher ratios, contrary to common assumptions, do not seem to lead directly to these other outputs. Therefore school officials would do well to keep looking further down the chain to find what the low student-teacher ratio is actually producing as an output.

Managers usually can find measures that are both accessible and yet well down the chain of outputs simply on a commonsense basis. But one way to strengthen and reinforce this process is to tie the management system to program evaluation.

Output chains, efficiency, and effectiveness   The concepts of efficiency and effectiveness are easily related to chains of output. Efficiency asks, "Did we perform the job without wasting resources?"; effectiveness asks, "Did the job achieve the desired result?"

Let us begin by considering the chain of outputs for a fire-fighting unit. With some links omitted, the chain might look roughly like this: number of alarms answered—number of fires fought—number of fires extinguished within a certain time—amount of property saved and number of lives saved—greater community peace of mind about fire—happier lives overall.

Because efficiency focuses on waste, it is usually measured by dividing immediate outputs by input (cost). For a fire-fighting unit, an efficiency measure would probably be based on an immediate output indicator like "number of fires fought"; this indicator would produce the efficiency measure "cost per fire fought." Thus efficiency focuses on outputs that are in the early part of the chain. (Sometimes efficiency measures are even less ambitious. They are occasionally based on dividing a process measure by cost, which, of course, makes them a type of workload indicator.)

Effectiveness focuses on the last part of the chain because it is a measure of whether a program has achieved its desired results (i.e., intermediate and ultimate outputs). One effectiveness measure of the same fire-fighting unit might be "reduction in number for lives lost in fires."

Attempting to measure final outputs: The use of surveys
As we have discussed at length, it is very difficult to measure the long-range (effectiveness) outputs that lie near the end of the output chain. Program analysts have recently begun to use citizen surveys experimentally to measure such long-range outputs. The analysts have recognized that near the end of almost all output chains for public organizations, there could be a link entitled "increased public satisfaction with this program." Therefore program evaluators have attempted to survey citizens' or clients' opinions on program effectiveness and then to see how well the opinions reflected more objective indicators of effectiveness.

The results are mixed. Sometimes the survey results seem to mirror actual agency performance; at other times they do not seem to correlate with other, more "objective" indicators. Surveys are particularly untrustworthy if the public rarely has direct dealings with the agency. For example, most citizens who have not recently been victims of crime are unlikely to be able to make precise judgments about how well the police are performing. Yet asking only those who have recently been victimized is likely to produce a biased sample, too. Understandably, the victims may feel that police protection is inadequate, even though the number of crimes is actually down. Surveys also can be distorted by low public awareness of an agency or an overreaction to a single isolated incident that may have received publicity.

It is just because surveys are such an attractive feedback device that their shortcomings have been emphasized here. But these pitfalls should not obscure the many advantages of using surveys: If we wish to know how well an organization is working, why not ask its "customers"? The analogy to private sector feedback is strong and inviting. Surveys can be especially useful when they question people who *directly* and *frequently* interact with the government program. Thus people leaving a post office can be polled on how long they had to wait and how courteously they were treated. Similarly, patrons of a public golf course, patients treated in a public clinic, and home owners who receive municipal garbage pickup are all likely candidates for a meaningful survey.

In sum, then, surveys can sometimes be very useful as *one* measure of organizational output. Although their use in the public sector has been increasing rapidly, they should still be used much more than they are. Nonetheless, survey results are often flawed or incomplete, and so they cannot stand alone as total, all-encompassing measures of agency performance.

The importance of chains   The entire concept of chains of outputs suggests a rather abstract, other-worldly approach to the

A few key considerations in citizen surveys

A number of aspects of government service performance are nearly impossible to measure without obtaining direct feedback from the agency's customers. Surveys can provide *customer ratings* of various service characteristics. They can indicate the views and perceptions of citizens on such matters as security from crime, accessibility of particular services, timeliness of government actions, and the responsiveness of government employees to citizen requests and complaints.

Mode of administration   To achieve acceptable response rates, certain modes of administration are better than others. Some recommendations are as follows:

- For household surveys, telephone interviews are likely to be needed, especially if the survey covers multiple services. In such cases, the questionnaire length will probably preclude mail surveying.
- For regular user surveys, mail surveys probably can be used, as long as multiple mailings or telephone reminders are used. Customers of a particular service are more likely to return a mailed survey about that service than the general population receiving a household survey.
- Local governments should seek at least a 50 percent response rate in surveys (thus achieving a response from a majority of those from whom the survey seeks responses).
- For services with substantial numbers of non–English-speaking customers, the questionnaires should be translated into the principal foreign languages.

Pretest the questionnaire   Before conducting the survey, each local government should have its questions pretested to check for possible bias and to ascertain local citizens' interpretation of the wording. The pretesting should screen out: long, awkwardly worded, or ambiguous questions; local language usage that requires a special choice of words; confusing or incorrect instructions to interviewers regarding "skip" patterns; redundant questions; wording that may offend or sound foolish to respondents; illogical or awkward sequence of questions; and difficulties encountered by interviewers in recording responses.

Size of sample   The size of the sample affects both the accuracy of the survey findings and survey costs. With properly drawn samples of about 400, for example, the percentages obtained should be within plus or minus five percentage points with a probability of about 95 percent. If a probability of 90 percent is acceptable (as it should be for most government purposes), then a sample size closer to 300 is adequate. However, local governments should identify the responses of various segments of their populations and not just measure aggregate responses. In general, public agencies should seek sample sizes of about 100 for each such segment. For example, if a jurisdiction has six geographical neighborhoods from which the government wants data, total sample size should be about 600.

Costs of surveys   Costs for telephone surveys contracted to professional survey firms are likely to be approximately $15 to $20 per interview. The annual out-of-pocket outlay for contracted telephone surveys, thus, is likely to range from approximately $9,000 to $12,000 for a sample of 600 households. For repetitive surveys, the costs could be as low as $10 per interview.

These figures cover pretesting, final questionnaire preparation and printing, interviewing, editing, card punching, and basic summary tabulations. Not included are such tasks as developing the initial set of topics for the questionnaire, the time of central staff or operating agency personnel, any special effort to develop the list of the population from which the sample is drawn, or any in-depth analysis of survey results. Local government personnel will need to work for many days to determine questionnaire topics and wording. Computer software is widely available for processing questionnaire data, but some special modifications may be needed for each individual survey application.

Small local governments can reduce their costs by using smaller samples and by seeking volunteer help from local professional or volunteer organizations or from local colleges and universities for such activities as telephone interviewing. A problem here is the undependability of free help and the need to train new volunteers each time the survey is administered.

Mail surveys such as those used for user surveys probably can be conducted for under $5 per person surveyed. Clerical help will be needed to undertake the various mailings, to keep track of responses, and for data entry.

Source: Excerpted from Harry P. Hatry, Louis H. Blair, Donald M. Fisk, John M. Greiner, John R. Hall, Jr., and Philip S. Schaenman, *How Effective Are Your Community Services? Procedures for Measuring Their Quality,* 2d ed. (Washington, DC: The Urban Institute and ICMA, 1992), 173–84.

nitty-gritty problems of measuring organizational performance. However this impression is misleading; the concept has some very real and practical uses in designing and analyzing management systems. Before taking any action on their management systems, managers should develop a chain for each of their programs. (Thus an agency with four programs would have at least four separate chains.)

Such an exercise has a number of beneficial results. For example, it forces managers to think through what they really want to measure and how measurable it is; this moves them away from the temptation to choose indicators on the basis of availability. Developing a chain before designing a management system also alerts managers to likely displacement problems (the

---

Examples of outcome questions for client surveys

Listed below are examples of topics that service or facility users are often asked about on client surveys.

- Frequency of attendance at or usage of a facility or program
- Helpfulness of the service
- Cleanliness
- Physical attractiveness of the facility or area
- Safety conditions (and feeling of security)
- Accessibility/convenience of the service
- Adequacy of hours of operation of the service
- Condition of equipment or facilities
- Crowdedness
- Waiting times or delays for service
- Satisfactoriness of registration procedures
- Availability of specific types of programs
- Program enjoyability
- Satisfaction with program content
- New skills or other information learned
- Effect of program or participation on the individual—positive feelings about oneself, money saved because of program, changes made in personal behavior due to program, etc.
- Skills of program staff
- Staff courtesy and attitude
- Reasonableness of fees and charges required
- Adequacy of information/publicity provided
- Overall satisfaction with the program or facility

Source: Harry P. Hatry, John M. Greiner, and Maria Swanson, "Monitoring the Quality of Local Government Services," *Management Information Services Report* 19, no. 2 (February 1987): 9.

further left an indicator is, the more prone to displacement) and to measurability problems (the further right, the more difficulty in measurement). It alerts them to difficulties with environmental impacts on the indicator (the further right, the more outsiders can affect it) and helps them balance the system (the measurements should include at least some indicators toward the right). (These considerations are summarized in Exhibit 3.) Managers wishing to tie their management systems to budget systems—particularly program budgets—will find that these systems are based on an implicit chain of outputs. . . . It is almost impossible to understand clearly what the output indicators for a program are telling the manager without displaying them as a chain.

Indicator choice and measurement theory

Reliability, validity, and output measures   Our discussion of measures can be connected to the concepts of measurement theory. No measurement is totally error free, whether it is a measurement we make in the physical sciences, in management, or in everyday life. For example, even if our weight did not change,

Exhibit 3. Developing a chain of outputs.

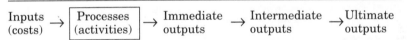

Inputs (costs) → Processes (activities) → Immediate outputs → Intermediate outputs → Ultimate outputs

Processes
Advantages in tracking: Extremely easy to measure (called workload measures)
Disadvantages in tracking: Little relationship to desired outputs

Immediate outputs
Advantages in tracking: Relatively easy to measure
                         Affected little by nonprogram forces and events
Disadvantages in tracking: Only moderate relationship to desired outputs, so prone to displacement

Intermediate outputs
Advantages and disadvantages in tracking: Midway between immediate and ultimate outputs

Ultimate outputs
Advantages: Represent desired outputs, so little displacement
Disadvantages: Because they are long-range and diffuse: difficult to measure, especially on a frequent basis; often affected by nonprogram forces and events

we would probably get some small variations in the result if we weighed ourselves many days in a row. But if error is inevitable, we nonetheless wish to recognize and minimize it to the extent possible. The two most important ways of categorizing and analyzing the errors associated with our measures are *reliability* and *validity*.

Reliability reflects replicability—whether the same results will be secured on repeated observations. If our scale in the preceding example continually showed the same weight, we would call the measure reliable. Reliability indicates that the differences shown by a measurement are actual differences and not illusory differences due to the measurement itself.

Validity, as the name suggests, is a determination of whether an indicator truly measures the concept it is intended to measure. A measure can be reliable but not valid. If our scales are consistently registering our weight as 20 pounds too heavy, we may constantly get the same number for our weight (reliability); but the measure is not valid (it does not reflect our true weight).

Thus useful measures must first of all be reasonably reliable; they are useless if they move around wildly because of random error in the measurement process itself. Once we have reliable measures, we next need to assure ourselves of their validity—are they truly reflecting what we really wish to measure? Only measures that are both reasonably reliable and reasonably valid will provide useful information.

We say "reasonably" reliable and valid because, as already noted, some error is unavoidable. The objective is to minimize the error, not eliminate it. Toward this end, it is often useful to employ multiple measurements, a process sometimes termed *triangulation*. As one measurement text notes, "Underlying the need for triangulation is the premise that any single measure carries with it its own characteristic sources of error. . . . [Accordingly] errors of reliability and validity are reduced through using multiple and overlapping measurement strategies."[3]

Our discussion of the chain of outputs can be recast in terms of reliability and validity. We can look at the validity of immediate output indicators (proxies) by judging whether they accurately reflect our primary organizational goals—the intermediate and ultimate outputs further down the chain. When we speak of the links in the chain holding, we are speaking of validity—that the immediate measures are accurately informing us about the intermediate and ultimate measures. Thus for a police department management system, the immediate output measure "number of arrests" is a valid measure of the ultimate output measure "public safety increase," if an increase in arrests leads to an increase in public safety. We want each of our proxies to be a reliable and valid measure of the intermediate and ultimate outputs that lie further down the chain.

Are the *immediate* output measures used by most public management systems likely to be both reliable and valid proxies? They are likely to be reliable because categories early in the chain of output are usually quite concrete—number of fires fought, number of students graduated, number of people arrested. Because they are so concrete, they raise few problems of reliability; most fair-minded observers would probably count the same number of fires fought or students graduated. The results can be easily replicated. But items early in the chain have greater problems with validity. As long as we assume that what we "really" want is the ultimate output—safer lives from the police system, more productive citizens from the school system—the early items may sometimes be weak in validity.

Further down the chain, validity is less of a concern. However, because the desired outputs are so global—safer streets, greater productivity—operationalization problems and thus potential measurement error become much greater. Also, these outputs are often long range and thus often difficult to measure on a month-to-month basis. To the extent that we trust our measurements, intermediate and ultimate output indicators have greater face validity. The measurement problems are daunting, however, which again reinforces the point: Management systems need some measures drawn from the early part of the output chain and some drawn from later parts of the chain.

Employing a broad perspective on indicator choice   Any indicators chosen for a management system must be reliable and valid measures of what they purport to measure. But at the same time, managers need to take a very broad perspective because the choice of indicators often also carries additional *psychological* and *political* ramifications for the organization.

Indicators in management systems are not chosen simply to measure current performance; they are also carefully chosen to affect behavior. They thus serve a dual role of (current) measurement and (future) incentive. Tracking (and thus emphasizing) a particular indicator that carries symbolic import to organizational members may well change employee behavior and morale.

For most forms of scientific and social scientific measurement, the analyst is unhappy if the measurement process itself changes what it is supposed to measure. In contrast, such effects are deliberately sought when performance indicators are chosen. Thus managers must at least intuitively consider psychological effects when deciding the number and type of measures to be employed.

A second reason for employing a broad perspective is that some indicators also carry political implications. For example, many studies have indicated that an increase in the indicator "hours patrolled" by the police does not usually lead to an increase in the ultimate output of a "safer community." (Patrol presence has surprisingly little effect on crime.) Nonetheless citizens may demand frequent, visible police patrols in their neighborhoods. Thus the indicator "hours patrolled," although not a valid measure of "increased safety," should probably still be kept for political reasons.

The vast majority of proxy indicators do not have such political overtones, of course, and thus agencies should drop them if they do not lead to ultimate outputs. But public sector managers must remain aware that, occasionally, an indicator that does not validly measure the organization's professed ultimate output may nonetheless be useful because of its political importance. In sum, managers must utilize performance indicators that are reliable and valid. However, the fact that people's psychological and political values play such a central role in public management means that the manager must also be sensitive to these concerns in choosing particular indicators.

Setting objectives for performance monitoring systems

We have considered some ways of choosing which indicators the performance monitoring system will track. But once particular indicators (e.g., reduction in number of flu cases) are chosen, we are not done. We still need objectives or standards for those indicators (e.g., *how much* of a reduction in the number of flu cases?). Performance monitoring systems, by definition, do not use MBO-type negotiations to set standards for each output category. However, as with all management systems, standards are necessary because output data are meaningless without a yardstick (standard) for comparison.

There are four ways to set objectives or standards in *any* management system. We will begin by briefly recapping the use of MBO-type negotiations; we will then examine the other three means of standard setting employed by most performance monitoring systems.

Standard setting by negotiation   Negotiations between subordinates and superiors are the best way of setting objectives, for a variety of reasons, including greater commitment to goals and greater exchange of information. Even many hybrid performance monitoring systems use this approach. Of course, if a performance monitoring system is tracking twenty-five outputs, it would be too time-consuming to negotiate standards for each one. Many of these standards can be derived by past performance or engineered standards, as will be discussed later. But if twenty-five outputs are being monitored, only a handful are really important in evaluating units and making management decisions, and these important objectives should preferably be set through a joint superior-subordinate effort. Both sides in this negotiation will want to consider the past performance data and standard time data in setting goals, but other intangible aspects will also be reflected in their final agreement.

Standard setting based on past performance   Many organizations report current output data side by side with last year's or last quarter's output figures. In such cases, past performance is implicitly used as the standard. Sometimes, in a slight variation, an organization may set as its objective "last year's output plus 5 percent." Productivity systems use base years for comparison. Thus productivity systems implicitly use past performance as the output standard.

Past performance information is useful, but it should not be used by itself as a valid standard for current output. Some organizations may have performed so badly in the past that even if this year's performance is 20 percent better, it is still poor. Other organizations may have performed so well in previous years that simply equalling the previous year's output is a high achievement. As these examples indicate, past performance figures do not really indicate how efficiently the organization is performing. They should be considered in setting standards, but they should not stand alone.

Standard setting based on superior-assigned quotas   Sometimes the top manager simply assigns a performance target to each unit. There are problems with this approach: Agency workers do not feel committed to standards that they took no part in setting, and valuable information is lost without the give and take of negotiation. Nonetheless quotas are listed here because they are (unfortunately) often used in standard setting for performance monitoring systems.

Standard setting based on engineered standards (standard times)   Especially for routinized tasks such as street cleaning or garbage collection, many governments turn to traditional industrial engineering to help them set reasonable output standards. Standards set by any of this large group of techniques are sometimes termed *engineered standards*.

The basis of engineered standards is the concept of standard times. A *standard time* is the amount of time it should take to complete a particular task. Time standards can be set in a number of ways. Let us begin with the most famous: time and motion studies, which have most often been used with factory workers. Each action of the workers is broken into smaller motions, assigned a time (say, .5 seconds) and then added together to get a standard time for the whole procedure. Although they are famous (or infamous), time and motion studies are essentially irrelevant to public sector needs.

However, there are ways of deriving standard times that do have some application in the public sector; the most common is called *currently derived standard times*. Under this approach, a number of experienced workers are gathered and timed while they work through one unit of output, such as one client interviewed, one stoplight installed, or one application completed. The average time of these experienced, well-trained workers becomes the standard time for that output or procedure.

Uses of standard times   Standard times are generally used to compare our performance in the current year to what it "should" be. For example, if we know that we "should" pick up one ton of garbage every two hours, because our standard time has established that level, and we instead average one ton every three hours, the variance between the standard and actual performance suggests that we first investigate and then take remedial steps.

An organization can use individualized standard times to set objectives for larger organizational processes. If the standard times indicate that six clients can be processed by one worker in an hour, an agency with ten workers can easily set its agency-wide output standard for clients processed per hour (10×6). The resulting output goals—sixty clients processed per hour or one hundred tax forms reviewed per week—are sometimes called *work standards*. It is simply a matter of arithmetic to use standard times to establish monthly or quarterly standards for all sorts of agency-wide processes and outputs. The manager then knows that if output falls far below these standards, the organization is not performing at peak efficiency. As the name suggests, standard times set up a goal or yardstick by which performance can be evaluated.

Distortions of standard times   Many public agencies say they use standard times when in fact their standard times have been established in a distorted manner. The most common error is the use of *average* times for the whole organization. For example, if a form-processing organization wished to determine a standard time for completing its forms, it would take the number of forms that had been completed for the week, divide by the number of employee hours that had been worked that week, and call the result a "standard" time. The problem is that an average time is not an accurate standard time. If, for example, most of the work force had been recently hired when the measurement was made, the average-based "standard time" would embody all that inexperience. The same is true if the work force is less educated or less motivated than that of years past.

Standard times are accurate only if they are based on the measurement of well-trained, experienced workers. Simply taking an average of all workers means that standard times will shift as employee characteristics shift. This will result in a rubber yardstick—an unreliable measure that stretches and shrinks depending on how well the work force is doing instead of how difficult the work is. Managers can never be sure what they are measuring when they use average times.

Objections to standard times   Many public employee labor unions have long opposed standard times that are not based on average times. Clearly if average times are the only available standards, public managers must use them. Although they are better than no standards at all, they are a very poor second indeed. Standard times are controversial with other actors as well; in fact they comprise one of the touchiest areas of public administration. Even the advocates of standard times are made uneasy by their occasional misuse and misinterpretation.

The concept of standard times connotes the image of Taylorism. Working at the beginning of this century, Frederick Taylor helped establish the study of administration.[4] He has a not totally deserved popular reputation as someone who viewed workers as machines and who cared only about their efficiency without being interested in their psychological or sociological well-being. Today managerial theorists understand that nontangible psychological and sociological factors are the most important determinants of workers' performances. Yet for many people the entire concept of work measurement carries at least the faint scent of Taylorism—of standing over workers with a stopwatch.

Even those most committed to standard time measurements must not overemphasize their importance. Such measurements are only one component of a performance monitoring system, which in turn is only one measure of employee and organizational performance. However, if used correctly, standard times provide managers with information that is available in no other way.

Combining standard-setting techniques   We have considered the four major ways of setting standards for all management systems: negotiations, quotas, past performance, and engineered standards. As noted, the use of quotas (goals set unilaterally by the superior, based simply on personal estimation) is undesirable, though common. Each of the other three techniques is useful in its own sphere. More important, however, the three techniques also complement each other. For example, a manager who wishes to use past performance as the standard will feel far more comfortable if he or she knows that a unit's past performance ranked high when measured by standard times. Similarly, when standards are set by negotiation, both superior and subordinate must come to the standard-setting meeting with some idea of their preferred goal or standard. Their knowledge of past performance and (if available) of engineered standards will help both sides of the negotiation to decide what is "reasonable."

Current patterns of performance monitoring system use

As previously noted, 67 percent of all American cities use performance monitoring systems, a substantial increase since the early 1980s. A 1985 survey indicates that the municipal functions most often covered by such systems are police, fire, solid waste, public transit, health and hospitals, and social services.[5] More than 90 percent of the respondents felt that such systems were either "very" or "somewhat" effective. Surveys have also indicated that most of the cities using performance monitoring systems use MBO as well, and it is to a final comparison of these two systems that we now turn.

The political uses of performance monitoring systems

Politics is "who gets what." Therefore management systems have "political" effects because some groups win and others lose with each new, system-based decision. Even seemingly neutral goals such as "efficiency" have political implications. For example, when efficiency is increased by replacing meter readers with computerized, automatic meter-reading machines, some societal groups (such as middle-class taxpayers) gain, while other groups (such as low-skilled workers who might have held the jobs or aspired to them) lose.

Often the political thrust of a management system is more direct. Two short examples of the political understructure of performance monitoring system choices are provided by the Nixon AFDC drive and the North Carolina state trooper performance ratings.

The Nixon management systems and AFDC   The Nixon administration came to office on a pledge of cleaning up the waste in the Great Society programs that it inherited. One of the major programs targeted in the resulting efficiency drive was the main federal welfare program—Aid to Families with Dependent Children (AFDC). AFDC was financed in large part by the federal government but administered by the states. Its performance levels were tracked by a Nixon administration management system that followed two major categories: (1) overpayments and (2) ineligible recipients receiving aid. Standards for the two categories were set at 5 percent for overpayments and 3 percent for ineligible recipients, and states that exceeded these levels were threatened with a cutoff of funds.

Over a period of time the drive in fact lowered the error rates in these two categories considerably (although not, for most states, below the standards). This effort was applauded by a wide spectrum of the U.S. public, including many who were sympathetic to the poor, because "efficiency" is a much-respected, seemingly neutral goal.

In fact, however, the monitored categories were clear attempts to direct workers' behavior in specific political directions that had little to do with efficiency. Overpayments were sanctioned, but not underpayments. Moreover, the system focused on ineligible applicants who received payments, but it did not monitor the opposite problem, eligible applicants who were denied their rightful benefits. The management system therefore provided strong incentives for erring in these unmeasured categories. A local social services department worker with an ambiguous application now had an incentive to deny benefits. If the applicant was actually entitled to benefits, the mistake was nowhere tracked or sanctioned. On the other hand, if the applicant was admitted to the AFDC rolls and later proved ineligible, the mistake was recorded and punished. The choice of outputs monitored by the Nixon administration under the guise of neutral "efficiency" were in fact strong incentives to err on the side of underpayment and denial of benefits to the eligible.[6]

State trooper performance ratings   In 1981 a North Carolina newspaper revealed that the new state trooper performance ratings contained thirteen monitored categories, one of which was "number of tickets written." Legislators and their constituents raised a large cry, protesting that such a category constituted a quota. Speeding drivers began to complain that the only reason they received a speeding ticket was because the trooper had to meet a quota. The head of the Department of Crime Control and Public Safety defended his new performance measurement system, emphasizing that the ticket category was only one of thirteen. Such information was valuable, he said, but it would not greatly affect workers' behavior.[7]

Nonetheless, the state legislature showed a rare interest in management systems. It passed a law that said that not only could there be no quota but also that the state patrol could not even *consider* the volume of citations written when making decisions on promotions or granting merit pay increases. In response to the law, and over the objections of the department head, the category was discontinued. Months later, figures were released showing that at the time the new category of "tickets written" was added to the performance evaluation system, the number of tickets written increased by 45 percent.[8]

As illustrated by these two examples, management systems necessarily involve politics—who gets what. No matter what outputs are affected by a system, some people will gain while others lose. This result is both inevitable and, if handled correctly, desirable. But to handle it correctly, managers must realize these political effects; they should not be lulled into believing that management systems, by emphasizing efficiency, are therefore apolitical and "neutral." All government actions (whether based on systems or not) involve choices; designers and users of management systems need only recognize this, and proceed to make their choices on considered and defensible grounds.

Summary

All output-oriented management systems that are not MBO systems can be called performance monitoring systems. Such systems generally focus on units rather than individual managers and on routine, continuing tasks rather than on one-time projects. Because of these characteristics, they are often most valuable for dealing with the lower levels of organization, whereas middle managers and staff people are more often covered by MBO.

Valid output measures are often difficult to establish for performance monitoring systems. As with MBO, goal displacement and misreporting are also troublesome. Output indicators are more likely to be valid if they are multiple, chosen on grounds other than data accessibility, and if they register both immediate and long-range impacts. This final balance is made easier by the concept of a chain of outputs, which indicates the expected links between immediate actions and outputs and desired long-range impacts. To maintain the focus on results, the manager must constantly strive to adopt some indicators that are well down the chain of outputs.

Once the outputs to be measured have been determined, the manager must also determine how much of the output he or she expects—in other words, a standard. There are four principal ways of setting standards: negotiations (the basis of MBO), past performance, unilateral quotas (undesirable but common), and engineered standards. Engineered standards are usually based on a "standard time," which is the amount of time it "should" take an employee to complete a task. Often more than one of these four techniques is used in determining a standard.

These and other system choices almost inevitably have political effects. That is, some people inside or outside the organization fare better or worse than they would without the system. Users and designers of systems must acknowledge these effects, rather than hiding behind claims of neutrality, because no possible choice (including the choice of having no system) can be truly neutral.

Ultimately, a performance monitoring system can be judged by whether it provides the data that managers find most useful in deciding the hardest, most important, recurring questions, and also by whether it motivates employees to act in ways desired by managers and the public.

1. Gregory Streib and Theodore H. Poister, "Established and Emerging Management Tools: A 12-Year Perspective," *The Municipal Year Book 1989* (Washington, DC: International City Management Association, 1989), pp. 45–54.
2. The concept is discussed in Edward A. Suchman, *Evaluative Research* (New York: Russell Sage Foundation, 1967), pp. 51–73. A very useful and practical exposition is Michael Quinn Patton, *Utilization-Focused Evaluation* (Beverly Hills, CA: Sage Publications, 1978), pp. 179–198.
3. Allen D. Putt and J. Fred Springer, *Policy Research: Concepts, Methods and Applications* (Englewood Cliffs, NJ: Prentice-Hall, 1989), p. 135. I have transposed two sentences here, but without changing the authors' meaning.
4. Frederick W. Taylor, *The Principles of Scientific Management* (New York: Harper & Row, 1911).
5. These and the following survey figures are drawn from Streib and Poister, "Established and Emerging Management Tools." The 67 percent of cities that report such systems undoubtedly include at least a few cities that claim systems (be-

cause they know they "should" have them) even though their systems are fragmentary or little used. Still, there are a number of fine municipal systems. Another article cites notable performance monitoring systems in Charlotte, Cincinnati, Dayton, Dallas, San Diego, New York City, and Phoenix—and of course there are many more. "Cincinnati Measures Service Success," *Public Administration Times,* April 1, 1985, p. 4.
6. Ronald Randall, "Presidential Power Versus Bureaucratic Intransigence: The Influence of the Nixon Administration on Welfare Policy," *American Political Science Review* 73 (1979), 798–800. The process was paralleled by developments in California under Governor Reagan. It is discussed in John Mendeloff, "Welfare Procedures and Error Rates: An Alternative Perspective," *Policy Analysis* (Summer 1977) 3, no. 3, 257–74.
7. William M. Welch, "Ban on Quotas Seen Creating Review Trouble," *Raleigh News and Observer,* May 24, 1981, p. 33.
8. Pat Stith, "Tickets Up 45% Under Evaluation Plan," *Raleigh News and Observer,* October 7, 1981, p. 1.

Productivity Monitoring: Systems, Indicators, and Analysis

Theodore H. Poister

Editor's note: An effective performance monitoring system depends on careful design and conscientious implementation, including appropriate and timely analysis of data. Using local transit systems as an example, Theodore H. Poister illustrates several important issues in the design of such a system and offers a performance monitoring framework that is applicable to other local government services as well.

Performance monitoring, the periodic measurement and tracking of key indicators of organizational or program performance, has been a staple in the public manager's tool kit for some time.[1] Indeed, it is considered by at least one authority to constitute one of only two true management systems used in government, along with management by objectives (MBO) systems.[2] Yet, considerable confusion remains as to what performance monitoring systems are, and it is safe to say that in practice they are not utilized as effectively as they might be. The technique should be viewed as an ongoing evaluative activity which focuses on program outcomes and is tied in as a central element of other managerial direction and control systems.[3] Very briefly, the principal reasons for the failure of performance monitoring to reach its potential include faulty conceptualization of performance, poor design of measurement systems, and the lack of direct connections to decision-making processes.

Measurement systems are indispensable for effective productivity improvement efforts. In some cases, discreet evaluation re-

Reprinted by permission from Marc Holzer, ed., *Public Productivity Handbook* (New York: Marcel Dekker, 1992). Copyright 1992, Marcel Dekker.

search designs employing before and after measures or control/ comparison groups may well suffice. However, particularly with respect to comprehensive productivity improvement programs mounted by organizations over time, ongoing monitoring systems are especially advantageous because they can help to identify needs and target projects as well as track results over the long run. This article provides a conceptual framework for developing such productivity monitoring systems. Detailed examples drawn from various urban transit systems are used to demonstrate the operationalization of a productivity monitoring system with indicators and various forms of analysis. The approach, however, which is based on system models emphasizing indicators and analysis keyed to improving productivity, is applicable to all substantive program areas.

Productivity monitoring systems

A productivity monitoring system consists of (1) a data component, (2) an analysis component, and (3) an action component.[4] As shown in Figure 1, the elements of these components are established by managerial decisions that are part of the monitoring *process* but not part of the monitoring *system* itself. Policymakers and managers have responsibility for setting objectives and at least the outline of strategies and activities aimed at achieving them. Management is also responsible for developing consensus about the kinds of indicators to be included as well as

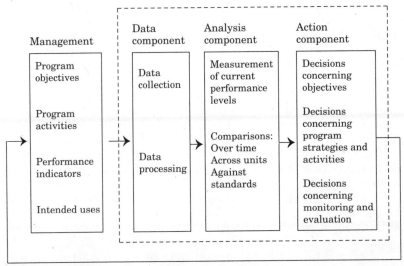

Figure 1. Performance monitoring system logic.

the kinds of analysis and intended uses of a productivity monitoring system.

The data component　Generating data that provide valid, reliable, and appropriate measures is essential in order for a monitoring system to impact on improved productivity. Furthermore, since data collection and processing consume the lion's share of the cost of implementing a monitoring system, the design must be geared to the selective acquisition of meaningful data in order to be cost-effective.

The most striking aspect of the data component is that in most program areas, relevant performance indicators come from such a wide variety of data sources. These range, for example, from internal agency records, accounting data, and administrative data reported to sponsoring agencies, through client-based or "caseload" data, observational counts and physical inspections, to citizen surveys. Fortunately, many of these types of data are readily available and incur relatively little additional cost for reformatting. While "external" data are usually desirable to complement these existing data sets, the overall monitoring system can be made more efficient by utilizing available data as much as possible. The most important consideration in developing the data component is what kinds of indicators to include, and this in turn depends on what kind of evaluative criteria are to be used to monitor performance. The relevant variables to be considered can be identified through a model of the program logic, illustrated in Figure 1, that clarifies the assumptions of cause/effect relationships by which a program is expected to produce its intended impacts.

The analysis component　The purpose of the analysis component is to distill the data into intelligible form, essentially to translate data into information. In part, this may be a matter of "data reduction," aggregating cases to fewer, larger groups or combining several indicators into composite indices, to deemphasize the detail and make the data comprehensible. For the most part, however, the data are given practical significance by analysis that focuses on the kinds of comparisons suggested in Figure 1. Given the function of a monitoring system to track comparisons suggested in Figure 1. Given the function of a monitoring system to track performance over time, the most natural kind of analysis is the comparison of current or most recent performance levels with similar figures for past periods. This facilitates an examination of current productivity levels against how well the program was doing six months or a year ago.

A second basis for comparison is an analysis of actual performance levels as opposed to budgeted amounts or specified productivity standards. Regardless of past performance, targets may have been set for the current or most recent period that were thought to be reasonably attainable. This "actual-vs.-plan" kind of comparison then provides a very direct indication of how well managers and/or programs are performing. Finally, managers often find it useful to have performance evaluated in terms of cross-sectional comparisons among geographical districts, organizational divisions, or operating units. These kinds of comparisons may serve to explain macroperformance trends, as when marginal improvement in an overall program turns out to be the net effect of substantial improvement in some areas or units, diluted by lack of improvement or retrogression in others. Furthermore, when operating responsibilities are decentralized to regional or organizational units, performance trends at this level are directly relevant to top management.

The action component   The types of decisions prompted by the results of productivity monitoring concern program objectives, program strategies, and the monitoring process itself. When results are uniformly positive, this tends to reinforce policies already in effect and generally would be interpreted as confirmation of a highly productive program. This is not a nondecision, but rather reflects a management-by-exception approach in which standing decisions are left in force unless challenged by negative results. Positive results, however, may prompt more proactive decisions along the lines of giving greater priority or increased financial support to intervention strategies that appear to be working well.

By contrast, negative results reflecting poor performance usually suggest the need for change, or at least looking into whether or not alternative approaches are in order. At the risk of oversimplification, the kinds of decisions suggested by negative feedback tend to fall into the following three categories:

• Modify objectives and/or standards
• Modify activities and/or pursue alternative strategies
• Change the measures included in the monitoring system.

The possibility of changing program objectives as a valid response to negative results should not be overlooked. Performance monitoring implies the use of "performance targeting" as a strategy for productivity improvement, whether as part of a formal management system such as PPB or MBO or not.[5] Not only does the monitoring track performance to determine whether objectives are being achieved, it also provides a frame of reference that can be helpful in establishing objectives for a productivity improvement program in the first place or modifying them later on.

Productivity models and measures

A workable performance monitoring system must be based on a clear understanding of the purpose of the program and the logic connecting its inputs, outputs, and intended effects. Figure 2 is a basic systems model of the logic underlying a conventional bus transit operation consisting of a primary service delivery component and two support components, (1) maintenance and (2) planning and marketing. The inputs into the system are resources such as employees, vehicles, facilities, equipment, and materials that can be measured individually or summarized as dollar costs. The program itself is a conversion process in which operational, policy, and design parameters—such as preventive maintenance procedures; routes and schedules; and fare structure—determine the system's outputs.

Outputs are the most immediate products of a program, and in the case of transit the principal outputs—those produced directly by the service component—are vehicle miles and vehicle

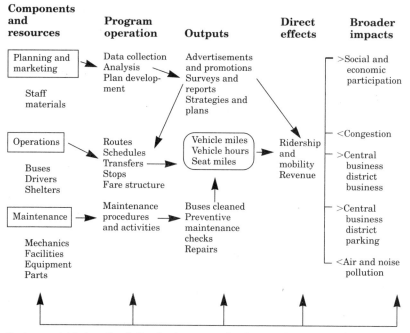

Environmental factors: Population density, topography, demographic characteristics, employment rates, street system, land use patterns, community values, automobile costs, travel patterns, parking availability, unionization, paratransit services, social service agencies, governmental regulation

Figure 2. Urban transit system program logic.

hours operated: measures of the amount of service offered to the community. Another output measure, bus seat miles of service provided, represents the capacity of the system. It is at the output stage of the system logic that interdependencies among the program components begin to appear. For example, the maintenance program outputs—buses cleaned, preventive maintenance checks, and repairs completed—contribute to both the ability to produce the service outputs, vehicle miles and hours, and the quality of these outputs. Similarly, some of the planning and marketing outputs such as service plan adjustments feed directly into the service component.

Output targets are immediate managerial objectives but do not represent the real outcome-oriented objectives, or benefits, of the program. While numerous and sometimes conflicting policy objectives are often assigned to transit, its overall objective may be best summarized as providing affordable mobility. Thus, the direct effects of a transit system, representing the attainment of this principal objective, are best summarized in terms of ridership levels. Increased mobility and transit ridership over the long run can also contribute to broader impacts relating to other community goals such as more widespread participation in social and economic activities, increased activity in central business districts, decreased traffic congestion and increased parking availability, and even reduced air and noise pollution. The model further recognizes the resource-dependent, open-systems nature of transit operations with the inclusion of numerous environmental variables, ranging from demographics and employment rates to land use patterns, travel patterns, and governmental regulations. While not usually built into formal performance monitoring systems, a strategic management perspective obviously requires keeping track of such factors as they may facilitate or impede transit performance.

Performance indicators   The conceptual framework provided by this system model of transit program serves as a guide for developing and selecting measures to be used in productivity monitoring. Managers are usually interested in tracking the status of several of the elements included in Figure 2 in absolute numbers, and ratios and rates computed by relating some of these to others provide indicators of productivity and overall transit performance. Figure 3 lists a number of performance indicators that are commonly used by transit managers grouped by performance dimension as keyed to the systems model. This is by no means an exhaustive list, but rather a selective set of indicators which illustrate the range of appropriate performance measures.[6] First, total expense is included in the list

Figure 3. Selected transit productivity indicators.

Resources and outputs	**Service quality**
Total expense	Percent on-time trips
Vehicle-hours	Percent transfers
Vehicle-miles	Accidents per 100,000 vehicle-
Seat-miles	miles
	Service interruptions per 100,000
Labor productivity	vehicle-miles
Vehicle-hours per employee	
Vehicle-hours per operator	**Service consumption**
Vehicle-miles per maintenance	Passenger trips
employee	Annual rides per capita revenue
	Revenue per passenger trip
Vehicle productivity	
Vehicle-miles per vehicle	**Utilization**
Vehicle-hours per vehicle	Passenger trips per vehicle-hour
	Passenger trips per vehicle-mile
Unit costs	Passenger miles per seat-mile
Expense per vehicle-mile	Revenue per vehicle-hour
Expense per vehicle-hour	
Variable cost per vehicle-mile	**Cost effectiveness**
Variable cost per vehicle-hour	Cost per passenger trip
	Percent cost recovery (revenue ÷
	expense)
	Deficit
	Net cost per passenger trip

because managerial performance is often keyed in part to cost-containment objectives. Similarly, the standard outputs such as vehicle-miles and vehicle-hours are basic operational elements that are often included in monitoring systems as scale factors. Measures of various aspects of the quality of service—such as the percent of bus trips that are on time according to printed schedules; the percent of trips requiring transfers; accident rates; and service interruption or "breakdown" rates—are critical to the concept of productivity as the relationship of quantity and quality to program cost.

Labor productivity indicators relate outputs to the employees contributing to their production. Because wear and tear on the buses is reflected more accurately by vehicle-miles as opposed to vehicle-hours, vehicle-miles per maintenance employee is an appropriate indicator of the labor productivity of the maintenance program, whereas the vehicle-hours of service generated by the bus operators better reflects the labor productivity of the service component. Vehicle productivity can be measured by either vehicle-miles or vehicle-hours per active vehicle in the fleet. Unit costs relate outputs to the cost of resources, as measured by such indicators as the cost per vehicle-mile and the cost per vehicle-hour.

Effectiveness is reflected first of all by consumption in terms of ridership. This is measured most directly by the number of passenger trips made on the system, but for comparative purposes the annual number of rides per capita may also be of interest. Consumption may also be measured by the amount of revenue generated by the system and/or the revenue per passenger trip, as at least a partial reflection of the value of the benefit received by patrons. Overall productivity can also be viewed in terms of utilization rates, the extent to which the system is utilized relative to the amount of service provided. Thus, the number of passenger trips per vehicle-hour and passenger trips per vehicle-mile are often tracked, as well as passenger miles traveled per seat-mile provided, which is the percent of capacity that is utilized. In addition, the ability of a system to generate revenue in relation to the amount of service provided is represented by the measure of revenue per vehicle-hour.

Finally, cost-effectiveness indicators relate the direct effects of the system to the cost of the resources going into it, most directly the cost per passenger trip. Although most transit systems are not expected to totally finance themselves from earned revenue, in the business enterprise sense of the "bottom line," cost-effectiveness is expressed in terms of the relation of revenue to expense, or the percent cost recovery. In addition, the operating deficit incurred and the net cost per passenger trip are other frequently used indicators of cost-effectiveness.

Selecting indicators   The choice of specific indicators to be included should depend primarily on the particular purposes for which a performance monitoring system is being instituted. Other factors include the expense and relative ease of collecting valid and reliable data as well as sheer manageability and the potential consequences of reporting particular measures. One research effort used factor analysis or aggregate data reported to the Urban Mass Transportation Administration (UMTA) to reduce a list of 48 measures to seven "marker" variables which consistently represent the larger set.[7] However, such abbreviated lists of indicators may be useful for making intersystem comparisons and yet fail to capture many of the more subtle aspects of the productivity of a particular system.

Managers using performance measures to monitor the status of their individual transit systems are likely to prefer a somewhat more comprehensive set of indicators that more fully represent the various dimensions of performance of concern to them. One observer points out that performance measurement systems in the public sector often need to balance varying information demands from different constituent groups, and suggests that in such situations the scope of the system can best be determined by gearing it to what potential users want to know about the program.[8] For a local transit system this would mean a measurement system that would allow the flexibility to provide summary information on key performance areas on a comparable basis to UMTA, and perhaps state agencies, while tailoring additional indicators to serve the presumably more specific needs of the individual transit manager.

Performance indicators are usually thought of as rates or ratios, and in making intersystem comparisons this is necessary in order to standardize for widely differing scales of operation. One system may experience many more service interruptions than another, for instance, but in terms of service interruptions per 100,000 vehicle-miles operated it may be exhibiting superior performance. On the other hand, tracking a single system's performance solely with rates and ratios often will not provide optimal feedback because the basic reasons underlying changes that are observed will not always be apparent. If, for example, a system experiences increases in the number of passenger trips per vehicle-hour over a particular time period, does this reflect actual growth in ridership, a cutback in service levels, or both? Thus, it is often helpful to report trends in terms of absolute magnitudes as well as performance ratios.

Table 1 summarizes outputs and operating expenses from fiscal 1984 through fiscal 1989 for the Metropolitan Atlanta Rapid Transit Authority, or MARTA, a major bus and rail system in Atlanta, Georgia. While the vehicle-hours and vehicle-miles operated by the bus system over this period have remained very stable, unit costs rose steadily as operating expenses increased from $76 million in fiscal 1984 to $106 million in fiscal 1988, owing to wage increases and the higher prices of other factor inputs. However, unit costs decreased substantially in fiscal 1989 as output increased marginally, whereas operating expenses were cut down to $96 million.

In contrast, unit costs of the rail system tended to decrease over several years, and at $2.80 per vehicle-mile in fiscal 1988 were actually lower than $3.90 per vehicle-mile in fiscal 1984. The explanation for this is that operating expenses on the rail system slightly more than doubled from $17 million in fiscal 1982 to $40 million in fiscal 1987, and then dropped back a little to less than $38 million in fiscal 1988 as power costs decreased. However, during this same period vehicle-miles operated more than tripled, from 3.9 million to 13.5 million, as track was added to the system and new stations opened. As rail outputs in-

Table 1. MARTA outputs and expenses.

	Fiscal year					
	1984	1985	1986	1987	1988	1989
Bus system						
Vehicle-hours (000's)	2,079	2,121	2,155	2,192	2,155	2,208
Vehicle-miles (000's)	29,018	29,393	29,770	30,323	29,872	30,265
Accidents	696	678	755	657	667	742
Accidents/100,000 VM	2.4	2.3	2.5	2.2	2.2	2.5
Operating expense (000's)	76,466	82,030	84,279	90,880	106,480	96,066
Expense/vehicle-mile	$2.64	$2.79	$2.83	$3.00	$3.56	$3.17
Expense/vehicle-hour	$36.78	$38.68	$39.11	$41.46	$49.41	$43.52
Rail system						
Vehicle-hours (000's)	314	448	531	529	561	624
Vehicle-miles (000's)	6,144	10,038	12,156	12,549	13,494	14,795
Accidents	N/A	291	451	377	326	315
Accidents/100,000 VM		2.9	3.7	3.0	2.4	2.1
Operating expenses (000's)	23,965	29,847	38,840	40,488	37,727	59,311
Expense/vehicle-mile	$3.90	$2.97	$3.20	$3.23	$2.80	$4.01
Expense/vehicle-hour	$76.32	$66.62	$73.15	$76.54	$67.25	$94.99

creased faster than expenses, the net effect was substantially improving operating efficiency. Nevertheless, in fiscal 1989 operating expenses rose dramatically to $4.01 per vehicle-mile, even though output increased slightly, as total expenses jumped up to $59 million.

One common negative effect of measurement systems is goal displacement, whereby organizational behavior reacts over time to maximize performance on those dimensions emphasized by the system, at the expense of other equally or more important objectives. Thus, the selection of indicators is critical in terms of avoiding a boomerang effect in which overall productivity improvement is actually impeded by the use of a monitoring system. This requires a well-balanced set of indicators to offset potential dysfunctional incentives created by any one measure. Often measures can be paired, in a checks and balances approach, by trying to anticipate the problems likely to be created by focusing too narrowly on some performance criteria while neglecting others.

For example, maintenance managers can most readily maximize the number of vehicle-miles operated per maintenance employee simply by reducing the number of employees in their divisions, but if they are no longer able to conduct essential preventive maintenance activities on a reasonable schedule, buses will begin breaking down and service quality will suffer markedly. To establish a balance between maintenance efficiency and service quality, then, a measure such as the number of service interruptions per 100,000 vehicle-miles operated should be included to assure that the real purpose of the maintenance component will not be ignored for the sake of cost control.

Monitoring transit system productivity

Since performance monitoring is the periodic measurement of key indicators at regular intervals, it accumulates time series data bases which lend themselves most readily to comparisons over time. For instance, MARTA develops a monthly statistical summary which tracks some 19 measures corresponding to its bus system and 34 indicators for the rail system, including outputs, operating efficiency, utilization, and cost-effectiveness measures. In addition to reporting these figures for the individual month and the change from the same month of the preceding year, this report shows most of the same information for a 12-month moving total and for the fiscal year to date, in each case comparing current performance with the preceding year.

Trends over time   Table 2 shows a selected set of these indicators for the month of June, 1988; since MARTA's fiscal year ends in June, the fiscal year to date entries also represent the entire fiscal year. At the beginning of this fiscal year the base fare was raised from $0.65 to $0.75, and the overall results are readily apparent from Table 2. Total vehicle-miles and vehicle-hours operated in June of 1988 were marginally higher than in June of the preceding year owing to continued expansion of the rail system, and total operating expenses were by up 11.6% to $14,185,563. However, ridership in June, 1988, was lower than in June of the preceding year, with a sharper decrease in linked passenger trips—down 6.0% to a little over 6 million—than in unlinked trips, down by 2.1%. This differential decrease reflects the conversion of some line haul bus routes to feeder routes for new rail stations, and may also suggest that the fare increase had greater impact on central city residents than on suburban commuters, who tend to make more multisegment trips. Utilization rates decreased to 3.42 passenger trips per vehicle-mile and 54.31 trips per vehicle-hour, and the combined effect of the increase in expenses with the loss in ridership was an 18.4% increase in the cost per passenger trip.

Yet, total passenger revenue went up by 20.6% over the same period to $3,861,778, as a result of the higher average fare

Table 2. *MARTA: Selected performance indicators.*

Indicator	This month				Fiscal year to date	
	Bus system	Rail system	Total system	Percent change last year	Total system	Percent change last year
Vehicle-miles	2,558,000	1,149,000	3,707,000	+2.8	43,893,000	+2.4
Vehicle-hours	184,900	48,100	233,200	+1.9	2,792,600	+1.0
Passengers (linked)	3,849,000	2,258,000	6,107,000	−6.0	71,959,000	−4.5
Passengers (unlinked)	7,109,000	5,555,000	12,664,000	−2.1	148,253,000	−1.1
Passengers/mile	2.78	4.83	3.42	−4.7	3.38	−3.4
Passengers/hour	38.45	115.01	54.31	−3.9	53.96	−2.1
Operating expense	$10,550,102	$3,635,461	$14,185,563	+11.6	$144,801,222	+10.2
Expense/vehicle-mile	$4.12	$3.16	$3.83	+8.5	$3.30	+7.8
Expense/vehicle-hour	$57.06	$75.58	$60.83	+9.5	$52.70	+9.1
Expense/passenger	$2.74	$1.61	$2.32	+18.4	$2.01	+15.5
Passenger revenue	$2,442,035	$1,419,743	$3,861,778	+20.6	$45,993,579	+17.9
Revenue/expense	0.2315	0.3905	0.2722	+8.1	0.3176	+7.0

being paid by the vast majority of patrons who were still using the system. As predicted by the underlying logic that calls for a fare increase, the net effect was an improvement in MARTA's revenue-to-cost ratio, which at 0.2722 in June of 1988 was 8.1% higher than in June of the preceding year. Such monthly comparisons, along with similar measures for the fiscal year as a whole, are obviously important for MARTA management to track, in particular with respect to the aggregate effects of service and fare changes. However, these particular data may obscure possible differential impacts on the bus system versus the rail system; for example, greater erosion of bus passengers than rail passengers as the result of a fare increase, which could be clarified simply by computing separately for each mode the percent changes from the same month a year ago.

For longer-term trend monitoring it may be more convenient to use quarterly rather than monthly data. Table 3, for example, shows selected indicators for the Peninsula Transportation District Commission, or PENTRAN, a medium-size bus system in Newport News, Virginia. These data pertain to each quarter of fiscal year 1988, with equivalent figures for each fiscal 1987

Table 3. PENTRAN revenue and expense comparisons.

Fiscal year	Fiscal year quarter				
	1st July–Sept.	2nd Oct.–Dec.	3rd Jan.–March	4th April–June	Total
1988					
Revenue	$ 674,179	$ 718,806	$ 771,982	$ 740,394	$2,905,361
Expense	$1,738,636	$1,729,036	$1,746,740	$1,967,623	$7,182,035
% cost recovery	38.8%	41.6%	44.2%	37.6%	40.4%
Deficit	1,064,457	1,010,230	974,758	1,227,229	4,276,674
Total passengers	1,016,584	1,284,230	1,297,977	1,215,595	4,815,048
Net cost/ passenger	$1.05	$0.79	$0.75	$1.01	$0.89
1987					
Revenue	$ 696,448	$ 798,107	$ 779,966	$ 776,394	$3,050,915
Expense	$1,575,496	$1,626,456	$1,751,343	$1,927,473	$6,880,759
% cost recovery	44.2%	49.1%	44.5%	40.3%	44.3%
Deficit	879,048	828,349	971,368	1,151,079	3,829,844
Total passengers	1,192,216	1,250,700	1,259,552	1,283,318	4,985,786
Net cost/ passenger	$0.74	$0.66	$0.77	$0.90	$0.77

quarter provided as a basis of comparison. Total ridership was higher in the second and third quarters and lower in the first and fourth quarters of fiscal 1988 as compared with fiscal 1987, but the net effect was a decrease in total passengers from 4,985,786 to 4,815,048 for the year as a whole. For each quarter of fiscal 1988 revenue was less than in the corresponding quarter of 1987, and overall revenue decreased from $3,050,915 to $2,905,361 for the year. Overall, revenue was down by 4.8% for the year, whereas total passengers were down 3.4%, indicating a slightly lower average fare on the system in fiscal 1988 even though the same fare structure was in place as in fiscal 1987. Since expenses were higher in fiscal 1988 in all except for the third quarter, PEN-TRAN's percent cost recovery factor slipped from about 44% in fiscal 1987 to roughly 40% in 1988, and the net cost per passenger trip increased from $0.77 in fiscal 1987 to $0.89 in 1988.

Longer-term trends are often presented most effectively in time series graphs. Figure 4 plots ridership trends on a quarterly basis from fiscal 1984 through fiscal 1989 for the Williamsport Bureau of Transportation (WBT) City Bus operation, a small transit system in Williamsport, Pennsylvania. First, some systematic seasonal variation is evident, with senior-citizen passenger trips tending to be lower and regular-revenue passenger trips tending to be higher in the third quarter of the fiscal year, January through March. Regarding long-term trends, the plots indicate that whereas senior-citizen trips have tended to decrease gradually over the past six fiscal years, regular-revenue passenger trips have increased over the same period. The net effect of the opposing trends has been a very slight increase in total passenger trips over the long run, averaging in the vicinity of 270,000 trips per quarter.

Intrasystem comparisons   As with the MARTA rail and bus systems, disaggregating the data down to the major components of a transit operation often provides additional insight as to how well these components, and the system as a whole, are performing. For example, in addition to its regular bus service with on the order of 2.6 million passengers per year, PENTRAN also operates some separate work "trippers" that carry more than a third of a million passengers per year and a "shipyard express" service to the largest single employer in the area, which carries more than a quarter of a million passengers per year. Furthermore, under contract with the local school system, PENTRAN also operates a separate school bus service that carries well over a million students per year to junior and senior high schools in the area. The school bus fare is only $0.40, as compared with $0.60 for the regular service, $0.75 for the work trippers, and $1.00 for the shipyard express.

Figure 4. WBT long-term trends.

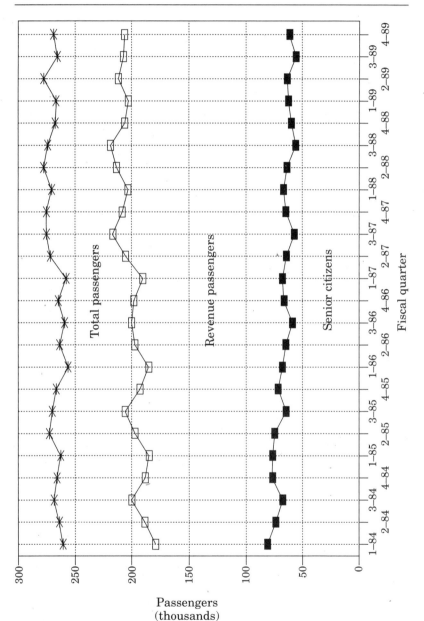

As shown in Table 4, tracking key indicators for these individual components reveals different trends in their ridership over time. Although all four components lost riders between fiscal 1986 and 1987, these trends continued through the next year on the first three components but not on the school bus service. Ridership decreased from fiscal 1987 to 1988 by more than 200,000 on the regular operation even as vehicle-hours increased marginally, and the work trippers lost more than 30,000 passenger trips, whereas the shipyard express carried 20,000 fewer riders. However, the school bus service, which is primarily sensitive to school enrollment trends, carried 110,000 more passenger trips in 1988 than in 1987. These countering trends resulted in the net loss of some 150,000 passengers systemwide and explain PENTRAN's lower average fare on the system as a whole and the decrease in aggregate revenue.

Especially on smaller systems, tracking many of these key indicators on a route-specific basis can be helpful in fine-tuning operations. In Williamsport, for example, WBT checks various aspects of individual route performance at least once a year, in addition to tracking most of the same indicators on a quarterly and annual basis for the system as a whole. Table 5 shows a few of these indicators broken down by route for a single week in September, 1989; the top eight routes listed in Table 5 are regular daily routes, whereas the remaining six are evening routes and trippers. The variable cost of operating each route was estimated by a model employing unit cost items for both vehicle-miles and vehicle-hours for the system as a whole.

The Newberry, Montoursville, Garden View, and Loyalsock routes are the real backbone of the system, operating the most service and incurring the greatest cost. However, ridership (not shown), and hence revenue, are also higher on these routes, and thus their operating deficits for the week are not far out of line with the other routes. By contrast, the West Third Street, South Side, and East End routes produce considerably less revenue but still have operating deficits comparable to the Garden View and Loyalsock routes. Looking at cost-effectiveness, among the regular routes the Newberry route has the lowest deficit per passenger trip at $0.19, followed by the Garden View route at $0.49, and the West Third Street route at $0.54.

At the other end of the spectrum, the South Side route incurred a deficit per passenger of $1.22, and the Montoursville and East End routes had operating deficits per passenger of $0.80 or more. Similarly, the percent variable cost recovery on the Newberry, West Third Street, and Garden View routes all exceed the systemwide average of 45%, whereas the Montoursville and East End routes recovered less than 40% of their operating

Table 4. PENTRAN ridership trends by service element.

	Fiscal year						
	1982	1983	1984	1985	1986	1987	1988
Regular service							
Vehicle-hours	90,123	96,954	99,303	99,061	98,628	101,869	104,054
Passengers	3,240,350	2,964,409	3,050,476	3,304,605	3,056,878	2,885,406	2,680,922
Passengers/vehicle-hour	36.0	30.6	30.7	33.4	31.0	28.3	25.8
Work trippers							
Vehicle-hours	17,466	17,036	14,760	14,477	15,693	16,948	14,965
Passengers	370,011	387,762	405,586	402,486	402,478	368,825	334,567
Passengers/vehicle-hour	21.2	22.8	27.5	27.8	25.6	21.8	22.4
Shipyard express							
Vehicle-hours	13,900	13,849	12,522	12,331	11,898	14,381	14,481
Passengers	292,057	303,576	308,360	290,471	294,760	291,325	268,350
Passengers/vehicle-hour	21.0	21.9	24.6	23.6	24.8	20.3	18.5
School buses							
Vehicle-hours	N/A	N/A	N/A	27,065	28,820	30,647	28,388
Passengers	1,328,964	1,398,922	1,450,031	1,389,700	1,287,543	1,261,743	1,373,356
Passengers/vehicle-hour	N/A	N/A	N/A	51.3	44.7	41.2	48.4

cost through the fare box, and cost recovery was only at 29% on the South Side route. While WBT planners have often focused on the Market Street route as needing attention because of its low absolute volume of ridership, these data show that the Market Street route performs relatively well and suggest that the Montoursville, East End, and especially the South Side routes may well be higher-priority candidates for modification in configuration and/or service levels.

Comparisons against standards   Monitoring systems often measure actual performance against fixed standards, targets developed in the planning process, or amounts set in the budget. For example, WBT has developed 29 standards relating to staffing ratios, labor productivity, operating efficiency, service quality, utilization, and cost-effectiveness and measures actual performance against these standards. A selected set of these standards is shown in Table 6, along with WBT's actual performance on these criteria for fiscal 1989. Statewide averages for the so-called medium-size systems in Pennsylvania are also shown as a basis of comparison. The percent employee attendance is defined as one minus the number of unexpected sick occurrences and

Table 5. *WBT expense, revenue, and deficit by route (September 18–23, 1989).*

Route	Estimated variable cost ($)[a]	Revenue ($)	Operating deficit ($)	Operating deficit/ passenger trip ($)	Percent variable cost recovery[a]
Newberry	3,218	2,293	925	0.19	71
Montoursville	3,517	1,187	2,330	0.95	34
Garden View	3,202	1,585	1,617	0.49	50
Loyalsock	3,034	1,317	1,717	0.64	43
Market Street	879	378	501	0.63	43
West Third Street	2,025	929	1,096	0.54	46
South Side	1,926	563	1,363	1.22	29
East End	1,922	735	1,187	0.80	38
Nightline East	305	137	168	0.57	45
Nightline West	382	177	205	0.55	46
PM Shuttle	61	57	4	0.02	93
Hill's Express[b]	67	31	36	0.60	46
Muncy/Mall Local	681	185	496	2.10	27
Lycoming Mall	475	181	294	1.40	38
Totals	21,694	9,755	11,939	0.60	45

[a]Estimated variable cost = ($0.89 × vehicle-miles) + ($16.26 × vehicle-hours).
[b]Saturday only.

Table 6. Selected WBT performance standards, fiscal year 1989.

Criterion	Standard	WBT fiscal 1989	Statewide average 1989
Percent employee attendance	≥97%	98.8%	NA
Vehicle-miles per employee	≥15,000	16,631	15,219
Vehicle-miles per maintenance employee	≥80,000	85,631	91,233
Vehicle-hours per operator	≥1,700	1,757	1,669
Vehicle-miles per vehicle	≥28,000	31,512	26,008
Expense per vehicle-mile	≤$ 2.75	$2.43	$2.75
Expense per vehicle-hour	≤$40.61	$34.57	$36.92
Vehicle-miles between road calls	≥3,500	5,596	5,024
Collision accidents per 100,000 vehicle-miles	≤3.0	0.84	2.42
Percent on-time performance[a]			
Peak periods	≥90%	93.3%	NA
Non-peak	≥95%	100.0%	NA
Percent transfers	≤10%	6.5%	6.2%
Passenger trips per vehicle-hour	≥28	27.5	23.2
Net cost per passenger	≤$0.90	$0.77	$0.78
Operating ratio (revenue/expense)	≥35%	43%	51%

[a]Percentage of trips departing from a bus stop within 5 minutes of scheduled time.

"missouts" as a proportion of the total number of report times for bus operators; all the other indicators have been defined elsewhere in this article. WBT's actual performance met or exceeded each of the standards with the exception of passenger trips per vehicle-hour, which was very close to the standard at 27.5 vs. 28. In addition, WBT outperformed the statewide average on nine of the 12 indicators for which comparable data were available, a profile which reflects very respectable performance levels while suggesting there is still some room for improvement.

Monitoring systems and productivity improvement

Many local government programs maintain monitoring systems for reporting to state and federal agencies but fail to translate the information provided into decisions and actions aimed at improving productivity. Results-oriented management requires tying monitoring efforts into other management strategies and systems, and the most direct means of accomplishing this is through the establishment of objectives which serve as standards against which productivity indicators can be evaluated.

In setting challenging yet realistic standards, transit agencies can analyze their own past trends in the context of key environmental constraints to gauge what fair expectations might be. For example, changes in the price of fuel will influence the cost per vehicle-mile, and current and anticipated employment patterns in the service area might temper expectations concerning the number of passenger trips per vehicle-hour. As suggested by the example involving WBT's performance standards, peer group comparisons with other transit agencies might also provide a frame of reference for developing reasonable objectives. In addition, technical analysis and prevailing industrial engineering standards may be helpful in setting objectives on such dimensions of productivity as on-time performance or the number of service interruptions per 100,000 vehicle-miles operated.

While MBO systems are now prevalent at all levels of government, one issue that frequently arises is that managers are justifiably reluctant to be held accountable for outcomes which they cannot control. Thus, for instance, operations managers are frequently concerned that on-time performance may be hindered by traffic congestion over which they have no control, and maintenance managers understandably resist being held responsible for the serviceability of equipment made with faulty components. At higher levels, transit managers may readily agree to be evaluated in terms of the quality of service they provide but not in terms of revenue generation, since so many factors beyond their control influence ridership.

However, such criteria clearly should not be omitted from managerial objective setting and performance monitoring systems because they in fact define what overall productivity is all about; to exclude such factors from consideration would be to deny management responsibility for performance. Rather, as pointed out elsewhere, the notion of shared responsibility should be the governing principle here.[9] Thus, managers need to take the relevant external factors into account in setting specific objectives and assume joint responsibility with subordinates for the reasonableness of these expectations. Furthermore, evaluations of individuals' performances in light of agency objectives should always be tempered by consideration of the factors beyond their control that might have influenced the results.

Programmatic and measurement changes

When productivity is found to be declining over time, or to be consistently below agency standards or "industry" averages, this should prompt investigation of the problem and analysis of whether programmatic changes are in order, at either the strategic or operations level. In the field of transit, such solutions play

out through changes in management policies, marketing strategies, maintenance practices, or the service plan of routes and
schedules. For example, PENTRAN's continued loss of ridership
over a three-year period led to the development of a new service
plan which reconfigured some routes, eliminated unproductive
runs on other routes, and provided for a 20% net increase in overall service aimed at reversing this negative ridership trend.

Problems that surface through ongoing monitoring can also
lead to the initiation of incentive systems designed to improve
productivity. WBT, for example, found it was consistently well
below standard on employee attendance, with frequent "missouts" and sick leave abuse driving up overtime costs to unreasonable levels. Management's response was to institute a quarterly
incentive program in which drivers and mechanics with a perfect
attendance record for the three months are given a $50 U.S. sav-
ings bond as a bonus. These attendance records are also factored
into decisions about a series of annual awards for drivers and
mechanics that also carry monetary rewards. The result of incentives has been a dramatic reduction in "missouts" and overtime
charges and marked improvement in overall employee attendance.

Finally, an unexpected or seemingly unreasonable result can
sometimes signal a measurement problem with the monitoring
system itself. Obtaining reliable data on ridership, for example,
which is so critical to monitoring transit productivity, can be particularly difficult for multimodal systems. This is especially true
when service quality is enhanced by barrier-free transfers that
leave no "paper trail" and when weekly or monthly passes are
used repeatedly in multisegment passenger trips, making it difficult to distinguish between originating trips and mid-trip transfers. On such systems, MARTA, for example, registered bus
boardings and faregate entries on the rail system may bear little
resemblance to the overall number of passenger trips. Indeed,
after its statistical summaries continued over several months to
produce ridership figures that seemed anomalous, contained in-
explicable fluctuations over time, and did not correlate well with
other system parameters, MARTA determined that its revenue-
derived passenger data were unreliable. Rather than modify system objectives or make operational changes based on faulty data,
MARTA decided to improve its own measurement system. The
result was a complex passenger estimation model that utilizes a
combination of electronic data, traffic checker counts, and parameters drawn from sample surveys to develop reliable estimates of monthly passenger trips and transfer patterns by mode
and fare payment category.

Conclusions

In summary, the regular monitoring of program performance is an indispensable element of strategic management which is concerned with productivity improvement at the operating level as well as enhancing overall effectiveness. Performance monitoring is very prevalent among urban mass transit systems, which readily lend themselves to illustrate the issues surrounding the design and utilization of monitoring systems. However, as is the case in many other program areas, transit agencies often fail to take full advantage of their monitoring systems to increase cost-effectiveness and improve productivity, largely because these systems have been implemented to fulfill reporting requirements but not designed to serve local managerial needs. While a handful of key indicators may suffice simply to track the status of system performance, for example, a balanced, more encompassing set of indicators may be better suited to assist in policy and managerial decision making.

Using urban transit systems as examples, this article has reviewed several issues concerning the selection of indicators to be included in monitoring systems and the kinds of comparisons that will facilitate effective utilization of this information in improving productivity. Taking full advantage of the potential of performance monitoring, however, requires designing and utilizing monitoring systems with direct linkages to other management strategies and systems regarding budgeting, personnel, and overall direction and control, which increasingly are found in the public manager's tool kit. The key to successful productivity monitoring is the use of systems frameworks, not only for delineating the underlying logic and performance indicators of the target programs, but more importantly to assure a logic in the design of the monitoring system itself which will translate the results of measurement and analysis into decisions that will lead to productivity improvement.

1. T. H. Poister and G. Streib, "Management Tools in Municipal Government: Trends Over the Past Decade," *Public Administration Review* 49, no. 3 (1989): 240–48.

2. J. E. Swiss, *Monitoring and Managing Government Performance: Output-Oriented Management Systems* (Englewood Cliffs, NJ: Prentice-Hall, 1991).

3. J. F. Wholey, *Evaluation and Effective Public Management* (Boston: Little, Brown, 1983).

4. T. H. Poister, *Performance Monitoring* (Lexington, MA: Lexington Books, 1983); S. Altman, "Performance Monitoring Systems for Public Managers," *Public Administration Review* 39 (1979): 31–35.

5. J. M. Greiner, H. P. Hatry, M. P.

Koss, A. P. Millar, and J. P. Woodward, *Productivity and Motivation: A Review of State Government Initiatives* (Washington, DC: Urban Institute Press, 1981).

6. G. M. Fielding, *Managing Public Transit Strategically* (San Francisco: Jossey-Bass, 1987); J. H. Miller, "The Use of Performance-Based Methodologies for the Allocation of Transit Operating Funds," *Traffic Quarterly* 34, no. 4 (1980): 555–74.

7. G. M. Fielding, T. T. Babitsky, and M. E. Brenner, "Performance Evaluation for Bus Transit," *Transportation Research* 19, no. 1 (1985): 73–82.

8. G. A. Grizzle, "Measuring State and Local Government Performance: Issues to Resolve Before Implementing a Performance Measurement System," *State and Local Government Review* (1982).

9. Ibid.

PART 3

Performance Monitoring in Action

In 1991, the business magazine *Financial World* published a report on the condition of America's thirty largest municipalities. A report card was compiled for each city, showing its grade on four "operating tools" considered important for proper management. One of those tools, labeled "performance evaluations," addressed key elements of performance measurement and monitoring:

Do the city's departments each have mission statements with clear goals? Are service measurements used in budget requests? Are targets for service contained in the budget? Are actual accomplishments compared with service measure targets? Does the city have a full-time performance evaluation staff? Are performance recommendations reported to the public or used internally? Do the city's performance evaluations calculate the cost of service delivered, the amount of service delivered, the quality of the service? To what degree are activities or departments affected by these evaluations? Are department heads' or any city employees' compensation tied to performance?[1]

Only five of the thirty cities were judged to have a performance evaluation system worthy of an A. Seven were awarded Bs, and eleven others earned Cs. Of the remaining seven jurisdictions—23 percent of the nation's largest cities—five earned Ds, one received an F, and one avoided a low grade by snaring an I (incomplete) on the strength of a system just being introduced.

Report cards compiled in subsequent years showed increasing attention to performance measurement among big-city governments and clear improvement in performance monitoring practices and the use of related systems. Many signs are positive—not just among the largest jurisdictions but among local governments of all sizes.

As noted throughout this volume, local governments that measure and monitor performance do so for many reasons. Several of the chief reasons are noted in the vignettes and case studies of local governments included in Part 3, "Performance Monitoring in Action." For example:

- *Accountability*   Local governments that measure their performance—especially those that systematically analyze performance data, financial trends, and citizen satisfaction—are better able to build public confidence through their documented stewardship of taxpayer dollars.
- *Planning/budgeting*   Sunnyvale, California, has long been recognized as a public sector leader in the collection and use of performance measures for planning and budgeting purposes. More recently, the city of Portland, Oregon, has received acclaim for its advances in service efforts and accomplishments (SEA) reporting.
- *Operational improvement*   Examples of operational improvements prompted by, or monitored via, performance measures are found throughout the case histories of local governments committed to their use. Savings on street maintenance in Sunnyvale, quality improvements by city mechanics in Charlotte, and advances in transit system inventory and logistics management in New York City are but a few of the examples documented on the pages that follow.
- *Program evaluation/MBO/performance appraisal*   Performance auditing conducted in Portland, Oregon, provides an example of systematic program evaluation in local government. Many other cities also rely on rigorous evaluations of selected departments or functions, sometimes conducted by outside consultants, sometimes by an internal, independent auditor's office, by analysts from the budget department, or by a separate unit sometimes referred to as an internal consulting group. Other evaluative uses of performance measures include their incorporation in management-by-objectives systems and performance appraisals.
- *Reallocation of resources*   Across-the-board budget cuts are increasingly decried as an inappropriate means of coping with resource constraints. Uniform percentage cuts punish lean departments harshly, while those with slack resources—or "fat"—more easily absorb the reduction. Facing a tight budget in the late 1980s but armed with good data on performance and demand, Charlotte, North Car-

olina, was able to identify a declining need for engineering
and development services and to devise a more appropriate
budgetary adjustment.

- *Directing operations/contract monitoring*   Suitable performance indicators, monitored in a timely fashion, tend to inspire a higher level of performance among those being
monitored—whether they are members of a local government
work unit or private contractors. Few better examples can be
found than the performance monitoring system used in Winnipeg, Manitoba, to provide daily feedback to municipal work
crews.

Skeptics may fear that elaborate performance measuring and
monitoring systems will permit and even encourage the centralized micromanagement of field operations by city hall executives,
other central staff, or legislative officials. Many proponents, however, note an opposite effect. Armed with valid information on the
condition of facilities, the output of crews and departments, the
quality of services, and the results achieved, officials and legislative bodies that are pleased with the performance record may be
less likely to micromanage operations through painstaking
scrutiny of line items and more likely to focus on policy and program objectives, priorities among those objectives, and resource
allocation decisions.[2] Rather than challenge each dollar allocated
for supplies or fuel, for example, elected officials in places like
Sunnyvale, a city renowned for the comprehensiveness of its performance measurement system, are more likely to challenge
managers to achieve desired results within resource constraints.
Empowered individuals are encouraged to devise better, more efficient ways to achieve those results.

Attempts to micromanage operations from the staff offices of
city hall or from the city council meeting room are unlikely to
produce results as favorable as those achieved through the initiative, insights, and creativity of operating employees in an atmosphere that values their ideas. Individual and group discretion is
important in fostering such an atmosphere, but employee discretion without accountability is inconsistent both with prudent
management and with democratic ideals. As articulated by Craig
Gerhart, Director of the Office of Management and Budget in
Prince William County, Virginia, "If we are going to give up control as a central organization, then we need to make sure that
those who have new flexibility and new autonomy can be held accountable for what they do."[3] And that is where performance
measurement and monitoring come in.

1. Katherine Barrett and Richard Greene, "American Cities," *Financial World* 160 (19 February 1991): 23.

2. Richard Napier, "Legislative Oversight," in *Managing for Results: Performance Measures in Government,* 1993 conference proceedings (Austin: The University of Texas, 1994).

3. Craig Gerhart, "Management Involvement," in *Managing for Results: Performance Measures in Government,* 1993 conference proceedings (Austin: The University of Texas, 1994), 80.

Experimenting with SEA Reporting in Portland

Richard C. Tracy
and Ellen P. Jean

Editor's note: The city of Portland has been a pioneer in service efforts and accomplishments (SEA) reporting, an approach that steps beyond the customary bounds of merely reporting expenditures and workload measures.

The performance of government is a continuing subject of debate between citizens, elected officials and government managers. For the most part this debate revolves around the amount of government spending and the level of taxes. In the past several years, however, interest in government performance has begun to move from what goes *into* government programs to what comes *out*. Citizens and government officials are concerned not only about the amount of spending but also about whether government programs are achieving intended results at a reasonable cost.

The need for better information to measure and monitor government performance has spawned a number of efforts at the federal, state and local levels over the past several decades. Some of these efforts have proved disappointing, while others have had continuing success and benefits for their governments. Although public interest in government performance is driven in large part by taxpayer dissatisfaction with the value received from taxes provided, public managers are also influenced by the quality revolution in the private sector and believe these new management principles should apply to public enterprises as well.

This article discusses the experiences of the Office of the City Auditor in Portland, Oregon, with performance measurement

---

Reprinted with permission from *Government Finance Review* (December 1993): 11–14.

and reporting. The article will describe the process used by the Portland city auditor and city departments to define, collect, audit and report information called service efforts and accomplishments (SEA) information. In addition, the article will assess impacts of SEA reporting to date, lessons learned and continuing challenges to successful implementation.

Designing the SEA Report

The elected city auditor of the City of Portland, Oregon, is authorized by the city charter to provide comprehensive auditing services in order to promote accountability and help improve the performance of city government services. In 1988, the audit services division of the city auditor's office was authorized to pursue experimentation with the concept of service efforts and accomplishments reporting.

A 1991 test of the feasibility of SEA reporting in Portland found that it would be possible. Auditors concluded that sufficient, reliable data existed in city departments to support an SEA reporting effort and that city managers generally were willing to

---

Government Finance Officers Association policy statement: Service efforts and accomplishments

The Government Finance Officers Association believes that performance objectives and measurement are critical components and key tools for use in budget planning and decision making and program management by all levels of government.

Good budget practice encompasses strategic, operational and financial planning that establishes performance objectives and results in the measurement of service accomplishments.

Service efforts and accomplishments (SEA) are one facet of effective use of performance objectives in planning and budgeting.

Performance objectives and measurement logically fall within the purview of budgetary practice, rather than financial reporting.

The Government Finance Officers Association directs its Committee on Governmental Budgeting and Management to develop recommended practices, budget award criteria, and budget guidelines for performance objectives and measurement in conjunction with the national task force on state and local government budgeting.

Adopted: May 4, 1993.

participate in the process. While better effectiveness and efficiency indicators were needed, the feasibility study recommended preparing an annual SEA Report that would include refined performance indicators and the results of a citizen satisfaction survey. Since the feasibility test, the audit services division has prepared and issued an annual report on the performance of the city's largest services in 1992 and 1993, with a third annual report due in January 1994. This report is issued not as a part of the city's annual financial report but as a separate document emanating from the auditor's office.

The City of Portland Service Efforts and Accomplishments Report contains information on the performance of the city's six largest services: police, fire, parks and recreation, water, wastewater and transportation. These services comprise about 75 percent of the city's staffing and spending. The report displays information on each service organized in four sections:

- A brief description of the service mission, goals, objectives and major activities
- Background information on service area spending and staffing levels
- Service workload and demand data
- Performance data on service results, outcomes and efficiency.

To aid the interpretation and evaluation of the information, several different kinds of comparison techniques are used. Spending and staff levels are compared to six other cities: Seattle, Sacramento, Denver, Kansas City, Cincinnati and Charlotte. Figure 1 shows a chart used in reporting these comparative data. In addition, five years of Portland data are displayed for each indicator so that trends can be seen over time. Most importantly, where possible, performance accomplishments are compared to planned goals, standards or benchmarks. Shown in Figure 2 is a report of five years of performance indicators for the fire bureau. If the data show unusual trends, poor or good performance, or very different spending compared to other jurisdictions, the report contains some explanatory information, if available.

The SEA Report also displays the results of an annual citizen satisfaction survey administered by the audit services division. The survey questions are intended to provide information on effectiveness and service quality from the citizens' or customers' point of view. Citizen opinions are reported for each of the seven major neighborhoods comprising the City of Portland.

The audit services division undertook the SEA reporting effort with two primary goals in mind: first, to improve the accountability of Portland by annually reporting to the public on the performance of city services; and second, to help make city programs

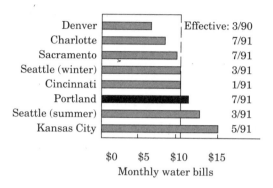

Figure 1. Comparable monthly residential water bills: Portland and six other cities.

Note: Based on monthly water use of 1,000 cubic feet plus service charge.
Source: *1992 Rate Survey: Water and Wastewater*, Ernst & Young.

work better by providing information to managers and elected officials that would help improve decision making. Consistent with these objectives, the division developed several working principles for carrying out SEA measurement and reporting.

1. Make it a cooperative, joint effort between city departments and the city auditor; focus on improvement, not punishment.
2. Make sure the information in the report is useful to managers and the public.
3. Use existing data and management information where possible; coordinate and link with other performance reporting.
4. Limit reporting to the largest and most visible services; do not overload citizens with data on all programs.
5. Keep terms simple and clear and the report easy to read; use a few well-selected indicators that are reliable and valid.
6. Aim for continuous improvement over time; do not expect perfection.

The SEA Report cycle

The working principles were carried out in each phase of Portland's SEA Report cycle. The cycle includes developing or refining SEA indicators for each service, collecting and auditing SEA data, analyzing and reviewing trends, presenting and reporting results, and improving indicators and reporting from year to year. Each phase of the cycle is described below.

Figure 2. City of Portland fire bureau performance indicators.

| | Fires/1,000 residents | | Lives lost/ 100,000 residents | Total fire loss per capita (in constant dollars) | Structural loss as % of value of property exposed | Percentage of travel times within 4 mins. | |
	Structural	Total				Fire	Medical
FY 1988–89	3.3	7.8	.7	$34.81	.48%	75%	81%
FY 1989–90	3.0	7.0	1.9	$40.26	.71%	75%	78%
FY 1990–91	2.9	6.4	3.2	$35.26	.39%	72%	75%
FY 1991–92	2.5	6.9	2.0	$49.74	.47%	72%	74%
Goal (91-92)	—	—	<1.9*	<$35.67*	<.51%*	70%	75%
Average annual % change	–9%	–4%	+67%	+15%	+8%	–1%	–3%

*No more than 97% of prior years' average.

Development and refinement of indicators   SEA indicators were initially developed and are continually reviewed and refined cooperatively with management and staff of service departments. A number of meetings were required during the first year of reporting, but subsequent reports have required less time and consultation between auditors and department staff. Audit staff help clarify service objectives, refine performance indicators and improve performance reporting where possible. The auditors critique indicators but generally rely on the departments to agree on a set of indicators for their service area. Auditors also work closely with each service manager to develop appropriate questions for the annual citizen satisfaction survey.

Collecting and auditing data   Data for the SEA Report are collected and submitted by service departments to the audit services division on forms provided by the division. The departments also provide information on the source of the data and a contact person to call if auditors have a concern about the data. Audit staff test and review the accuracy and reliability of the SEA data, collect information from comparison cities and administer the annual citizen survey.

Review and analysis of trends   After the SEA data are audited, auditors review and analyze trends and changing conditions. A draft report is prepared, and each service area receives a working draft to review and comment on. Usually the departments provide explanatory information to help clarify the outcome of their programs. While some of the SEA data are presented in narrative form, the report often uses graphs and tables to present the data. Some data are displayed in a map of the city by the seven neighborhood coalitions, as shown in Figure 3.

Dissemination of results   The final SEA Report is issued publicly to the city council, all city managers, citizen groups, the media, business and civic groups, neighborhood associations and other interested parties. A formal presentation is made to the city council, and a press release is issued to major print media and to television and radio stations.

Evaluation   After each year's SEA Report, staff of the audit services division meet with representatives of each department to get feedback on the report and to agree on modification and improvements for next year's report. Council members and managers provide suggestions on how to make next year's report more useful.

*Figure 3. Percent of residents rating their neighborhood
"safe" or "very safe" during the day
(significant changes from 1991).*

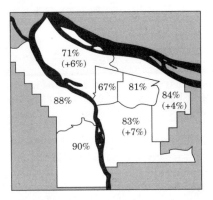

Source: City of Portland Auditor's Office, 1992 Citizen Survey.

Costs of SEA reporting

Each year since preparation of the initial feasibility study in
1991, the audit services division has spent less time and effort on
the SEA Report. Auditor and support staff hours have declined
from 3,000 hours for the first feasibility test to 1,800 hours for
the second annual SEA Report issued in 1993. Audit hours include indicator development; auditing of SEA data provided by
departments; collection of data from other cities; administration
of the citizen survey; and report writing, layout and production.

Time spent annually by service departments collecting SEA
data has varied from five hours in one department to 20 hours in
another. Average time spent by the six service areas represented
in the SEA Report averaged about 10 hours. Additional efforts
began in 1993 in some departments to design and implement
projects to collect missing management information which will
provide data for several SEA indicators. For example, the city's
parks and recreation department is spending several hundred
hours in 1993 to develop a process for trained observer ratings of
city parks and recreation facilities. This process will help the bureau measure its progress and performance in maintaining facilities and parks.

The annual citizen survey administered by the audit division
has cost about $17,000 per year. The anonymous, statistically

valid survey was administered by mail and included several features: three separate mailings to 10,000 addresses selected at random, telephone survey of non-respondents to test reliability of respondent information, data entry of returned surveys into a database for statistical analysis, and contracting-out for printing and mailing services.

Effects and benefits

After the first two annual SEA Reports, the audit services division has identified a number of preliminary effects and benefits. The SEA reporting process has had an impact on program management, the budget process, citizen accountability and audit effectiveness.

Better program management   The process of defining missions, clarifying goals and identifying performance indicators has encouraged managers to focus on the purpose of their programs and helped increase understanding of performance measurement in the departments. Many believe that if managers have a clear focus on intended results and outcomes of their programs, ongoing decisions have better connection with mission and more clarity of purpose, resulting in more coordinated and rational management.

Portland's SEA Reports have stimulated discussion leading to specific actions to improve operations in several departments. For example, the 1992 SEA Report showed a negative trend in water turbidity, an important indicator of the quality of the city's drinking water. The city council noted the trend during a public presentation of SEA results and asked for an explanation from the water department. After some review, it was discovered that some data in the department's annual public brochure on water quality were not comparable from year to year and needed to be revised.

In another case, auditor discussions with managers about developing better data to document achievement of employee empowerment goals caused the police department to design and initiate an annual employee job satisfaction survey.

Improved public accountability   While it is premature to assess the SEA Report's ultimate impact on public accountability, the report has been used on several occasions by citizen groups and the local media to assess and evaluate the performance of city government. The newly elected mayor provided dozens of copies of the report to her transition team to help formulate plans and recommendations for her administration. Hundreds of copies of the report have been distributed to local media, neigh-

borhood associations and civic groups. These groups have used
the report to prepare newspaper editorials, comment on the annual budget and educate themselves on the performance of their
city government. Because the document reports both positive and
negative performance information that is audited by staff from
the elected auditor's office, it is viewed as credible and objective.

Improved information for budget decisions   The SEA Report has been used in a variety of ways to assist the council, budget analysts and the public in the annual review of budget
requests. The report was used by the city council during a series
of budget workshops that preceded public hearings in 1993. They
found the report valuable in conducting budget oversight, as
well. Budget analysts use data in the report to analyze department budget requests and to prepare budget analyses. SEA data
and graphs also were presented in the adopted city budget.

More effective auditing   The annual preparation of the SEA
Report has indirect benefits for the audit services division. The
annual nature of the report helps audit staff stay in frequent contact with the city's major departments and keeps the spotlight on
major problem areas. Unexplained negative trends in a performance indicator may suggest the need for more focused performance audit work. Audit staff increase their knowledge of service
areas so that future detailed audit work in a department may be
more directed and require less time. The public reporting of SEA
indicators has encouraged managers to publicly commit to several program improvements that can be followed up on by audit
staff.

Lessons and challenges

A number of lessons have been learned from the SEA reporting
effort in the City of Portland. The auditors most involved in this
city's three-year process believe others may reach similar conclusions about the process.

1. Valid and objective SEA data can be collected, audited and
    reported. The relative ease of collection and audit may be due
    in part to Portland's experience with performance measure-
    ment in prior years and the availability of performance audit
    staff. SEA reporting may take longer to plan and implement
    in jurisdictions with little experience with performance re-
    porting or budgeting.
2. SEA reporting is an ongoing process that improves incre-
    mentally over time. The annual nature of the effort helps
    educate and "culturalize" managers and users, provides his-

torical trends and a longer-term perspective, and gives the organization time to refine and improve the product continually.

3. Consistent reporting of valid performance information creates a demand for more and better information. Users are requesting more conclusions and analysis of impact, more highlighting and explanations of warning trends, specific suggestions for council action and additional opportunities for public discussion of report results.

4. SEA reporting requires less time, effort and cost with each subsequent report. Routines become established, data collection is faster, and auditing methods are refined.

5. SEA information can complement and enhance traditional financial information.

SEA reporting in Portland also faces some continuing challenges that may reduce its effectiveness as an accountability tool for citizens, public managers and elected officials. These challenges include

- Developing better methods for communicating results to reach more citizens
- Devising new and creative techniques for presenting large amounts of data in easy-to-read and inviting ways
- Improving coordination with federal, state and regional performance measurement efforts to reduce duplication and inconsistency
- Creating more incentives to use the data.

Conclusion

The preparation of Portland's Service Efforts and Accomplishments Report has required significant staff effort and resource investment. The process of developing, collecting and reporting performance indicators is slow, and improvements are incremental. Early indications are, however, that the effort is justified. City analysts and citizen groups use it regularly, and city council members find it a useful tool in overseeing city programs. Department managers differ in their opinions; those most in need of performance information use it greatly, while others with better management information systems find the SEA Report too brief and simplified. A number of other local governments, state offices and the federal government have found Portland's report useful as an aid in designing their own experiments with performance reporting.

Portland's service efforts and accomplishments reporting has shown promise in helping improve accountability. The city's initial efforts indicate that the progress can benefit the organization. The concept remains experimental, and much needs to be learned about how best to carry it out. Continual experimentation and refinement by others will contribute to better understanding of effective ways to measure government performance.

GASB'S advocacy of service efforts and accomplishments (SEA) reporting

In 1986, the Governmental Accounting Standards Board (GASB) issued its first concepts statement, which establishes concepts of financial reporting for state and local government entities. That statement sets forth the types of information the board considers necessary if financial reporting is to cull useful information for users. Included among the concepts is the objective that financial reporting should provide information to help users assess the service efforts, costs, and accomplishments of the government.

Subsequent research led GASB to conclude that measures of service efforts and accomplishments (SEA), especially measures of results (outcomes), were essential to measuring and reporting on the performance of government services and were being developed and used, though not widely, in each of twelve services of state and local government selected for examination. The types of SEA measures recommended for external financial reporting were:

- Inputs (resources applied)
- Outputs (services or products being provided)
- Outcomes (objectives achieved)
- Efficiency (the cost per unit of output or unit of outcome).

Researchers also identified the need for explanatory factors that would measure factors, other than the service outputs being provided, that influence the outcomes of services being provided. [The two figures that follow show sample SEA measures.]

Source: Excerpted from James Fountain, Jr., and Mitchell Roob, "Service Efforts and Accomplishments Measures," *Public Management* 76 (March 1994): 6–12. *Public Management* is published by ICMA.

Categories and examples of SEA measures.

Categories of SEA measures	Examples
Measures of efforts	
Financial information	Cost of salaries, benefits, materials and supplies, etc.
Nonfinancial information	Number of personnel, equipment to be used, other capital assets, etc.
Measures of accomplishments	
Output measures	Lane-miles of road repaired, number of crimes investigated, number of commuters on public transit, etc.
Outcome measures	Percentage of lane-miles in excellent or good condition, clearance rate for serious crimes, percentage of citizens rating their neighborhood as safe or very safe, etc.
Measures that relate efforts to accomplishments	
Efficiency efforts to outputs	Cost per lane-mile of road repaired, cost per transit passenger, cost per serious crime investigated or per arrest, etc.
Efficiency efforts to outcomes	Cost per transit passenger arriving at destination within specific time schedule, cost per lane-mile of road maintained in excellent or good condition, cost per serious crime cleared by indictment, etc.
Explanatory information	Includes both factors substantially outside the control of the entity and factors over which the entity has some control. For example, the density of the population, the percentage of trucks in vehicle traffic, and the unemployment rate are all factors outside the control of the entity. The type of construction used for high-ways, the number of police officers per capita, and the number of buses per route-mile are all explanatory factors over which the entity has some control. Also includes narrative information provided with SEA measures about the reason for a given level of performance or how results may have been affected by explanatory factors.

Source: *GASB Exposure Draft of a Proposed Concepts Statement*, Service Efforts and Accomplishments Reporting (Norwalk, CT: GASB, September 15, 1993), 21–25.

A sample set of service efforts and accomplishments indicators: Solid waste collection.

Indicator	Rationale for selecting indicator
Inputs	
Expenditures	
Current dollar[a,b]	
Constant dollar[a,b]	Provides information on total resources input
Number of personnel[b]	
Number of vehicles[b]	Provides a breakdown of resources by labor and capital
Outputs	
Number of customers served[a,b]	
Tons of waste collected[a,b]	Provides a measure of workload; enables comparison over time; provides data for unit costs
Outcomes	
Percentage of scheduled collections missed[a,b]	
Percentage of scheduled collections not completed on schedule[a,b]	Attempts to quantify whether service goals were reached, data are readily available
Percentage of streets rated acceptably clean[b]	Objective assessment of service goal
Average customer satisfaction rating[a,b]	
Number of customer complaints	Assesses customer satisfaction with the service
Efficiency	
Cost per ton of solid waste collected[a,b]	
Cost per customer served[a,b]	Indicates efficiency; already widely used; will enable comparisons with other jurisdictions
Tons of solid waste collected per employee[a,b]	Useful in assessing employee efficiency

continued

A sample set of service efforts and accomplishments indicators: Solid waste collection (continued)

Explanatory information
Frequency of collections[a,b]
Location of collections[a,b]
Composition of solid waste
Climatic conditions
Terrain
Average wages of employees
Type of agency(ies) providing the service
Type of contract with service provider (if relevant)
Average number of customers per collection route-mile[a]
Types of vehicles
Average crew size on vehicle
Type of containers used by customers
Percentage of recyclable waste recycled
Transfer costs

Indicates level of convenience to customer; usually readily available

Source: Marc A. Rubin, *Sanitation Collection and Disposal: Service Efforts and Accomplishments Reporting—Its Time Has Come* (Norwalk, CT: GASB, 1991), 38–39. Reprinted by permission.

Note: The recommended indicators presented in this exhibit are illustrative. They are intended to serve as a starting point for use in the development of a comprehensive set of SEA indicators for external reporting of an entity's results of operation. This exhibit does not provide illustrations of indicator disaggregation or of comparison data such as trends, targets, or other comparable entities. Both disaggregation and comparison data are important aspects of SEA reporting.

[a]Designates an indicator for which it would be desirable to disaggregate by customer type (commercial, single-residential, multiple-residential).

[b]Designates an indicator that should be disaggregated by district.

Silicon Valley Civics

Allan E. Alter

Sunnyvale, Calif., is an anomaly in the nation's IT breadbasket. True, the city has attracted national attention for its performance-measurement systems. True, it has achieved financial stability and a satisfied citizenry through the masterful gathering and deployment of data. Located in the heart of Silicon Valley, Sunnyvale owes most of its achievements to information—but not to information technology.

Sunnyvale's 19-year-old "information-driven system of calculating performance," as former Mayor John Mercer described it, has received rave reviews for helping deliver high-quality services at low cost to taxpayers. The city was lavishly praised by David Osborne in *Reinventing Government,* his best-selling book on public-sector innovation. A joint study by the four major U.S. budget and accounting offices, including the Office of Management and Budget, concluded that Sunnyvale offers the best example of a comprehensive approach to performance measurement in the United States. And experts on government voted Sunnyvale onto *CIO*'s High-Performance 100 list (see "The People's Choice," August 1992) for efficiency and effectiveness.

City Manager Thomas F. Lewcock credits the city's management information system with helping Sunnyvale reduce the cost of government by 20 percent from 1985 to 1990, run a budget surplus of at least $500,000 annually for the past 15 years and win a 90 percent satisfaction rating on its most recent survey of residents. And Sunnyvale has weathered the fiscal crunch

Reprinted through the courtesy of *CIO*. © 1992, CIO Communications, Inc.

in California without cutting programs or laying off staff, according to *San Jose Mercury News* reporter Leland Joachim.

Sunnyvale appears as an oasis of efficiency at a time when cries of government mismanagement are on everyone's lips. But the city also has a startling message for CIOs: Don't be seduced by technology. The soul of a true management information system is not the machine—it is process, culture and information. Do it right, and you may not need expensive, flashy technology at all.

Not that Sunnyvale is afraid to deploy advanced technology. Tree-pruners use hand-held computers to enter data into an inventory system of the city's 38,000 trees. Officials can tap into a system that tracks zoning, inspections, construction permits and other data by parcel of land. The library boasts a bilingual computerized catalog system. And the public safety department (Sunnyvale's combined police-and-fire force) pioneered computer-aided dispatch systems back in 1975 and is currently piloting a computerized fingerprint ID system that focuses on local suspects.

Yet the computer systems that help managers run day-to-day operations and plan for the future are based on old technology and archaic data-processing practices. Remote data entry? Most city employees track their work and hours on time cards; these are shipped to the city's Finance Department where the data is entered manually into a minicomputer. Online, real-time information? The data, once processed, comes back in the form of printed monthly status reports. LANs? The city is experimenting with downloading budget data from the minicomputer to the department managers' PCs. But Sunnyvale's department managers still submit their budgets on paper, receive data in the form of paper reports and are not obliged to use computers to prepare their budgets and calculate citizen-satisfaction indices.

What Sunnyvale calls its "management information system," then, is really an occasionally computer-assisted managerial process with many interlocking parts: long-range planning, a biannual budget process (see related story, page 142) and two feedback loops—one for quality of service, one for tracking costs and auditing. By setting spending ceilings and quantifiable, measurable service objectives, the process drives managers to be rigorous and methodical, results-oriented and cost-conscious.

It also empowers them. Line managers must make their numbers, said Lewcock, "but we give our department heads lots of management freedom to marshal their forces to get the best result. A typical governmental organization controls how people do the job but doesn't hold them accountable for results. We've reversed that."

Sunnyvale's management process is reinforced by financial incentives. The city provides bonuses to managers who exceed the budget's objectives and—more radically—cuts 5 percent from the salaries of managers who come in below plan, unless there are mitigating circumstances. (Managers who have their salaries cut usually leave government, according to Larry Stone, a member of the city council for 15 years.)

The process can be tough on managers in other ways as well. Marvin Rose, who became the city's director of public works in 1989, said the process can intimidate new managers: After six months on the job, they become frustrated by all the reporting, planning and budgeting. Jess Barba, the recently retired public safety chief, agreed. The process's downside is that it requires "lots of work," he said. "It doesn't just happen."

Some managers "work too hard, put in too much time" trying to keep up with its demands, said Lewcock. "You have to be real sensitive to your people, or they can easily push themselves over the side."

This results-oriented approach to management fits well with Sunnyvale's political culture, which reflects Silicon Valley's eagerness to embrace innovation and a typically suburban, Western belief that the government's role is to provide high-quality services as efficiently as possible. Sunnyvale employs a council-manager form of government that restricts the elected city council to setting goals and approving budgets. Day-to-day operations are managed by a non-elected bureaucracy led by an appointed city manager. Political partisanship, patronage and careerism are further checked by term limits for council members and a California law forbidding political parties from participating in local elections.

Thus, while strategic issues remain the province of elected officials, Sunnyvale's bureaucrats are able to counter political hot air with hard facts. This is nowhere more obvious than in Sunnyvale's performance-based budgeting process, which encompasses long-range planning, financial and performance budgeting and expense-tracking. The budget, which establishes service objectives and spells out what it will take to meet them, ensures that the city is working toward attainable goals and that it is, in fact, attaining them.

The city's streets offer impressive evidence of this process's concrete benefits. At a time when everyone is complaining about America's crumbling infrastructure, Sunnyvale is simultaneously saving money on road maintenance and getting better roads, thanks to a plan initiated eight years ago by then-Public Works Director Ed James (now assistant city manager).

"We evaluated every road in the city," said Lewcock. "Streets were rated in four levels. An 'A' street was in good shape, a 'D' street in poor shape." Based on that study, James suggested that

What do we want, how do we get there?

"Performance-based budgeting" may sound jargony, but in Sunny-vale's case it is accurate. The budgeting process is at the heart of this California city's unusual approach to government and management.

Conventional budgets are organized by line item. In Framingham, Mass., for example, where *CIO* is published, the Highway Division's budget lists salaries, operations and snow removal, among other things. But Sunnyvale's budget lists service objectives instead. These set the level of service to be delivered, performance indicators for measuring how well goals are met, a list of tasks that must be performed to meet each objective and the maximum allowable cost.

For instance, one service objective is to "ensure a safe and orderly flow of pedestrian, bicycle and vehicular traffic . . . to achieve a ratio of [no more than] 3.42 accidents per million miles traveled." This objective includes five tasks: conducting traffic and bicycle safety operations and providing pedestrian traffic enforcement, crossing-guard services and traffic enforcement.

Altogether, Sunnyvale's budget contains approximately 300 service objectives and 1,500 tasks. "That's 1,500 mini-budgets," said City Manager Thomas F. Lewcock. "That would be impossible without a fairly involved computer system to do the calculations and measurements." Computers process the data used to track these items and issue monthly updates on whether budget goals are being met. The system calculates cost per unit of work and tracks some service goals—such as the percentage of 911 calls the public safety department responds to in under five minutes.

Not only must managers balance revenue and expenditures for the two-year period covered in each budget; they must project a balanced budget for the next 10 years. Lewcock acknowledged that the projections—based on "guesstimations" of demographic shifts and inflation rates—are fallible. Nevertheless, "this approach has been of incalculable value over the past decade," he said. "You quickly find that things you think you can afford today are unaffordable over the long term."

That's a big help for elected officials, said veteran council member Larry Stone. "We can say, 'Wait a minute, constituents, that sounds good, but do you know this thing loses money in year seven or eight?' It allows you to say no to public expenditures."

–A. E. Alter

the council approve a new objective for road maintenance: Improve each street to level A. He defined each level according to a set of measurements of road conditions (amount of elasticity in the asphalt, number of surface cracks, bumpiness). And he set cost ceilings for improving roads at each level.

James and Lewcock justified their proposal before the city council by projecting costs over 10 years. While the project would require that an additional $500,000 be spent on road improvement in the first year, the projections showed long-term savings.

Road workers now regularly measure road conditions and report on how they compare with the service objectives. Every day, maintenance crews record hours and work performed on their time cards. Every month Lewcock and the public works director look over a report to see if maintenance costs are on-track. Occasionally they send out an auditor to make sure the work reported on the time cards is actually being performed and that the roads are in the condition public works department officials claim.

The result? "Today the annual street-maintenance budget is $500,000 less, and the streets are in [better] condition," said Lewcock.

That level of performance not only makes Sunnyvale a better place to live (and drive)—it also makes the politicians look good. Elected officials recognize the value of having ready answers to their constituents' questions—especially when those answers are good news. "I constantly get calls [saying things like], 'My street was perfectly fine, and people are putting a new surface on it. Why do we spend so much money on it?'" said Stone. "The answer is, we spend less on surfacing because we maintain our streets before they get potholes."

Sunnyvale's approach to projects like the road-improvement plan dates back to 1973, when the federal Office of Management and Budget cosponsored pilot performance-measurement programs in a dozen cities. Sunnyvale's was the only one to survive. It took root, according to ex-mayor Mercer, because the city combines a performance-oriented political culture with Silicon Valley's infatuation with innovation and information. "In Sunnyvale, if our staff came up with an idea no one else was doing, we got more excited about it," said Mercer, who is now chief minority counsel on the U.S. Senate Committee on Government Affairs.

Former Public Safety Department Chief Barba has lived with this process longer than anyone else in town. His department hosted the original OMB pilot, and over the years he's combined those principles with his own passion for measuring customer satisfaction.

As Total Quality Management advocates know, quality is largely in the eyes of the customer. Accordingly, one way the city ensures quality service is by measuring customer satisfaction. Like other branches of Sunnyvale's government, the public safety department mails out citizen-satisfaction surveys to see if residents are happy with the service it provides; at least six areas of service within the department are studied each year. After the surveys have been filled out and mailed back, the results are added up on a calculator and converted into a citizen-satisfaction index, which the department uses as a guide for improving procedures and policies.

Barba has been known to really push the envelope in the name of customer service. Once, when his department surveyed every motorist involved in an accident during an entire month, he calculated the satisfaction index for the one-third who were slapped with a citation. "[The city manager] told me, 'You are either gutsy or stupid,'" Barba laughed. It turned out he was gutsy; 73 percent of motorists who received citations said they were satisfied with the professionalism and quality of service provided by officers at the accident scene.

"Isn't it nice to put in eight hours of hard work and know that's what people want and appreciate?" said Barba. "Nothing is worse than working hard and finding out what you're doing isn't what people want. That's a waste of time, money and life.

"And what a wonderful tool—if you subscribe to the principles of behavior modification—to get people to improve their performance," he went on. "Years ago, the only letters we received were complaints. Now the ratio of letters commending our service to complaint letters is four-to-one."

The focus on customer service and on measuring and tracking performance are also evident in Sunnyvale's IS function. Four years ago, Lewcock handed responsibility for IS to his library director, Beverley J. Simmons. As Simmons put it, Lewcock believed that "if I could lead an organization that was good in providing information, then I must be able to provide an interesting perspective on the technology that provided the information." Since then, Simmons has also been given responsibility for records management—thus consolidating responsibility for all information under one title: director of libraries and information services.

IS operates by the same principles as other departments: performance-based budgeting and long-range planning. Service objectives cover percentage of uptime, speed of repairs and user satisfaction with reliability, service quality and timeliness of response. For example, last year IS achieved its goal of responding to 98 percent of all requests for assistance within one working day. The only area where users give IS poor marks, said Simmons, is in the cost of service to users.

Lewcock is tough-minded about spending more on technology. Line managers who want a new application fare best if they can prove it will save the city money over 10 years while improving service levels. "You go in with a Nordstrom appetite but operate on a Kmart budget," said Barba.

Lewcock is also tightfisted when it comes to the city's central computer system. He has already set aside money for modernizing it and authorized Simmons to lead an interdisciplinary group to create a new strategic plan for IS. But other than agreeing to upgrade the system from three Hewlett-Packard 3000 minicomputers to an H-P 9000, and managers' PCs to '386s, he's kept the purse strings tight.

Sunnyvale is not everyone's idea of democracy. Tom McEnery, the former mayor of nearby San Jose, does not put much faith in an enlightened bureaucracy, and many Americans would agree with him that "the well-laid plans of bureaucrats often run contrary to what Joe and Martha want to see happen." Besides, while San Jose has also received praise for being well run, it is a bigger city with different, often more-complex problems. As McEnery pointed out, it's easier to go from plan to implementation "in a rather homogeneous community that doesn't have the problems you see on the six o'clock news."

Proud as he is of his city's accomplishments, Lewcock does not think that others should blindly copy Sunnyvale; each city must find an approach that best fits its culture and population. But he believes that a city staff guided by clear goals and good information can usually manage to please the average citizen. Sunnyvale officials, for example, consistently meet 95 percent of the city's service objectives. And Sunnyvale's information-rich approach to management "reinforces a fundamental belief I have," said Lewcock. "Tell people what the objective is, and they will be incredibly creative in getting it done."

Performance Auditing: Catalyst for Change

Richard C. Tracy

Editor's note: Performance auditing is a narrowly targeted and extremely systematic form of performance monitoring. Usually, it involves a detailed examination of a limited number of functions, conducted as an ad hoc study rather than on an ongoing basis more typical of other forms of performance monitoring.

Like most bureaucracies, local governments resist organizational change. Government officials and managers seeking innovation face formidable obstacles, not the least of which is organizational inertia—"that's the way we have always done it." This natural resistance to change is compounded by the provisions of negotiated labor contracts or by long-standing political agreements that can limit flexibility to try new, more effective methods for delivering services. Plans for overhauling outdated administrative systems also can be frustrated by the lack of objective information on organizational performance. Performance data often is unavailable because of local government's preference for funding direct services rather than staff functions that can analyze and report on how well services are provided.

The City of Portland, Oregon, has adopted a method of bringing about operational and administrative change—performance auditing. Approved and funded in July 1983, the performance audit program has issued a string of 25 audit reports and studies on many aspects of Portland's government. Major studies were conducted on police staffing and deployment practices, employee pension and disability costs, and the fiscal impact of city annexations. Each audit report has contained recommendations and in-

Reprinted with permission from *Government Finance Review* (February 1988): 7–11.

formation to help managers improve program efficiency and effectiveness. Many of the studies issued have helped management make significant changes in the way programs are administered. This article describes the audit program and discusses three case examples that illustrate the catalytic effect of performance auditing on organizational change in Portland.

Program description

Responsibility for the performance audit program rests with the independently elected, nonpartisan city auditor. Audits are conducted by the Internal Audit Division of the Office of the City Auditor in accordance with generally accepted governmental auditing standards developed by the Comptroller General of the United States. These standards, also referred to as the "Yellow Book," require due professional care in conducting audits, freedom from impairments to independence and objectivity, and professionally qualified auditors. Amendments to the city charter passed by the voters in 1985 gave the audit program full access to records for audit purposes and require departments to respond in writing to audit recommendations.

The division's primary goal is to promote accountability to the public and to improve the efficiency and effectiveness of city government. Since the inception of the audit program, it has identified more than $6.6 million in potential savings and increased revenue. Other audits, while not identifying measurable dollar savings, have provided objective performance information to managers and the city council. The scope of audit work includes:

- Evaluating organizational efficiency and effectiveness
- Checking compliance with legal and administrative requirements
- Evaluating the adequacy of internal control systems
- Assessing the potential for loss or abuse of resources.

The annual budget for the program is approximately $500,000, of which 90 percent is for salary and benefits. The program has 10 full-time positions including an audit director, seven staff auditors, one electronic data processing (EDP) auditor and a secretary.

Selection of audits to be conducted by the internal audit division is done in advance of each fiscal year. Council members, managers of city bureaus and other interested parties are consulted as to what areas would benefit from performance audit review. These suggestions are combined with a list of programs which have potential for cost savings or increased revenue and then rated on the basis of established selection criteria. The city auditor oversees audit preparation and publicly releases the audits conducted by the division's professional staff. Through the audit activities of the internal audit division, the elected city auditor can help ensure the proper handling and use of public funds in Portland's commission form of government. Figure 1 illustrates the role of auditing in the City of Portland.

Change through auditing

Audits conducted by Portland's performance audit program have changed city organizations in varying degrees. While some managers have implemented new administrative systems consistent with audit recommendations, others have taken different approaches to address audit findings. In many cases, organizations have gone much further in making organizational change than was suggested or considered in the audit report.

Figure 1. Role of performance auditing in the City of Portland.

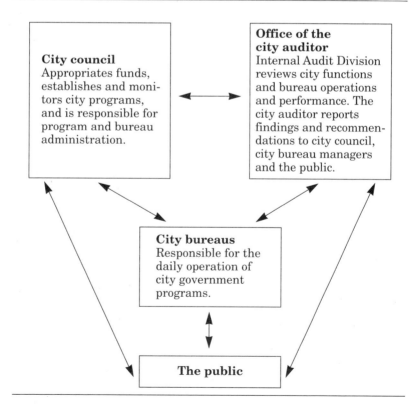

City council
Appropriates funds, establishes and monitors city programs, and is responsible for program and bureau administration.

Office of the city auditor
Internal Audit Division reviews city functions and bureau operations and performance. The city auditor reports findings and recommendations to city council, city bureau managers and the public.

City bureaus
Responsible for the daily operation of city government programs.

The public

The three case examples discussed below are examples of organizational change that has occurred following performance audits. Each example discusses the audit findings and recommendations, actions taken to address problem areas, and the change or improvements in organizational performance accomplished by managers.

Case 1: Improving city risk management   In October 1985, the internal audit division completed an audit of the Bureau of Risk Management and its program to protect the city from workers' compensation and liability losses. The audit found that the city had a high number of claims and a deficit in the reserve funds needed to pay future claims liabilities.

Auditors reported that too little was being done to prevent workers' compensation claims from occurring and that liability claims costs increased by 100 percent in a four-year period. Analysis showed that Portland had substantially more disability claims and experienced a higher level of lost workdays than other jurisdictions. City workers submitted 5.7 claims per 100 employees, while workers with the State of Oregon and with other Oregon localities had 1.7 and 2.3 claims respectively. The audit also revealed that the city's reserve fund for paying future claims had a deficit of $1.9 million, and the ability to pay future obligations was threatened.

To address these problem areas, the performance audit report recommended a variety of actions, including the following:

- Strengthen the existing loss control and prevention program
- Help city departments to develop plans and training to control claims
- Provide statistical reports on claims rates and costs to city council
- Make reserve funds actuarially sound
- Make departments more accountable for losses through revised cost allocation systems.

In large part due to the findings of the performance audit, city council and managers initiated a major overhaul of the risk management program. Based on recommendations from a loss control committee composed of city managers, the council passed an ordinance to strengthen the city's approach to preventing and controlling disability and liability claims. The plan included setting claims reduction goals, obtaining written plans from all city organizations on how goals would be achieved, and reporting to council on the progress of meeting targeted reductions. Following passage of the ordinance, each city bureau worked with risk management representatives to develop individual loss control plans to address the particular risk exposure and loss experience unique to its operation.

The result of this major planning and assessment effort is a July 1987 publication, *City of Portland Loss Control Plans.* The book includes historical claims counts and costs, targeted reduction goals and goals for claims costs in 1990. The book also contains specific descriptions of the loss control programs for each city department. Overall the city set annual cost reduction goals for three years at 9 percent for workers' compensation and 10 percent for general and fleet liability. Increased attention to loss control is expected to produce as much as $900,000 per year in cost savings to the city.

To shore up the claims reserve fund, the council also transferred more than $1 million from contingency reserves and made several supplemental appropriations to meet requirements. Self-insured funds are now actuarially sound and able to meet future claims obligations.

Although it is too soon to judge the full impact of the revised loss control program on Portland claims, initial indications in FY 1986–87 show that the heightened awareness of safety has slowed the growth of claims in some bureaus. Disability costs were $200,000 lower than expected, while liability claims have remained largely stable. The Risk Management Bureau also has revised its cost allocation methodology so that the bureaus with the highest loss exposure and experience must budget for higher "premium" costs than city organizations with lower claims, thereby reducing appropriations available for direct services. The revised cost allocation process is expected to create additional incentives to control liability and disability costs.

Case 2: Controlling employee health costs   In late 1986, the internal audit division issued a performance audit report entitled "Containing the Costs of City Health Care Programs." The audit was the third in a series of reviews of city employee health benefits. The chief reason for the audit was that health benefit costs had tripled, from $3.6 million in FY 1976–77 to $10.8 million in FY 1985–86. The audit evaluated the reasons for rising health care costs, compared the cost of Portland's plan to other government health programs and described various ways to control future cost increases.

The auditors found that while inflation accounted for more than 50 percent of the increase in health costs, the city's major health plan was more generous than other government health plans surveyed nationwide. The survey, conducted under contract by a consulting firm, found that the city provided a higher dollar level of health coverage than 90 percent of 22 state and local governments reviewed. Moreover, the city also provided more total employer-paid benefits (i.e., pensions, insurance) than 75 percent of other governments.

The auditors found that after inflation, the major factor influencing the 200 percent increase in health costs was the liberal plan coverage. For example, no adjustments had been made over the years in employee-paid deductibles or maximum out-of-pocket expenses. Consequently, the city had absorbed all of the inflationary cost increases over several years. More importantly, the city provided very generous coverage, including 100 percent of all basic services ("first dollar coverage"), and special, high-cost services, such as chiropractic visits and full vision care.

In order to suggest ways to control rising health benefits costs, the auditors evaluated a number of alternatives. The major techniques suggested in the audit report were:

- Plan redesign: Introduce more employee participation in the cost of the plan through higher deductibles or copayment provisions. Limit special coverages such as those for prescriptions and chiropractic services. Require employees to share a portion of the annual premium. Auditors projected potential savings of $200,000 to $1.1 million annually through various redesign methods.
- Alternative services: Introduce alternative services to lower hospital and surgery costs, such as outpatient surgery, pre-admission testing and preauthorization of certain treatments.
- Negotiate lower hospital rates: Explore opportunities to lower hospital rates by negotiating directly with hospitals to obtain lower rates.
- Initiate employee wellness programs: Encourage employees to maintain their own health. Programs could include annual health assessments, smoking cessation programs, exercise and nutrition education.
- Develop and use improved management information: Produce better data to track health expenditures, monitor high-use providers and evaluate the effectiveness of cost containment efforts.

City managers took a number of actions to respond to the recommendations contained in the audit report. For example, the Bureau of Personnel Services proposed bidding claims processing in order to encourage competition and lower the administrative costs of the program. Also the bureau developed several lower-cost health plan alternatives, including a preferred provider organization (PPO).

Bureau management also received city council approval to negotiate a redesigned health benefits program with one of the city's labor unions. The resulting labor contract eliminated many of the high-cost plan provisions, while providing employees with a wider choice of other benefits to suit individual needs. The bureau also contracted with a health consulting firm to help develop improved financial information to assist in monitoring and managing the city's health program.

While management generally has been responsive to the recommendations in the audit report, they have chosen a variety of different approaches to contain health costs that were not considered or analyzed by the auditors. The major effort is the implementation of a "cafeteria style" health program that provides employees a choice of five different health plans and four different dental plans. This program, covering nonrepresented employees, was implemented shortly before the audit commenced and was expanded and modified during 1987 and 1988. The program allocates a set dollar amount of benefits for each eligible employee and allows individual choice on how to expend benefit dollars. Rather than spend their benefit allocation on health coverage, employees may elect to receive cash or a variety of services, such as child care or expanded life or disability coverage. Managers expect employees to shift to lower-cost health plans in order to free up benefit allocations for other services that better meet family needs. In the long term, city officials believe this approach will have a more significant impact on benefits costs than those proposed in the audit report.

Recent data on health expenditures has shown that employees are switching from the original, high-cost program to other programs that have higher deductibles or copayments. It is believed that employees are making this conversion, in part, to take advantage of cash-back options or to purchase more life or disability insurance. The city also has experienced a slowdown in claims costs in its primary plan that may be due to other efforts to control claims costs, such as preadmission testing, outpatient surgery and limits on chiropractic care.

Case 3: Reducing delinquent special assessments   A performance audit of the city's process for collecting special assessments was issued in September 1985. The audit evaluated the city's methods for collecting lien payments resulting from special assessments. Special assessment charges are used to recover costs from property owners for city services associated with sewer and street improvements, sidewalk repairs and nuisance abatement.

The audit revealed that more than $3.5 million in assessment payments were at least 30 days past due. Approximately $1.1 million of this total was owed by 16 large property owners, less than 2 percent of all delinquent owners. Auditors found that delinquencies were growing, with $900,000 becoming delinquent in the current year.

Analysis by the audit team showed that unpaid assessments were reducing available cash in several city funds that was needed to pay for new street and sewer projects and to repay improvement bonds. While the city retained a lien on all assessed properties and would eventually collect delinquent amounts, unrecovered debts were creating cash flow shortages and making it difficult to fund improvement projects.

Auditors found special assessment delinquencies were caused not only by depressed economic conditions, but also by inadequate city collection policies and procedures. Specifically, the city lacked effective collection methods, notification procedures and management information to ensure timely payment of assessment amounts. Additionally, the city had discontinued selling property as the final step in the collection process. Without this ultimate sanction for nonpayment, there was little motivation for property owners to pay their assessments on time.

The audit report recommended several steps to reduce assessment delinquencies and strengthen the assessment process. Major recommendations included:

- Implement more aggressive collection techniques
- Provide for penalties and fees to recover administrative costs and to discourage nonpayment
- Improve communication with property owners to clarify obligations and consequences of nonpayment
- Develop management information to track age and status of liens
- Reinstate foreclosure as a final sanction for nonpayment.

Response to the audit report was immediate and comprehensive. Foremost was the hiring of a liens collection supervisor and the reclassification of several existing positions to focus staff effort on the delinquency problem. An Assessment Collection Task Force was created to recommend to city council ways to improve the timeliness of lien payments. The council reviewed and approved a comprehensive collection process that included foreclosure as a final option. City code amendments increased the responsiveness and flexibility of the collection process by imposing fees and penalties for nonpayment.

A number of administrative changes also were implemented by the managers of the special assessment program. For example, all assessment forms and notices were rewritten in more concise and clear language to help communicate the requirements of assessment payments and to reduce property owners' confusion about their payment responsibilities. A variety of expanded financing options were created, including monthly payment plans with terms as short as five years. Also, management instituted a number of enhancements to the existing automated lien accounting system in order to provide more current and accurate management information on collection efforts and accounts status. Finally, the collection program placed more emphasis on personal contact with owners of delinquent assessments. Phone calls and visits were made by two full-time collection specialists.

A recent review of the condition of special assessment payments shows considerable improvement in reducing the level of delinquencies. Total delinquencies have declined approximately 20 percent, and the percent of payments delinquent more than 90 days has dropped from 90 percent to 40 percent. The improved collection program also has recovered more than $1.2 million in past due payments from 15 of the 16 largest property owners. Further, the threat of foreclosure on several delinquent accounts has resulted in partial payments of overdue amounts.

Conclusion

Performance auditing in the City of Portland, Oregon, has had a positive influence on organizational change since its inception in 1983. Completed audits often have played an important role in helping city managers make needed changes in administrative systems and operational procedures. Audits have helped the city council and managers focus on problem areas by providing objective analysis and quantified performance information to guide action. The public release of performance audit reports has provided sufficient visibility to encourage innovative and comprehensive solutions to problems.

The success of the program is in large part due to the commitment of the city council to effective and efficient city management. Council members have taken an active role in addressing audit findings and have directed managers to make positive responses to audit recommendations. Tangible improvements in reducing disability and liability claims, controlling health care costs, and lowering delinquent assessment payments are evidence of this commitment. (See Figure 2 for a summary of audit changes.)

In addition to council member support for the function, the success of the program is dependent on four factors:

• Independence: The audit function reports to an elected city auditor. Auditors are free to analyze and report on any operation in city government without undue influence on the audit scope and conclusions. While auditors closely consult with

Figure 2. Summary of changes following three City of Portland performance audits.

Audit findings	Management actions	Outcome/current status
Risk management audit—October 1985		
City workers injured more frequently than workers in comparable jurisdictions.	City council passed an ordinance strengthening loss control and prevention program.	Disability costs decreased by $200,000 in FY 1986–87.
Liability claims costs increased 100 percent over four years.	Loss control plans were developed by all city organizations.	Liability costs have stabilized.
Insurance reserves not adequate to pay future claims liabilities ($3–$4 million underfunded).	Contingency funds were transferred to reserves.	Reserve funds actuarially sound.
Health benefits audit—September 1986		
Benefit costs increased by 200 percent over 10 years, from $3.6 to $10.8 million.	Developed proposals for collective bargaining.	Negotiated revised benefit coverage with one union.
City provides higher level of benefits than 90 percent of other health plans.	Developed plan to implement lower-cost, preferred provider plan.	Employees shifting to lower-cost plans.
Plan includes high-cost specialty coverage (chiropractic, prescriptions).	Instituted utilization and cost controls (hospital bill audits, preauthorization).	Claims costs increasing at lower rate.
Special assessments audit—September 1985		
$3.5 million in special assessment payments past due.	Developed revised procedures for accounting and reporting on special assessments.	Collected more than $1.2 million in past due assessments.
Street improvement funds experiencing cash flow problems.	Council approved revised foreclosure policy.	Delinquent payments declined by 50 percent.
No sanctions to encourage timely payment.	Implemented new collection methods: demand letters; phone solicitation; payment terms.	

management on areas to be audited, the final authority for selecting audit topics rests with the city auditor.

- Adherence to auditing standards: Audit activities comply fully with generally accepted governmental auditing standards. These standards require due professional care in collecting and evaluating information, adequate supervision and planning of audit work, and fair reporting of audit findings.
- Professional, qualified audit staff: Performance audit staff members have advanced academic degrees or certification as public accountants or internal auditors. Previous work experience includes program evaluation, public accounting, internal auditing, and general business and government experience. Educational backgrounds include public and business administration, accounting, economics, law and social sciences.
- Cooperative and constructive relationships with management: The effectiveness of the performance audit program can be judged by the degree to which audit reports can assist management to make improvements in program performance. Cooperation and teamwork are key in achieving this change. Reports must be objective and fair—they must recognize accomplishments as well as identify areas needing improvement.

Performance auditing holds great potential to assist local government in making needed organizational changes. A successful program must stress its independence, objectivity and professionalism, as well as its availability to city council and managers in their efforts to ensure greater accountability, effectiveness and efficiency.

The Power of Performance Measurement

James R. Griesemer

In the popular book *Reinventing Government,* authors Osborne and Gaebler describe the power of performance measurement. In their words, "Organizations that measure the results of their work . . . find that the information transforms them." Research in developing performance measurement concepts and working with local governments to implement measurement systems suggests that Osborne and Gaebler are correct. Performance measures do indeed possess considerable power to help officials make better decisions and use resources effectively. How they do this is the subject of this article.

The goal of performance measurement is to improve the quality of management and policy decisions by providing a clear picture of the activities and accomplishments of the organization. This is done by providing information about the performance characteristics of the organization, usually in the form of trend and ratio data. These data typically describe where the entity has been in terms of performance, where it is today and how it compares with other, similar organizations. If it is done correctly, such an analysis results in a detailed picture of performance, painted in graphical and statistical terms. It is this picture that helps officials to make more informed policy choices and managers to make better decisions.

The use of modern performance measurement tools allows governmental officials to manage with much higher degrees of precision than has traditionally been the case. Through the consistent use of such instruments, it is possible to monitor changes,

Reprinted with permission from *Government Finance Review* (October 1993): 17–21. This article was originally entitled "The Power of Performance Measurement: A Computer Performance Model."

identify potential problems and take timely corrective action. Equally important, these tools allow officials to support activities that are successful, to allocate resources based on what works well and to build public credibility by being able to demonstrate the effective use of taxpayer dollars.

A tool for shaping performance

Perhaps the most surprising thing about measurement is its ability to shape the future performance of organizations. Performance measures do not simply describe what has happened; they influence what will happen, as they provide information for decision makers and affect the behavior of employees. When an organization establishes an ongoing measurement program, performance and productivity almost inevitably improve. The reasons for this have to do with organizational focus, resource allocation and achievement recognition.

Scholars have long recognized the central role that focus plays in organizational performance. High-performing organizations—be they public or private—have clear goals and a strong focus. The process of establishing departmental performance measures requires that department goals be clearly identified, because one cannot measure performance until desired results have been defined. This seemingly simple act of defining results to be achieved has enormous power to focus the organization. Because measures have great power to direct activity, it is important that departmental performance measures be consistent with broad organizational goals and policy.

Performance measures not only focus the organization's activity toward defined goals, they strongly influence employee behavior. The reasons, again, are straightforward: People react to what is measured. When goals are identified and employees know the basis on which they will be measured, they perform.

For elected officials and top managers, one of the most tangible benefits of performance measurement is its ability to help in resource allocation decisions. Without the ability to measure accomplishment, the budget process can become a no-win game of slicing a shrinking fiscal pie into ever-smaller pieces. Performance measures provide officials with new tools for evaluating resource allocation decisions on the basis of demonstrated accomplishments rather than solely on the basis of traditional funding or political clout. Measures provide the foundation for a new approach to budgeting built around an investment-management philosophy.

Finally, performance measures have the ability to recognize the achievements of employees, departments and the government as a whole. For employees, recognition of demonstrated achievements provides motivation and builds self-esteem. At the departmental level, performance measures can help identify successful activities and encourage their further use while steering managers away from less effective approaches. For the government as a whole, performance recognition builds trust: Demonstrated achievements can enhance credibility with citizens, taxpayers, the press and potential new businesses.

A measurement system

To be successful, a performance measurement program needs to be built around a common conceptual theme and continued over time. If the measurement is done on a one-time basis, it will neither highlight key trends nor identify important changes in performance over time. The performance program described in this article was designed around resource management concepts, since resource limitations constitute a serious problem for many governmental organizations. Thus, the system looks at where resources come from (the economic characteristics of the community), how they are allocated (the financial characteristics of the government), and how efficiently and effectively they are being used (the performance characteristics of departments).

This performance measurement system, developed by the author, employs a computer technology called performance analysis modeling (PAM), which is illustrated in the schematic diagram in Figure 1. The local government provides the data for the model; items such as population, assessed value, building permit activity, department staffing levels and financial information are derived from the annual audit. Simple data-input software designed for personal computers is used to enter the information into the performance model.

The computer model conducts analyses of the economic, financial and departmental performance characteristics of the local government. It provides an in-depth picture of performance trends which, if desired, can be expanded to include citizen satisfaction information and comparative data from other communities. The results of the analyses can be compiled into reports covering performance trends, citizen satisfaction information or comparative data. In terms of output format, the model can provide statistical data and graphical information.

In practice, the computer modeling approach has proven to be an effective and economical way to provide performance information in a format that officials can use to make decisions. The illustrations of performance measures in the sections that follow are drawn from actual reports of a group of Colorado cities that have been actively using performance measures for up to three years. Among the group are Fort Collins, Grand Junction, Loveland, Lakewood, Thornton and Westminster.

A benchmarking case study:
The New York City transit authority

Few benchmarking efforts in the public sector have been as exciting as those that took place in the early 1990s at the New York City Transit Authority (NYCTA). By 1994, NYCTA was in the advanced stages of implementing the recommendations of a detailed benchmarking analysis of inventory and logistics. The benchmarking of NYCTA's inventory and logistics management activities deserves a close look, as it illustrates an extremely successful benchmarking effort: one done for the right reasons, planned with the right focus, and executed with the right tactics.

In the 1970s and 1980s, the New York City Transit Authority, one of the world's largest multimodal transit systems, experienced a slew of operating problems that brought the service to its knees. Its state-of-good-repair, inventory readiness, and response-time performance bordered dangerously on "fall-apart" levels. In the early 1980s, through generous capital funding, however, NYCTA was able to throw a great deal of money at the problem, with noteworthy results. The transit authority was able to fix many of its problems and to boast solid improvements in track maintenance, rail car repair, and bus maintenance—all within impressively upgraded facilities. On the surface, NYCTA seemed to be flying high, but not without cost. Inventory had been swelling to excessive levels, and the resulting problems of obsolescence and storage costs were getting worse.

The capital funding sources dried up, and the operating funding grew tighter. In an effort to provide more service with less resource consumption, NYCTA embarked on a detailed study of inventory management. This study, which had a largely internal focus, enabled NYCTA to achieve some reduction of inventory levels and an increase in the through-put of supplied parts. Old, obsolete inventory was discarded and written off. But the progress went only so far, then began to plateau. NYCTA, seeing at first hand the potential value of continuous improvement in inventory and logistics management, called upon a multidisciplinary inventory consultant to conduct a benchmarking analysis of world-class inventory and logistics management organizations. The goal of the analysis was ambitious but simple: Through a cost-effective approach, NYCTA sought to elevate its inventory and logistics management capabilities to world-class performance levels.

Benchmarking analysis extended far beyond the realms to which NYCTA had become accustomed in prior studies. Examined in detail were not only the best practices of other leading multimodal transit authorities but also those of single-modal transit authorities (Houston and Detroit), foreign transit authorities (Montreal, Tokyo, and Stockholm), and private-sector companies (Federal Express, United Parcel Service, and Delta Airlines). Major insights came from analyzing companies and organizations not directly comparable to NYCTA. Like the transit authority, many of these companies were operating under severe budgetary constraints forced by both economic and market pressures.

NYCTA studied a wide variety of variables, both quantitative and qualitative. For example, certain aspects of maintenance and materiel organizations were rendered in detail, including their lines of accountability, skill levels, and job requirements. Inventory costs per bus and rail mile also were analyzed at NYCTA and at the best-in-class.

The analysis showed NYCTA both the short- and the long-term improvements achievable through adopting the best practices of these organizations. The detailed study tied these improvements to specific actions and strategies with explicit deadlines. Among the most valuable new programs applied to NYCTA were a balanced scorecard for transit authorities that detailed inventory and other operating statistics; a program tying employee and manager accountability to specific inventory management objectives; and a framework for balancing inventory targets with service goals throughout the organization.

Because the benchmarking results were only beginning to be implemented by 1994, benefits would take some time to manifest themselves in full. But remarkable results were already becoming evident. Standards of service performance and inventory efficiency had been set far higher than even the most ambitious NYCTA employee could have predicted. The transit authority had found many public- and private-sector best practices that were readily applicable to their own situation, even taking into account the profoundly different realities of the respective operating environments.

The project's success extended further, beyond the concrete measures and deliverables that benchmarking had brought to NYCTA. Morale had soared because all employees and managers close to the activities being benchmarked were involved throughout the process, some through interviews and others through day-to-day responsibility and accountability for results. The organization faced tremendous challenges in bringing its inventory and logistics operations to world-class levels, but it was excited by the prospect of this change. Employees were witnessing the beginnings of short- and long-term improvements that, if pursued diligently, could cause NYCTA to become a leading benchmarking candidate in its own right.

Source: Kenneth A. Bruder, Jr., and Edward M. Gray, "Public-Sector Benchmarking: A Practical Approach," *Public Management* 76 (September 1994): S10.

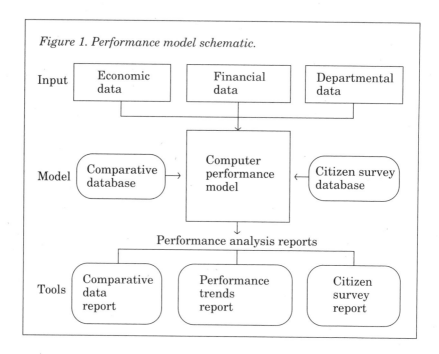

Figure 1. Performance model schematic.

Input — Economic data — Financial data — Departmental data

Model — Comparative database → Computer performance model ← Citizen survey database

Performance analysis reports

Tools — Comparative data report — Performance trends report — Citizen survey report

Economic performance measures

Economic performance measures monitor the tax base, business, employment, population, land-use and development characteristics of the community.

Information on economic performance has many uses in local government. It can, for example, be used as a tool to develop economic strategy by tracking changes in the composition of the tax base. Economic data also can be used to monitor the success of an annexation program through a measure called area revenue density, which tracks the relationship between revenue and the physical size of the community. By monitoring the average revenue per acre, the city can see the financial impact of its annexations. For example, an aggressive annexation program that initially reduced net revenue as undeveloped land was annexed was shown to be ultimately successful when revenue density was restored to earlier levels but based on a much larger and more diverse economic base.

Economic performance data also can be used to evaluate the success of economic development efforts. Figure 2 tracks the impacts of a policy decision by a Colorado city to expand its sales tax base while trying to maintain its strong manufacturing and nonretail business base. The success of this city's efforts is

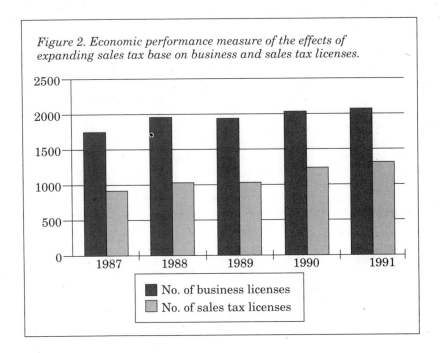

Figure 2. Economic performance measure of the effects of expanding sales tax base on business and sales tax licenses.

clearly shown, as the number of business licenses holds steady as that of sales tax licenses expands significantly. The magnitude of such an accomplishment should not be underestimated nor unrecognized, and one of the most important benefits of performance measurement is that it allows a local government to document its achievements.

These illustrations show just a few of the many ways that cities can use performance measures to develop economic strategy, track progress and evaluate the results. Some cities are using economic measures to evaluate development activity, project the long-term impacts of various land uses and monitor business activity.

Financial performance measures

The ability of a community to meet the needs of its citizens is directly related to its financial health. Financial performance measures allow local governments to monitor their fiscal condition and document responsible stewardship of taxpayer dollars. Where problems do exist, performance measures help provide early warning signals and suggest strategies for corrective action.

Analysis of the general fund revenue trend, for example, may indicate that, while nominal revenues exceed the inflation rate, real revenues in inflation-discounted (constant) dollars are barely keeping up with inflation. Where financial problems threaten to become acute, tracking and reporting performance measures can offer a clear picture of an issue and help convince citizens of its legitimacy. Figure 3 depicts just such a situation. In this case, a city's water fund revenues were unable to keep up with inflation, in spite of good departmental efficiency as documented in the department's productivity measures. Recognition of the problem by officials and citizens alike provided a basis for corrective action taken in 1990. The impact of the 1990 decisions concerning the financing policies for the water fund is seen clearly in the 1991 revenue data.

Performance measures not only help diagnose and correct problems, they also help to assess how well policy decisions are being implemented. Their ability to demonstrate superior performance can help build credibility with citizens and taxpayers. The use of performance measures enabled one Colorado city to improve its fund balance through a program of contracting services in some areas and using job-sharing and part-time personnel in other areas. Performance measures aided in tracking the effectiveness of management decisions as well.

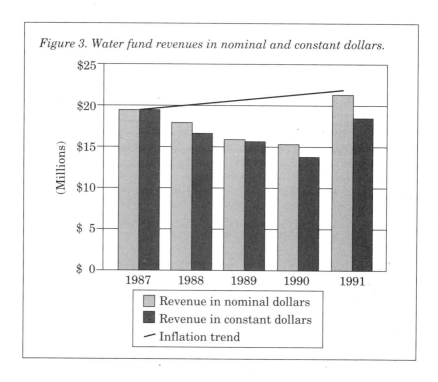

Figure 3. Water fund revenues in nominal and constant dollars.

Departmental performance measures

Few measures are more important than those that track and compare departmental performance. It is in city departments that most money is spent, and it is departmental output that most directly affects citizens and their satisfaction with community services.

Because the measurement of departmental performance is not a simple matter, the performance model examines departmental activity in three dimensions. First, the model measures departmental inputs by tracking the costs and human resources associated with department operations. Second, for cities using the citizen satisfaction survey, the model tracks both satisfaction and cost data to provide measures of effectiveness. Finally, the model measures efficiency by tracking specific departmental performance measures and relating those outputs to changes in costs. This provides an important index of departmental productivity.

These measures of departmental performance—costs, effectiveness and productivity—are indicators of value. The challenge for governments is demonstrating value, that is, letting citizens know that various public services are worth the tax dollars they pay. Performance measures are well suited to this task because they can identify the quality of departmental performance. The example that follows, drawn from actual measurement data, provides an illustration of the way in which measures can be used to monitor performance and to document the value being created by a city department.

A police department case study

Few departments elicit more interest among both officials and citizens than the local police department. Police departments are both important and expensive, sometimes consuming a significant portion of the entire city budget. As a result, policy departments are often the subject of debate among council members, citizens and even within the administration itself. Is the department doing its job? Are costs under control? How does this police operation compare to those in other cities? Performance measurement helped answer these important questions.

An analysis of the cost history of the police department over five years indicated that costs of the department's operations had risen moderately during the period, increasing slightly faster than the rate of inflation. Cost relationships, such as internal personnel demand (personnel costs as a percentage of total department costs) and total department demand (total department costs as a percentage of total general fund expenditures), were also tracked. These types of cost relationships depict the overall pattern of resource consumption and show the degree to which resource allocation decisions are consistent with community goals. In this case, the police department's personnel costs were holding steady at about 80 percent of total department expenditures and 37 percent of total general fund personnel expenditures. In addition, the police department's share of total general fund expenditures was holding steady at less than 20 percent of total general fund expenditures, a comparatively moderate level of resource consumption.

Although the police department's cost relationships had been maintained at generally stable levels, departmental performance had been anything but static. Productivity measures showed that arrests had increased significantly during the five years. Analysis of the relationship between the change in departmental costs and the change in the number of arrests revealed that the relative cost of this output actually had declined slightly, indicating that output was rising faster than cost. Another measure showed similar performance in the area of serious offenses cleared, showing that output was up, while the relationship between costs and outputs was stable. The same pattern was reflected in a measurement that showed total calls for service rising while relative costs remained steady over the five-year period.

All of the performance indicators cited above demonstrated that technical performance in this police department was on the rise. They also showed that improved performance in the department had not been achieved simply by throwing money at the problem, but rather that department productivity had remained solid as outputs rose as fast as, or faster, than department costs.

While technical performance in this police department was clearly improving, there still remained the issue of effectiveness. Did the public recognize the value being created through superior performance in this police department? Five years of citizen satisfaction surveys showed steady-to-rising citizen satisfaction levels with police service. Not only were satisfaction levels stable within the community but they were above the national average.

As impressive as this department's performance was from productivity and citizen-satisfaction perspectives, the real "bottom line" for value is shown in Figure 4. This measure, called satisfaction cost, compares changes in the level of satisfaction with changes in the cost of department operations. Satisfaction cost, an effectiveness measure developed by the author, is the per capita cost of departmental operations divided by the satisfaction rating. It technically expresses the per capita cost of each 1 percent of satisfaction. It is particularly useful for trend analysis since it shows the relationship between inputs, *discounted for growth,* and effectiveness as measured by citizen satisfaction. In

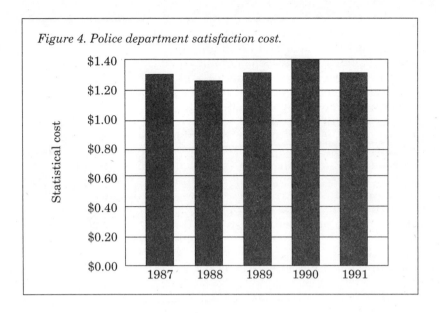

Figure 4. Police department satisfaction cost.

this case, the result from an effectiveness point of view is that the department's costs of operations had remained consistent with its satisfaction rating. From a cost-effectiveness viewpoint, this police department continued to create value for citizens of the community.

Information from departmental performance measures, such as those used in this case, can have a powerful influence not only on decision makers but on the community at large. At the community level, performance measures can help governments affirm value by showing the costs and results of operations, by examining performance trends and by comparing performance with similar jurisdictions.

Focusing organizational effort

This article has taken an introductory look at the use of performance measurement in local government. Today's new measurement tools are a direct result of modern computer technology that makes possible the production of easy-to-understand performance analyses at low cost. This information, in turn, makes it possible for officials to make management and policy decisions at much higher levels of precision than was possible in the past. The low cost of modern computers extends these benefits to even the smallest local governments, which encounter many of the same resource limitations faced by larger cities.

Performance measures do much more than simply record what has happened. The picture they paint influences the future by shaping decisions and directing activity. Measures have the ability to clarify goals, focus organizational effort, guide resource allocation, evaluate performance and recognize achievements. They are powerful tools that have the ability to transform local governments in very positive ways.

As officials continue to work with performance management tools, they are constantly finding new uses for the information that measures produce. These uses include applications as concrete as evaluating performance and allocating resources and as diverse as supporting a community visioning program, monitoring the effectiveness of an economic development effort, measuring the results of a total quality management program, reexamining proposed land-use patterns and much more. As public officials and managers find new ways to use these new tools, they not only are discovering the power of performance measurement, they are creating it.

Customer-Based Performance Management in Charlotte

Pamela Syfert

The performance system of the city of Charlotte, North Carolina, is a management-by-objectives (MBO) system and is very budget-oriented. We implemented management by objectives back in the early 1970s and have had a strong program focusing on quality measures and effectiveness since the mid-1970s. We have rarely given our councils over these past few years a line-item budget. The budget is debated and developed as a program or performance budget. We consider performance issues as well as some of the other cost issues that come up at budget time. Now we are trying to develop measures that are more change-oriented and customer-oriented. One of the questions we are asking ourselves about performance measurement is whether the MBO system is relevant. What measures are relevant to meeting the vision and strategy for the community and for our organization?

We have over 500 objectives for our departments, and we measure our services on a variety of measures. We rate some on effectiveness measures and establish efficiency standards. We measure activity and workload. And we use the objectives in the performance measurement program to establish contracts with outside agencies. We do not provide many social and human services, but wherever we do, such as community development and housing, we have established a very strong contracting and performance budget for those agencies. In setting efficiency standards, we have used many different measures.

Excerpted from Pamela Syfert, "The City of Charlotte, North Carolina: Customer-Based Performance Management," in *Managing for Results: Performance Measures in Government,* 1993 conference proceedings (Austin: The University of Texas, 1994), 61–71.

For example, in our street maintenance program, we have established a rating system. We use trained observers; in fact, we contract with trained observers to rate our streets based on their condition, such as the prevalence of potholes and the possibility for base failures. We have an objective that tracks our progress in having an average life expectancy of twelve years for 95 percent of our streets. This rating system is one of the key factors in the process of allocating resources for street maintenance. We have also used trained observers to rate the cleanliness of parks, and we sometimes use them now for street-cleaning. We used to depend heavily on broad citizen surveys; we are now doing more targeted customer surveys on a particular service.

I'd like to offer some examples from our program to illustrate the dynamics of the performance measurement process—how it can work and how it has been helpful to us. The first example concerns a goal that sets the standard for what we will tolerate in repeat repairs for equipment serviced by our equipment services division, which is responsible for the maintenance and repair of almost all our vehicles, such as police cars, garbage trucks, and heavy equipment. Several years ago, during the budget process, the departments identified a real problem with the frequency of repeat repairs. Vehicles that had just been serviced in the preventive maintenance program were showing up with problems, or they were breaking down again a week or two after they had been repaired. The departments complained that this situation was a real detriment to productivity and service effectiveness. So we brought the issue up in the budget process and asked the head of equipment services to set a goal to address the problem.

One thing we often do in our budget process is to identify data collection as an objective simply in order to set a goal. In other words, we institute a record-keeping system to track a problem that has been identified primarily from customer complaints or some other informal evaluation. This case is especially interesting because the department collected the data, set a goal, and involved employees in solving the problem. The result is that once you highlight an issue and start collecting data, people get more interested in trying to solve the problem. In this instance, one of the employees who was trying to determine the cause of so many repeat repairs on garbage trucks came up with the suggestion to improve the fender. They made that improvement, saved a great deal of money, and solved one of their problems. And the employee became a winner in our suggestions award program. This did not happen because we set the objective; rather, the performance measure and the objective helped focus attention on a problem, especially from the customer's perspective, and on the need to take action and engage in some diagnostic work.

Another example of success in the use of quality measures is solid waste services. In Charlotte we still have weekly backyard refuse collection—city employees go into the backyards of all our single-family homes and empty garbage cans, regardless of the size of the yard. There is tremendous potential for missing a pickup, spilling trash, or damaging property. Once a week we also collect at curbside all recyclables, yard waste, and household trash. Again, there is potential for spilling trash. So we chose a very simple outcome for refuse collection. We wanted to ensure that all the trash was picked up, that it was picked up when we said it would be, and that we were dependable in this service. One of the ways to measure this outcome is in customers' calls. If you miss a pickup, if you spill trash, or if you damage property, you will get complaints. So we identified an acceptable number of citizen complaints, which was lower than the number we had been receiving. Thus we use a budget performance measure as well as a quality measure and tie them to individual performance measures, either for the refuse collection team or the individual workers. In this case, we have emphasized team performance measures, not just individual performance measures. When our employees work in teams to get things done, we look at the team performance and set performance standards based on the team.

Another example is response time, that old standby. We have not made much change over time to meet this objective. At budget time, there will be discussions with the police department and city council about what is wrong in the Baker team area, where we are consistently unable to meet the objective for response time to emergency calls. The resources that would be necessary to solve the problem are not thought to be worth the particular outcome; that is, there are other ways to spend resources on police services that do not necessarily have to do with the response to emergency calls. The response time to emergency calls is good information, but the council and the community would rather see more resources allocated for community policing, and we have done just that.

A performance measurement system can point you in the direction of a consideration of problems and issues as well as more discussion and diagnosis. In the area of police services, we track clearance rates, the effectiveness of their training, and a number of different aspects of police services. Our police department gets very good marks on meeting its objectives and performance standards, but this may have nothing to do with whether citizens actually feel safe. What we have learned in measuring police services is that you are not evaluating the total criminal justice system or some of the other components outside the police department that make people feel safe in the community. In the

1970s we conducted a major victimization survey, and we will continue to do so from time to time. What it demonstrated was that Charlotte has a very high rate of [reporting]. People feel confident about calling the police department and reporting a crime, but this does not say anything about why people continue to feel unsafe in their communities.

In the late 1980s a task force chaired by the chairman of Nations Bank studied some of our performance systems—how we were rating employees and our objectives program—and made several key suggestions. While we were doing a very good job of making high quality and service effectiveness top priorities, we were not doing a good job of addressing efficiency—what citizens were getting for their money. You may have a wonderful refuse collection service, but what is it costing and how are those costs changing? The task force suggested that we begin to develop efficiency or productivity standards, which we began doing in the late 1980s; it also suggested that we integrate them into the MBO program and also tie them into our planning. For example, we identified a problem in the collection cost for solid waste services and set a goal for what we wanted the unit cost to be. We explained what that problem was and why we were having it, which helps track the cost of solid waste. It is a part of other measures that we report to the council and the community on our solid waste program.

In our MBO program, we present our objectives report to the council twice a year. During the budget process, the departments submit their budget and their budget objectives along with some of their problem areas. This does not cover all 500 objectives and measures; it just highlights some of the key issues. Some of the measures are more important for internal operations than for reporting to the council and the community. Sometimes we make a report to the council at a meeting or workshop, and sometimes we send the report to the council, but we have regularly reported on objectives achievement for the last eight years of the program.

One example of efficiency measures is the cost per ride of transporting the disabled. Having these cost-per-unit measures in our department is very important in determining what we do in the future. We are now preparing ourselves for competitive bidding. We are going to bid out one-quarter of the city's refuse collection sometime next year. The city is going to bid on that contract, which is similar to what Phoenix has done.

We are also preparing our organization for competition. We are not calling the effort privatization, because that is not necessarily the goal. The goal is competition, whether it is competition among private entities bidding for a service or competition between the city and the private sector. The goal is to get the best value for the taxpayer. It is very important that we have these measures in terms of both performance outcomes and cost as we make service contracts and find ways to evaluate them. We set this particular objective in response to the suggestion that we begin developing efficiency standards; we set an objective to collect and analyze data toward this end. We have been tracking this information for a couple of years, and it became important when we were considering expanding our transportation services for the disabled. Our department determined that the expansion could not be done as efficiently with in-house resources as it could be contracting it out because the expansion pertained to night and weekend services. This was helpful in making a budget recommendation: we knew we could not maintain our cost and the private sector could match it.

When we first began developing an objectives program, we were told not to have workload indicators, just outcome measures. However, we use workload indicators and will probably continue to use them. At times they become very important in the budget deliberations. For example, in our engineering and development departments, we staff to meet construction increases. In the late 1980s, when our construction efforts were gearing down, workload indicators gave us the kind of information we could use to downsize until we needed to start gearing up again. Workload measures should not be the only measure you have, but you should not dismiss them as unimportant, especially if you are trying to integrate them into your budgeting process.

We set performance standards in all of our contracts. For example, we have a contract with a partnership whose goal is to build low-income housing and help promote home ownership for low-income people. We target a lot of people who can move out of public housing as clients for low-income home ownership. The program's goal is to provide counseling, build the housing, and place those individuals who meet the eligibility guidelines. We do not dictate how the program is structured or run; but we do expect certain outcomes for the money we give the program. One outcome that is very crucial is that 50 percent of the applicants will have purchased a home. In other words, we do not want more than 50 percent of the applicants wasting their time with the program, and the program does not want that either. We also expect the quality of the program to be high enough that the homebuyers will not default on the loan within a certain time period. Those contracts are evaluated at the end of the contract period, the report is sent to the city council, and next year's contract is renegotiated based on the results of the contract evaluation.

Along with developing efficiency objectives in the late 1980s, we began to identify ways to measure the changes we wanted to bring about. In 1987 we defined our mission as six core values: providing public services, learning what the customer wants, learning what the community wants, being responsive and accessible to the citizens, being accountable for our work, and being productive. Quality and excellence were no longer enough; we also had to consider accountability and productivity. We also identified three core values with a more internal orientation: how we do work, how we are organized to do the work, and how we treat and motivate employees.

As I said earlier, in the mid-1970s we did some major crime victimization surveys. They were very expensive, and we concluded that the expense did not justify the results. We found that we used the information we had gathered internally much more effectively than we used public survey information. Sometimes program managers are a little reluctant to use sample data. So we found an unusual way to obtain that information. The Urban Institute at the University of North Carolina branch in Charlotte began conducting an annual citizen survey. City and county governments, the school board, nonprofit agencies, and businesses are allowed to buy questions on the survey, although there is a limit. The institute ensures that the methodology is accurate and helps you structure the questions to get the information you want. It is a much cheaper and more effective way of getting that information. So in the last few years, when we have wanted a citizen survey of broad information, we have bought questions on the Urban Institute's surveys.

On these surveys we usually ask about police contacts. Sometimes we ask questions about victimization: was the respondent a victim of a crime? did he or she report it? if not, why not? and so on. We usually ask people whether they were satisfied in their contacts with city government: did they get the information they needed? did they get the runaround? did they get their problem solved or their question answered? have trash collectors missed picking up their garbage? The problem with citizen survey questions is they give you a broad overview but not much specific information about a particular department or service. So we have moved toward more direct contact with people who actually come to us for service or who have contact with us on regulatory issues.

Through our customer service center, we started sending out cards asking for feedback. When we have contact with a citizen, we try to follow up and ask how we did. Sometimes we will do this kind of follow-up for a defined period or on a regular basis. Our departments also conduct internal customer surveys. Once a year our purchasing, human resources, and budget departments send a questionnaire to other departments asking how they are doing, whether they make service delivery easier, and whether their information is accurate. The surveys are all tied to the specific issues that a particular department is trying to address. We also conduct an employee survey that is part of our mission process to establish benchmark data. These are all ways in which we have expanded our MBO system by gathering more information on performance in order to see what we are doing and what some of the issues are.

A survey sent out from our engineering department gathers information from developers and others who come in for information about compliance with the tree ordinance, or people who need maps or help with storm drainage issues. Customers are asked whether their concern was treated seriously; if the question was not answered or the problem was not solved, the customer is asked whether he or she understood why. We don't ask whether we solved the problem completely because this isn't possible in many cases. There is a difference between good customer service and saying yes to everything anybody wants. In fact, all of us in the public sector must struggle with what customer service means. We also ask for comments or suggestions. This information is used in the engineering department to help identify problem areas. It does not provide the solution, but it does pinpoint areas needing diagnosis and improvement, particularly when people feel they are not being treated well or are receiving inaccurate information.

Internal customer surveys vary depending on the department. For example, the planning department works a lot with other city departments, such as engineering and transportation, and county departments; it works with all of our departments in identifying our ten-year capital needs. Their surveys target the employees they actually work with. In contrast, the budget office is more likely to send its survey to the department head and maybe the budget analyst. With internal surveys, we try to target the people we work with, and the questions are phrased to address the kinds of problems or issues that are being dealt with. For example, are employees given the autonomy to make decisions? Are departmental representatives given the proper authority to be effective in representing the department in meetings? Are the department's services timely?

The engineering department sends out an internal survey that asks such questions as whether its information is accurate, whether the staff listens, and whether the department is adaptable to special situations. In other word, are we trying to solve the problem or are we just ignoring it? So different questions go to different people to gather feedback on how performance is being viewed by the people using the service. Many of our strategic efforts in the last few years have examined our internal operations—specifically, what we are doing that may be keeping other city employees from getting their job done. That is a big issue with some of these customer survey questionnaires.

Are we treating customer service seriously? are we trying to be productive? are we open? are we promoting empowerment? We are preparing to do a follow-up survey in the next year or so. If our goals and strategic vision are to be more customer-focused, we must know whether we are giving our employees the right tools. We need to determine whether we are successful in providing internal support for employees who are actually doing the job.

To measure change, we start with a list of expectations for a management-by-results program at the beginning of each fiscal year. For example, our 1994 expectations include accountability, quality customer service, and increased productivity. In the performance planning process, we ask employees what goals they can set and what results they want to achieve to show they are participating in meeting the expectations. Another expectation is the use of teamwork. We want some examples of when employees will use teamwork and what result they want it to have. So the employees and the supervisors are responsible for developing their performance plan and producing the results that will meet expectations. Performance planning is done primarily with technical, professional, and managerial employees; it is also done with performance planning and support employees. For our field employees, performance planning focuses more on performance standards, many of which are related to safety, attendance, workload, and quality, which result in a number of complaints. They are held accountable for those, often within the context of the team they work on.

One of the objectives in the performance plan for our customer service center concerns the percentage of citizen calls that are resolved with just one conversation. This is a response objective. Another objective is based on ratings from cards that customer service representatives send to customers as follow-up that asks their opinion about the services provided. Another goal of the plan is to encourage empowerment of employees. When the employee meets with the supervisor, the employee is responsible for identifying what he or she has done to facilitate empowerment—such as a training plan, a set of guidelines, or teamwork on empowerment.

As part of our right-sizing effort, we conducted a services assessment to determine what menu of services the local government should be providing for the community. We wanted to know whether we had the right menu or whether there were services we should be providing or providing differently—or not providing at all. To help answer this question, we used a process of forced pairing of services: we inventoried the hundreds of services and grouped them into forty-one key services that involved some kind of customer contact. We compiled a services inventory handbook, which identified the need for a service, a description of some of the characteristics of the service (if we had the performance information), and its cost and staffing requirements. There were three different rating groups: senior management staff, the mayor and the council, and a citizen focus group. They went through each of the key services and rated their importance in pairs: is police patrol more important than fire suppression? is fire suppression more important than solid waste services? is police patrol more important than cable enforcement? You can probably argue about the methodology, but it revealed what community leaders and decision makers considered important. Then the services were rated on their effectiveness: is police patrol more effective than fire suppression? A service might be perceived as very important but not effective.

The result was a rank ordering of the forty-one services, and the top five were police patrol, firefighting, criminal investigations, street drug interdiction, and pickup of household waste and recyclables. When we looked at costs, we found that most of the dollars were going for these top services. Services ranked as less important were receiving fewer dollars. We found we were pretty much in sync with what was considered important and how the resources were allocated. For follow-up, the council evaluated the twenty services ranked lowest in terms of need, performance indicators, and cost, and the allocation of resources was still probably right in sync. A major finding from the services assessment was that too many resources were probably being allocated for refuse collection, so the council has voted to convert backyard collection to curbside collection in the summer of next year. This has been a major service issue in Charlotte for the last ten years.

With performance measurement, we are now starting to ask questions about where we want to be in the future. If our vision is to be competitive, how do we get there? If our strategy is to improve customer service and give customers what they want from the community, how do we do that? How do we reach our strategic objectives through performance measurement? Is our current MBO system relevant? What performance measures are relevant to meeting our strategic objectives and realizing our vision? For example, in customer service, we need to identify measures for how customers perceive us. If we want a goal of competition, what must we excel at? How can we continue to improve and be an organization of continuous learning? What are the city council's policies for the budget, and how do those policies relate to the organization's visions and strategies?

I call this concept a balanced scorecard. We are trying to have a set of measures—these may be the performance measures from our MBO program, customer service measures, as well as new measures—that give us a quick look at our progress in moving toward our vision and meeting strategic objectives for the organization. It is a bigger picture than service delivery. Our first crude attempt to have a scorecard for the community is a state-of-the-city report. If customer service and empowerment are two of the things we want to develop and make a part of our organization, what measures should we use? We have already established goals for timeliness in serving customers, whether they are internal customers or citizens; quality, such as the repeat repair failure rate; performance; service; and cost. We cannot leave cost out of the customer service ratio because our citizens want value for their tax dollars.

So this year, in addition to the usual objectives report to the council, we also are doing a budget and a report on council policies, a state-of-the-city report. These quarterly reports give key information to the community about what its government is doing. The state-of-the-city report does not supplant any performance measure or budget reporting, but it puts it in a different perspective. The first such report addressed value-oriented issues—the real cost of operating city government and the reshaping of the workforce to meet the challenges of the 1990s. This is the kind of information the citizens said they wanted to know about their local government. Then we dealt with some of the ways we focus on innovation and productivity in our right-sizing effort. The second state-of-the-city report came out right after the budget and focused more on the issues of the tax rate and council policies on competition. The third report will focus more on what the community wants from public safety and performance requirements related to public safety. We are trying to develop a set of measures and a way of reporting to the community that meets citizens' needs as well as our vision of city services. If we are competitive, how are we evaluating and measuring that competitiveness, and what are we actually doing in terms of providing service to the community? We are not supplanting our MBO program, but we are looking at ways to make it more relevant to and more integrated with the way we measure where we are going, what our employees are doing, and where we want to be.

Performance Chart Increases Crew Productivity

Stanley Y. Siu

Productivity management plays an important role in the improvement of quality of service and efficiency in public works. This study describes the water crew performance chart, a simple productivity measurement method that was developed in Winnipeg's Operations Department. Using a simple formula, maintenance crew supervisors calculate the productivity index of their crews and plot the results on the chart daily. Since 1987, when use of the chart began, productivity of crews has increased. Management sees the chart as a way workers can get daily feedback on what they do. Deviation from typical performance is easier to detect, and crew members are motivated to improve their performance.

Winnipeg is one of the few cities in Canada that use the services of industrial engineers in their public works. The engineers specialize in improving work methods, which can lead to increased productivity as well as better service to customers.

In 1987, the industrial engineer in Winnipeg's Operations Department was assigned to the water subsection and given the task of improving the work methods and productivity of the 11 water system maintenance crews. The project began with a series of studies in various districts and included field observations so the engineer could become familiar with the operations. On the basis of his analysis, the engineer developed and implemented an easy-to-use device, the water crew performance chart, to measure the crews' productivity. Since 1987, when the chart

Reprinted from *Journal of the American Water Works Association*, Vol. 84, No. 2, by permission. Copyright © 1992, American Water Works Association.

was implemented, continued improvement in productivity has been noted. The purpose of this article is to describe development of the chart and its positive effect within a relatively short period of time.

Geographic divisions facilitate service

The Operations Department of the city of Winnipeg is responsible for the delivery of various municipal services including public works, in-house construction programs, control of new subdivision development, supply and maintenance of an equipment fleet used by several city departments, and provision of primary materials and supplies.

To facilitate the effective delivery of municipal services to Winnipeg's 625,000 citizens, the Operations Department has divided the city into six geographic districts. Each district provides street maintenance, water distribution, and refuse and sewer services, as well as technical and administrative services and control of development of new subdivisions.

Crews share same structure

Each district has one or two maintenance crews responsible for the repair and maintenance of the water distribution system, including mains, valves, hydrants, and services. Table 1 shows the distribution of maintenance crews in the six districts. Except in district 3, all crews are made up of four workers: a senior pipelayer, a junior pipelayer, a skilled laborer, and a backhoe operator. All crews are assisted by district support staff members, who are responsible for materials, logistics, and turning the water mains on and off.

There are 3,762 mi (2,338 km) of water mains in Winnipeg. The inventory of the city's water distribution system is summarized in Table 2. In 1990, maintenance crews repaired 2,300 water main breaks, an activity that generally requires nearly half of their time. The workload distribution of the 11 crews by service programs based on 1990 total work hours is summarized in Table 3.

Performance chart implemented in 1987

The water crew performance chart developed by the industrial engineer was implemented in all six service districts in November 1987 to measure productivity of work crews. Charts cover two-week periods, coinciding with the city's pay cycle. Using a formula to be described, crew supervisors calculate the productivity index of their crews and plot the results on the chart daily. The process, which takes less than a minute a day, enables supervisors to pinpoint how productively their crews perform and

Table 1. *Makeup of water system maintenance crews.*

District	Number of crews
1	2
2	1
3	2
4	2
5	2
6	2

Note: District 3 has one water main crew and one service crew. The structure of the water main crew is the same as that of crews in other districts. The service crew has three workers: two skilled laborers and a backhoe operator.

Table 2. *Inventory of water distribution system: Winnipeg, 1990.*

Item	Number
Water meters (⅝ in. to 2 in.)	172,751
Water meters (3 in. to 8 in.)	310
Services (2 in. and under)	175,577
Services (more than 2 in.)	3,436
Service boxes	178,916
Valves (mains)	22,490
Valves (hydrants)	17,378
Hydrants	17,391

Note: Length of water mains: 3,762 mi (2,338 km).

Table 3. *Workload distribution of water maintenance crews.*

Service program	Workload distribution
Water mains	46%
Services	35
Valves	11
Hydrants	8

Table 4. *Water excavation tasks and their respective work points.*

Water task number	Description	Work points
910	Excavated repair to service boxes	25
912	Service excavation and repair (more than 2 in.)	70
913	Service excavation and repair (2 in. and under)	62
922	Service renewal (2 in. and under)	82
929	Planned valve installation	80
930	Excavated valve replacement	84
932	Excavated valve box repair	25
933	All excavated valve box repairs	53
942	Excavated hydrant repairs	62
943	Planned hydrant installation	100
944	Hydrant replacement	100
949	Water main repair (pavement)	84
950	Water main repair (grassy area)	69
957	Water main mini-renewals	*

*Work points for task 957 are calculated by multiplying by 2 the length in feet of the renewed water main.

to determine the best use of crews for various maintenance tasks. If the chart indicates that performance is lower than usual, it prompts supervisors to take appropriate corrective action. See Figure 1 for a sample of a completed chart.

Chart created to resolve particular issues

The water crew performance chart was developed with a specific set of objectives in mind.

- It must enable daily measurement and monitoring of crew productivity.
- It must assist in enabling maintenance crew supervisors to schedule work more effectively.
- It must enhance among both management and staff personnel awareness of productivity improvement in the Operations Department.

The Operations Department uses a mainframe-supported maintenance management system (MMS) to track the total work accomplished and the total cost of that work by each district for the pay period. However, from the perspective of productivity management, a productivity measurement system was needed to effectively monitor the performance of individual water maintenance crews. The measurement method was originally developed to address two weaknesses that were identified in the MMS:[1]

- The MMS did not measure the productivity of individual water crews. Primarily, it gave biweekly cost and budget information for each MMS task.
- Results generated by the MMS were not readily available until four days after the end of each pay period. This weakened the system's effectiveness as a management tool because feedback to workers and managers was delayed.

Chart earned management's approval

The introduction of the performance chart in the Operations Department has met with the approval of managerial personnel. Performance has improved, crew members can get daily feedback on what they do, performance deviation is easier to detect, and crews are motivated to improve their performance.

Using the performance chart does not imply that vital job performance factors—job safety, standard work procedures, job supervision, and quality of work—are being sacrificed to higher productivity. A long-term sustainable productivity improvement program always depends on the successful amalgamation of all of these factors.

Figure 1. Crew performance chart for 1991.

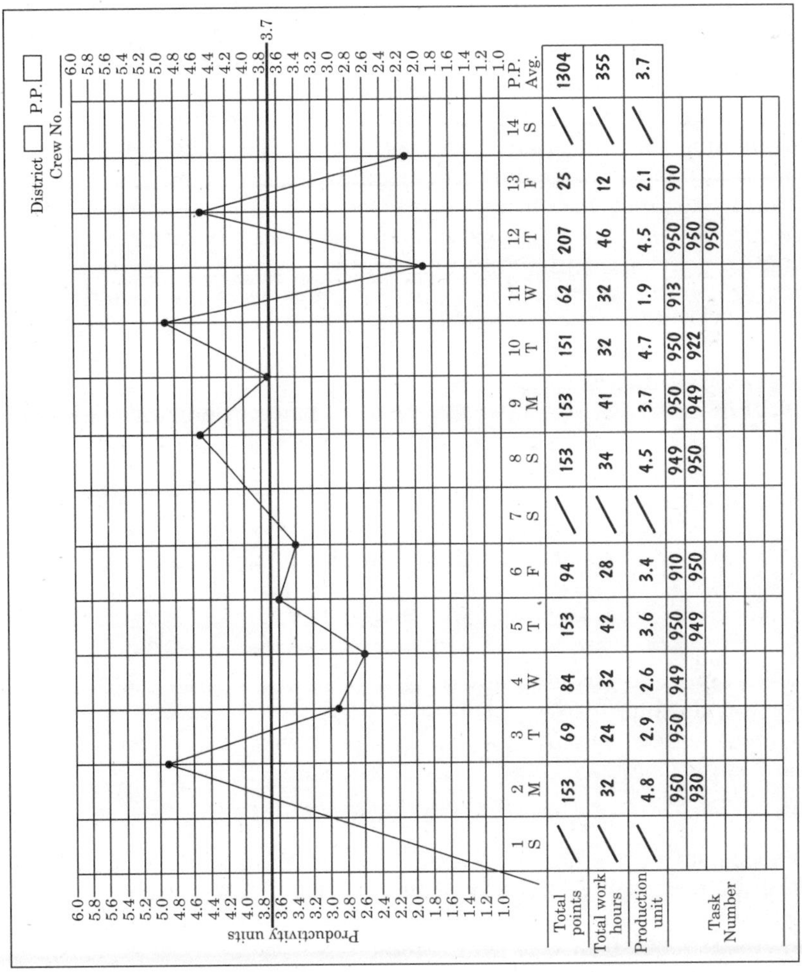

District ☐ P.P. ☐   Crew No. ____

Productivity units: 6.0, 5.8, 5.6, 5.4, 5.2, 5.0, 4.8, 4.6, 4.4, 4.2, 4.0, 3.8, 3.7, 3.6, 3.4, 3.2, 3.0, 2.8, 2.6, 2.4, 2.2, 2.0, 1.8, 1.6, 1.4, 1.2, 1.0

	1 S	2 M	3 T	4 W	5 T	6 F	7 S	8 S	9 M	10 T	11 W	12 T	13 F	14 S	P.P. Avg.
Total points	\	153	69	84	153	94	\	153	153	151	62	207	25	\	1304
Total work hours	\	32	24	32	42	28	\	34	41	32	32	46	12	\	355
Production unit	\	4.8	2.9	2.6	3.6	3.4	\	4.5	3.7	4.7	1.9	4.5	2.1	\	3.7
Task Number		950	950	949	950	910		949	950	950	913	950	910		
		930			949	950		950	949	922		950			
												950			

Productivity assessed daily

Kendrick defines productivity as "the relationship between outputs of goods and services and the inputs of basic resources—
labor, capital goods, and natural resources."[2] For purposes of
the performance chart, productivity is defined by the following
formula:

Productivity index = equivalent work points/work hours

Each crew's productivity is assessed daily by the crew's supervisor, who determines how many and which maintenance tasks were completed on that day and divides the total by the work hours required to complete the tasks. For each completed task the crew is credited with equivalent work points, which are derived from statistical analysis of the historical labor usage data. The labor usage data are extracted from the MMS. No work points are given for incomplete tasks; the work hours continue to accumulate until the task is completed. (To make the performance chart as simple and practical as possible for daily use by water crew supervisors, the calculation of work hours is limited to water crews only. Support staff do not enter into the picture: it is difficult to keep track of their hours because they work on a variety of tasks each day.)

For example, if a crew has spent 8 hours repairing a broken water main on pavement (task 949; 84 work points) and a service box (task 910; 25 work points), its productivity index that day is calculated as follows:

$$Productivity\ index = 84 + 25/4 \times 8$$
$$= 109/32$$
$$= 3.41$$

Overtime is treated as straight time in the index calculation so that productivity is not unfairly penalized or misrepresented. The 14 water excavation tasks and their respective work points on the performance chart are listed in Table 4.

Chart has some limitations

The performance chart method was designed to be economical, simple, acceptable to the staff members who use it, and capable of achieving all of its objectives. However, like many other management tools, it has its limitations.

- To keep the calculation simple, the performance chart measures productivity on excavation tasks only. Nonexcavation tasks such as cut maintenance are not monitored. The total labor hours reported by the MMS for 1990 indicated that more than 90 percent of water system maintenance activities were related to excavation tasks such as repairs of water main breaks.
- Cost data are not included in the performance chart, which is designed specifically as a productivity indicator. Such data

are, however, available in the MMS. The monitoring process and the information gathered thereby are intended to complement the information provided in the MMS for assessing how effectively labor and equipment resources are used in water system maintenance activities.

Productivity increased yearly

Since the water crew performance chart was implemented in November 1987, water maintenance crews have continuously improved productivity (Figure 2). The 1990 productivity index of the 11 individual crews and their averaged productivity are shown in Figure 3.

The average productivity of all district crews rose from 2.90 in 1987 to 3.59 in 1990. The 0.69 increase in productivity is equivalent to a $1.4 million cost savings in labor and equipment costs in 1990 dollars over three years. The breakdown of the cost savings is 70 percent in labor costs and 30 percent in equipment costs. There were a number of other positive results.

- The number of water excavation tasks completed by a crew in two weeks increased from 13 in 1987 to 18 in 1990.
- From 1987 to 1990, the work hours required to repair a water main on pavement and on a grassy boulevard declined by 16 percent and 12 percent, respectively (see Figures 4 and 5).
- Increased awareness of productivity improvement among the water subsection staff was a significant intangible benefit.

Chart leads to continued improvement

The chart developed to monitor the productivity of Winnipeg's water system maintenance crews has led to continued improvement in productivity. Use of the performance chart broadens the data base that managers use to analyze productivity, and the data it provides complement the information provided by the MMS. With modifications, the method can be applied to other public works operations, such as street maintenance and refuse collection.

1. Siu, S. "How Industrial Engineering Improves Productivity in Winnipeg." Proc. Canadian Public Works Congress and Equipment Show, Winnipeg, Manitoba (1990).

2. Kendrick, J. W. *Understanding Productivity*. The Johns Hopkins University Press, Baltimore, Md. (1977).

Figure 2. Growth in crew productivity
(productivity = equivalent work ÷ work hours).

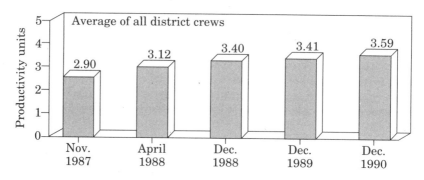

Figure 3. Productivity of crews, 1990.

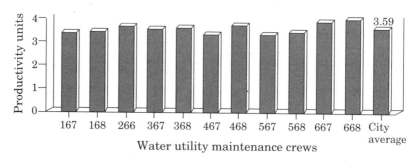

Figure 4. Decline in work hours
spent on repairing a water main
break on pavement.

Figure 5. Decline in work hours
spent on repairing a water main
break on a boulevard.

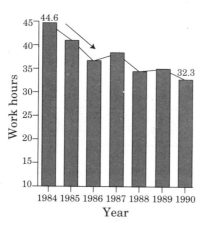

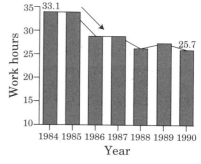

Management Involvement

I firmly believe that where one sits determines what one sees. It will be useful for you to understand where we are in Prince William County and, just as important, where we are not. We have a decentralized, bottom-up approach that has threatened middle managers to a degree. We have made efforts to deal with this, but not all of them have been successful.

I am a management and budget director. We do budgets and strategic planning. Performance measurement came our way about a year and a half ago. It is something we are doing in the course of business. I am certainly no more of an expert than any of you, probably not nearly as expert as many of you. Prince William is struggling with performance measurement, and we have a very long way to go.

We began performance measurement for five reasons. The first is related to political changes in our locality. We had a veteran board of supervisors throughout the 1980s that was responsible for overseeing government growth that nearly tripled our budget during the decade. Our community was also adding population, and commercial and residential development was happening quite rapidly. The board members were not interested in rehashing budget decisions but rather in implementing most of the budget that we brought to them every year. They really did not want to deal with any new services we were proposing; they were fairly content with the existing services. In the late 1980s we had a fairly complete turnover of board members.

Craig Gerhart, "Management Involvement," in *Managing for Results: Performance Measures in Government,* 1993 conference proceedings (Austin: The University of Texas, 1994), 79–83.

Some chose not to run again; others were defeated. We acquired some board members who had not participated in the government's growth to this point. They were not content to just look at the incremental pieces that we were accustomed to bringing to the board. They wanted instead to start examining existing services to see whether any needed change or reduction. That whole discussion ended up with the adoption of a local ordinance that requires the routine evaluation of all county services. We cannot hope, given our staffing levels, to do a full-blown performance review of every service that we provide during that cycle. We are turning to performance measurement to tell us which services are acceptable and which services need a little more analysis and investigation.

A second reason that we are in the business of performance measurement is that we were hit by the same fiscal change at the end of the 1980s that I'm sure many of you saw. Our double-digit revenue growth stopped; in fact, it went down for a few years, and we realized that we had to change the way we funded our local services. We were robbing Peter to pay Paul, and in some cases we were shooting Peter altogether. We wanted more objective tools to make sure that the services we were changing or cutting out were the right ones. That led us to look for performance measures.

A third reason has to do with the county strategic plan. In 1993 the board of supervisors adopted a community-based strategic plan that requires us to develop a performance measurement system. It also forces us to look at customer-based performance measurement. Not only does the strategic plan guide us to develop a performance measurement system, but so does our customer-service philosophy, which is the fourth reason why we are pursuing performance measurement.

We have, like many of you, been wrestling with changing the attitude of our bureaucracy. We are trying to make sure that we are delivering services that people need and want, not just the ones we think ought to be delivered. We really cannot tell if we are doing a better job for our community unless we measure satisfaction with our services.

The fifth reason we began performance measurement has to do with reinventing government. One message of Osborne and Gaebler's *Reinventing Government* is that central bureaucrats like me have to get out of the way of service deliverers. We have to get rid of our archaic control systems and let people do their jobs. We need to offer flexibility in the areas of personnel management. We are interested in doing this, but we also recognize that accountability is essential. If we are going to give up control as a central organization, then we need to make sure that those who have new flexibility and new autonomy can be held accountable for what they do.

We see three uses for performance measurement. First, we want to make better decisions for service delivery. Second, we want to use it to evaluate program performance. We realize that measurement does not evaluate programs, but it does provide a clue to which programs need further analysis. Third, it facilitates communication about program information. This appears to be something that is often overlooked. We do a lot in Prince William County, and some of it is done pretty well. Performance measurement, if appropriately handled, can help us get that message across.

There is nothing revolutionary about the measures that we are trying to develop: inputs, outputs, efficiency and service-quality measures, and outcomes. [Although] we often talk about results-oriented measures and outcome measures, it is going to be difficult to persuade the community or governing body to spend more money to achieve greater outcomes if they are not convinced that you are efficiently using the money you have now. We should not be ignoring those other categories of measurement.

We knew all along that this would be a multi-year process. In our first year, we had three good accomplishments and an awful lot of short-term failures. First of all, we developed program measures for each program and category of measurement in the county government. We have a program budget structure consisting of about 200 or 250 programs. By the end of the first year, each one of those programs had developed measures in each of those categories. Mid-management came into the picture at the very outset. Early on we concluded that we wanted our measurement development effort to be decentralized. The department heads, the division managers, and the program managers became the point people for developing these measures. We asked them to get together with their employees and to bring customers to the table to determine what the public believed would be most appropriate. We discovered that, with this approach, you are going to get a lot of bathwater with the babies. We acquired some really bad measures, and we still have some. You can't have a decentralized process—one that relies on mid-managers and their employees—and say, "I'm sorry, that measure is no good. You should use this one instead." We are gambling that time and the test of using these measures will be the controlling factor in getting rid of bad measures and developing new ones.

In our first year we also developed a Performance Analysis Measurement System (PAMS) to collect and analyze the measures that are being gathered throughout the government. We applied technology in this effort, and it was like pulling teeth.

The data processing staff was involved as well as department management and clerical support. It was a real struggle to come up with a system that would allow data to be entered at the department level, then transferred through our networks and reformatted so that we could actually produce a report.

Performance measurement served as a lightning rod. Lots of people were uncomfortable with performance measurement because it was a very tangible report that was the object of everybody's angst or anger. So we beat ourselves up pretty badly as we developed that report.

The third and most important achievement is that we completed our first annual citizens' survey. That survey gets at very basic levels of satisfaction with globally grouped services: police, fire, public safety in general, parks, libraries, financial management planning, land use, economic development. This should establish a baseline of data.

In the second year we hope to develop targets for each of the performance measures by refining some of those measures to create actual service-level targets that capture more of the essence of the service than each of the measures alone might. We did not use targets in the first year, although we are trying to develop them this year. We had also hoped to begin auditing measures that were being collected to test them for validity and reliability. However, we are in a slight budget crunch again, and the audit program is under fire. It will probably not survive at a level to continue a regular auditing program for the measures that are being collected. We will wait and see how it turns out.

In the third, fourth, and fifth years we plan to refine what we have already been doing. We will improve our data collection methods and help people learn new methods. We will refine measures and targets, and we will begin to help the government learn how to use measures in making decisions. One dream is to use these measures in the future to develop contracts between departments and the governing body or the community. For example, for a certain amount of money, we would produce a certain outcome. A more ambitious outcome would require more money. A lesser outcome would cost less. This principle can be applied to the evaluation of individual performance—specifically, department directors, program managers, and groups of program employees.

When and where did mid-management begin to feel threatened in this process? There seem to be six threats that mid-management is likely to experience.

The first threat seems to be accountability. We talked to people early on in the process and explained that performance measurement was going to help make people accountable for their resources and the way they delivered their services. Many people expressed concern about this concept. At first we thought they did not want to be held accountable. Actually, most people are willing to be held accountabie, but they do not know exactly what that means—accountability has become a buzzword. From their perspective, they want to know whether it means they are going to get raises or be fired. Because of our inability to state what accountability clearly is and translate it to something more than a buzzword, we have scared many people.

The second threat relates to workload. None of our departments have planning and evaluation teams. They have department heads, some clerical support, maybe a staff assistant, and sometimes an administrative unit. By and large, those in the department who have to deal with performance measurement are the same people who have to run the enterprise—filling the potholes, catching the bad guys, dealing with human services and case management, counting the dollars. Many are concerned that we have asked a lot from them but have not given them any additional resources to perform those tasks.

A third threat to mid-management is the fear of appearing stupid. Like many of us, the people that I work with are pretty sharp. They care, they believe in what they do, and they are proud of what they accomplish. People who are smart do not like to feel stupid. Performance measurement is not new and has become much touted in recent years, but there is no reason for many of the people running our departments and managing our programs to know a great deal about it, and many of them do not. Nevertheless, they do not like to feel or appear stupid.

This feeling manifested itself in several ways as we worked with departments. For example, in a meeting on performance measurement we would be making good progress; then we would get to some element that was fairly complicated and difficult to explain well, and a cloud would come over the manager's face. The wrist would pop up and the manager would say, "You know, I forgot all about it, but I need to be somewhere else right now." And the manager would actually leave. Another indication that people are feeling stupid is that they begin attacking the performance measurement project. They say, "This is a stupid waste of time and no one is going to use it. You don't know what you're doing and I don't understand why we're doing this, anyway." Another reaction is that managers will take their glasses off, heave a sigh, and put their head down on the table. It doesn't happen very often, but when it does, it's a sign that they are not feeling good about themselves or this exercise.

A fourth threat involves the downsizing of many departments. In Prince William County, performance measurement is inevitably associated with our need to cut budgets. People firmly believe that, while I am formally the performance measurement manager, I am really the budget director in disguise. They believe that when performance measurement is instituted, it will somehow be used to cut their budgets.

A fifth threat arises when they recognize that a number of external variables beyond their control are affecting their measures. They are concerned that we are using performance measurement as an accountability tool but that we are measuring things they cannot control. They believe they are being set up, and we are struggling to deal with that attitude.

The sixth and final threat to mid-management is mixed messages. They are concerned that performance measurement is just a management trend that is in vogue this year, that we will change things later and they will have wasted a lot of energy. They are also concerned when we say, "Don't worry about that part of it, just worry about this part." They're afraid we're going to come back in a year and say, "Well, look, you didn't do anything about this." Some department heads are sending mixed messages to their mid-level managers by telling them not worry about performance measurement—just fill the potholes. We, on the other hand, are telling them that, yes, they have to fill the potholes but that we need measures.

The tools that we have used to allay some of these fears have not all been successful. To allay the fear of being held accountable for something uncertain, we told people not to worry about targets in the first year. We asked them to collect data first and establish their current level of success before we asked them to project targets for an upcoming year. We also tried to deliver a lot of training, using outside speakers and in-house exercises and activities. The training was well received and offers people some degree of comfort. However, we did not do enough training overall. The single most effective tool we used was consulting internal to the organization. We have a small management consulting unit in my shop, and those staff members helped people work out their measurements in a group consulting environment.

Almost without exception, the departments that created the best measures were those where the department, the middle managers, and the Office of Management and Budget have all been actively engaged in the process to develop measures. There were two consequences of this interaction. First, we were able to help guide them, and they were able to use us as a feedback loop. Second, we represented real people they could work with, not just forms. It took some of the intimidation out of the system. People benefited psychologically from the human contact. We continually emphasize that performance measurement is evolving and that it is a long-term process.

Beginning in the second year, we tried some other things with mid-managers. We invited all the program managers in the government to participate in small focus groups that used group tasks to wrestle with key questions: what is good about the effort to measure performance in this county so far? what is bad about it? what needs improvement? what needs to be eliminated altogether? what can we capitalize on? We had great suggestions using this training format, and the managers realized that we empathized with them. Whenever we have been able to maintain personal contact with agency staff members, we have ended up with better results.

We also asked for volunteers from the mid-managers to help us design the second year of the process. We asked them which forms we should use and what kinds of instructions should be given. We asked what kinds of training were necessary. We received great feedback for ways of simplifying the instructions as well as the number of measures we were looking for. We learned to be more flexible at the central agency. For example, we did not force an agency to have measures for each category if the category truly did not fit.

I want to describe some of the mistakes that mid-managers have told us we have made. The first is that we did not focus the effort very well at the outset. We started on our measures without spending much time in thinking practically about the whole process. We were not able to help people understand how all of this was supposed to fit together.

Our second big mistake was that our consultant resources were inadequate. I mentioned that consulting was perhaps our best tool for making people comfortable with creating measures. Unfortunately, we have only a couple of consultants. We tried to use budget analysts and other staff to spread out the consulting load, only to discover that some of them did not know any more about performance measuring than the people they were consulting with. We suffered some loss of credibility at that point.

Another mistake was in not managing our customers' expectations well. We identified different levels of customers, but we did not specify whose expectations we were going to meet first. As a result, all of our customers believed they were going to be the first group to receive meaningful data out of these measures and that other groups would benefit in the subsequent years.

Perhaps our most glaring mistake was getting lost in the data. We overcounted; we overmeasured. We measured a lot of things because they were countable, and we mistook that for progress.

Our final mistake was that we were incredibly impatient. We want the entire system to be there and to be there now, but it never can be.

One series of measures is for a unit that does nothing but manage the contracts for road construction. The second series of measures is for a long-term care program for the aging. In our first year of measurement, we instituted efficiency and effectiveness measures. These were mostly input items that did not measure how well we were performing our services. In the second year, we instituted some cost and workload measures. The road unit does not design the road, determine its capacity or location, or approve development that feeds into that road. We needed to know whether this was affecting people's lives. Does building this road result in better transportation? Can people get from point A to point B quicker? Can we measure and reduce congestion at critical intersections? Yes, we found that we could measure these elements but that a completely different public works unit was responsible for each of them.

In 1989 our program for long-term care was slightly better than our transportation program. In our first year, we produced some good outputs in terms of number of clients, number of client needs, number of contacts. When we looked at our outcomes, we got lost in identifying which aspects of the program were most important. We simplified outcomes and came up with one: has the person been able to maintain an independent living situation because of the program? We are pretty comfortable with that as an outcome.

Let me offer these observations on performance measurement:

1. This is a long-term process. Sticking with the program is critical.
2. The worst time to start a performance measurement program is when you are downsizing and cutting budgets. Unfortunately, we are now all downsizing.
3. Begin the measurement from the bottom up and recognize that you are going to get some bad information for a while.
4. An effective, focused consulting team is the most effective tool for working with mid-managers and allaying their fears.
5. Expect setbacks. You will make lots of mistakes before you see any benefits from many of your measures.
6. Before you even start, try to determine whether a performance measurement can even survive in your agency. Do not bother if you think the odds of survival are pretty slim.
7. Start with a citizen survey before you develop your measures. After we did our survey, people began to see how the measures related to the customer. They also began to see the need for some balancing measures to offset what the public was saying about their programs.

8. Target a couple of key programs and start a pilot measurement effort. We didn't do this, but I wish we had. We started with a countywide effort. We started fast and made credibility mistakes that have been hard to reverse.

9. Figure out whether it will be better for you to start measuring and decide how to use the data later, or whether it is better to identify a use for the measures and then measure accordingly. Logically, the latter approach would be better. The problem is that many people do not know how to use information until it is in front of them.

10. Establish a vision. Ours was sketchy, and people were constantly wondering why we were doing all this. If you can explain to mid-managers the purpose of the process before you start, then it will help them to believe in the measures.

11. Elected officials can help: they can use and reinforce measures, they can pat folks on the back for doing measurement.

Let me close by noting that you cannot build buildings or have economic development in your community without first zoning land and providing water and sewer services. Performance measurement is much like that physical infrastructure, but it is only for decision making and management. It is a price we have to pay early on in order to reach better decisions down the road.

Appendix:
Service Efforts and
Accomplishments
Reporting

Governmental Accounting Standards Board

Editor's note: The Governmental Accounting Standards Board (GASB) strongly advocates improved performance measurement in the public sector. GASB encourages government units to report information pertaining not only to inputs and workload but also to outputs and outcomes— hence the label "service efforts and accomplishments (SEA) reporting." Following are excerpts from a key GASB document explaining the essentials of SEA reporting.

The objective of service efforts and accomplishments (SEA) reporting as stated in the Governmental Accounting Standards Board's (GASB) Concepts Statement 1 is founded on the belief that SEA information is an essential aspect of the measurement of governmental performance, and is necessary for assessing accountability and in making informed decisions. Therefore, to be more complete, a general purpose external financial report (GPEFR) needs to include SEA information.

SEA reporting provides more complete information about a governmental entity's performance than can be provided by the operating statement, balance sheet, and budgetary comparison statements and schedules to assist users in assessing the economy, efficiency, and effectiveness of services provided. The measurement of a governmental entity's performance requires information not only on the acquisition and use of resources, but also on the outputs and outcomes of the services provided and the relationship between the use of resources and outputs and outcomes. By focusing on a variety of financial and nonfinancial measures of inputs, outputs and outcomes, and measures that relate efforts to accomplishments, SEA reporting provides additional information needed to provide a basis for users of general purpose external financial reports to more fully assess governmental performance.

To meet its objective, SEA information should focus primarily on measures of service accomplishments (outputs and outcomes) and measures of the relationships between service efforts and service accomplishments (efficiency and cost-outcome). Because the reporting of SEA information is directed at providing users with information about the results of the governmental entity's services, the measures reported should emphasize performance. The performance of governmental entities is primarily measured by output, outcome, and efficiency measures. These measures report what services the entity has provided, whether those services have achieved the objectives established, and what effects they have had upon the recipients and others. This information when compared to service efforts (inputs) also provides a basis for assessing the efficiency with which the entity operated.

Categories of SEA measures

SEA reporting elements consist of the categories of SEA measures and certain explanatory information. Three board categories of SEA measures have been identified in GASB research: those that measure service efforts, those that measure service accomplishments, and those that relate efforts to accomplishments. Although a clear division cannot be made in all cases among these categories of measures, they are helpful for understanding what an SEA indicator is designed to measure. SEA measures should be reported for services the entity is responsible for providing, whether the governmental entity provides the service itself or contracts for it.

Measures of efforts   Efforts are the amount of financial and nonfinancial resources (in terms of money, material, and so forth) that are applied to a service. Measures of service efforts also include ratios that compare financial and nonfinancial resources with other measures that may indicate potential demand for services, such as general population, service population, or lane-miles of road.

Financial information   This information includes financial measures of expenditures/expenses. These measures include the cost[1] of salaries, employee benefits, materials and supplies, contract services, equipment, and so forth, for providing a service. For example, measures of efforts may include the amount spent for education and the amount spent per full-time–equivalent student; the amount spent on public transit and the amount spent on public transit per commuter; the amount spent on road maintenance and the amount spent per lane-mile of road on road maintenance; and the amount spent for crime investigations and the amount spent per capita on crime investigations.

Nonfinancial information
    Number of personnel   Because personnel are the major resource, indicators that measure the number of full-time–equivalent employ-

ees or employee-hours used in providing a service often are appropriate measures of resources used. These measures have the effect of removing wage, benefit, and cost-of-living differences from the resource inputs, and may facilitate comparisons over time and with other organizations. For example, measures may include the number of teachers in total or per student; the number of road maintenance workers in total or per lane-mile of road; and the number of uniformed officers assigned to crime investigations or the number per capita assigned to crime investigations.

Other measures These may include the amount of equipment (such as number of vehicles) or other capital assets (such as lane-miles of road or acres of park land) used in providing a service.

Measures of accomplishments Accomplishment measures report what was provided and achieved with the resources used. There are two types of measures of accomplishments—outputs and outcomes. Outputs measure the quantity of services provided; outcomes measure the results of providing those outputs.

Output measures
Quantity of a service provided These indicators measure the physical quantity of a service provided. For example, measures may include the number of students promoted or graduated; the number of passenger-miles provided by public transit; the number of lane-miles of road repaired; and the number of crimes investigated.
Quantity of a service provided that meets a certain quality requirement These indicators measure the physical quantity of a service

provided that meets a test of quality. For example, measures may include the percentage of students graduated or promoted who have met a minimum prespecified standard of achievement; the percentage of buses meeting a prespecified on-time standard of achievement; the percentage of lane-miles of road repaired to a certain minimum satisfactory condition; and the percentage of criminal investigations performed that result in the identification of a prime suspect. In some cases, meeting a quality requirement may turn an "output" indicator into an "outcome" indicator.

Outcome measures These indicators measure accomplishments or results that occur (at least partially) because of services provided.[2] Results also include measures of public perceptions of outcomes. For example, measures may include the percentage of students achieving a specified skill-level gain in reading; the percentage of the population being served by public transportation; the percentage of lane-miles of road in excellent, good, or fair condition; and the clearance rate for serious crimes or the percentage of residents rating their neighborhood as safe or very safe.

Outcomes measures are particularly useful when presented as comparisons with results from previous years, entity-established targets or goals and objectives, generally accepted norms and standards, other parts of the entity, or other, comparable jurisdictions (both public and private). For example, measures may include 75 percent of the students achieving a specified skill-level gain in reading when the school district's objective is for at least 70 percent of the students to achieve the specified skill-level gain in reading or where 65 percent of the students statewide achieve the specified skill-level gain; 25 percent of the population being served by public transportation when the transit system's objective is to serve at least 35 percent of the population or where the norm for similar transit systems is that 30 percent of the public is being served; 88 percent of the lane-miles of road in excellent, good, or fair condition when the entity's objective is for at least 85 percent of the lane-miles of road to be in excellent, good, or fair condition or where an average of 80 percent of the lane-miles of road were in excellent, good, or fair condition for the previous five years; and 25 percent of serious crimes cleared by indictment when the entity's objective is to clear 35 percent or where the national average is 21 percent.

Sometimes the secondary effects of a service on the recipients, state, or community may be identified and may warrant reporting. These measures include significant indirect consequences, intended or unintended and positive or negative, that occur as a result of providing a service. For example, measures may include a decrease in the unemployment rate in a community as a result of a decrease in the school dropout rate (more students are staying in school and are not looking for employment); a decrease in traffic accidents because of an increase in the percentage of the population using public transit; a decrease in vehicle repair costs because of an increase in the percentage of lane-miles of road in good condition; and an increase in the reported crime rate because a new street patrol system results in a larger percentage of committed crimes being reported. These measures often are difficult to identify and to relate to the actual service being provided. This occurs because of an inability to establish a definite correlation between the secondary effects and the service and because extraneous factors may affect the results.

Measures that relate efforts to accomplishments

Efficiency measures that relate efforts to outputs of services   These indicators measure the resources used or cost (for example, in dollars, employee-hours, or equipment used) per unit of output. They provide information about the production of an output at a given level of resource use and demonstrate an entity's relative efficiency when compared with previous results, internally established goals and objectives, generally accepted norms or standards, or results achieved by similar jurisdictions. For example, measures may include the cost per full-time–equivalent student or the cost per student promoted or graduated; the cost per transit passenger or per passenger-mile; the cost per lane-mile of road repaired in total or repaired to good condition; and the cost per serious crime investigated or per arrest.

Cost-outcome measures that relate efforts to the outcomes or results of services   These measures report the cost per unit of outcome or result. They relate costs and results so that management, elected officials, and the public can begin to assess the value of the services provided by an entity. For example, cost-outcome measures may include the cost per student who achieves a specified skill-level gain in reading; the cost per transit passenger arriving at his or her stop within a specific time schedule; the cost per lane-mile of road improved or maintained in excellent, good, or fair condition; and the cost per serious crime cleared by indictment.

Explanatory information

In addition to the preceding categories of SEA measures, the elements of SEA reporting also include explanatory information. Explanatory information includes both quantitative and narrative information that can help users to understand reported SEA measures, assess the entity's performance, and evaluate the significance of underlying factors that may have affected the reported performance.

There are two primary types of quantitative explanatory information that can be reported with SEA measures:

1. Factors substantially outside the control of the entity, such as environmental and demographic characteristics. For example, measures may include the number of students in families below the poverty level; the density of population in the area where public transit is being provided; the percentage of trucks in vehicle traffic; and the unemployment rate.
2. Factors over which the entity has significant control, such as staffing patterns. For example, measures may include the teacher-pupil ratio; the number of buses in service per

route mile; the type of construction used for highways; and the number of police officers per capita.

Narrative information provided with SEA measures can provide explanations of what the level of performance reported by the measure means, the possible effects that explanatory factors might have on performance, and actions that have been (or are being) taken to change reported performance. Explanations are particularly important when comparisons with other jurisdictions or among similar components within the same jurisdiction are reported. They are also important in conjunction with reporting secondary, unintended effects of a service.

Desired characteristics of SEA measures

SEA information should meet the characteristics of relevance, understandability, comparability, timeliness, consistency, and reliability. The application of these characteristics to SEA information is discussed in the following paragraphs.

Relevance SEA information should include data that are essential to provide a basis for understanding the accomplishment of goals and objectives of the entity that have potentially significant decision-making or accountability implications. As with any other information provided in GPEFR, SEA information should be management's representations of performance. Because the purpose of governmental entitles is to establish and enforce laws, regulate activities, and provide services economically, effectively, and efficiently—not to earn profits—no single measure of performance is readily available to assist users in assessing accountability and in making economic, political, and social decisions. A broad variety of SEA measures may therefore be required to meet the diverse needs of the different users; report on the many goals and objectives of different agencies, departments, programs, and services;[3] and address the issues being considered for different decisions and levels of accountability.

Understandability SEA information should be communicated in a readily understandable manner. It should communicate the performance of the agency, department, program, or service to any reasonably informed interested party. To enhance user understanding, different forms of reporting such as tables, charts, and graphs may be needed by different state and local governmental entities and for different services.

SEA information should be concise yet comprehensive with regard to which (and how many) measures of SEA are reported. Both conciseness and comprehensiveness in reporting SEA measures are important because of the number, diversity, and complexity of state and local governmental agencies, departments, programs, and services. SEA information should be provided at the most appropriate level of aggregation or disaggregation. A balance should be achieved among the number of services reported, the SEA measures reported, and the capability of users to understand and act on the information.

SEA information may be accompanied by a description of the way in which the SEA measures should be used. This could include comments on the need to consider SEA measures in conjunction with explanatory information, the need to consider the multiple aspects of performance when assessing results, instances where surrogate measures are being reported because of an inability to measure an outcome of a service, and the difficulty of using SEA information to assess policy accountability. The descriptions could also contain additional information about SEA measures that could assist users in understanding the reasons for the reported level of performance and actions planned or being taken to change results.

Comparability SEA information should provide a clear frame of reference for assessing the performance of the entity and its agencies, departments, programs, and services. SEA measures, when presented alone, do not provide a basis for assessing or understanding the level of performance. Therefore, SEA information should include comparative information. This information may take various forms; for example, reported measures of SEA could include comparisons with (1) several earlier fiscal years; (2) targets established by the entity, such as targets established as part of the budgetary process; (3) externally established norms or standards of performance; (4) other parts of subunits of the same entity, or (5) other, comparable entities.

Timeliness SEA information should be reported in a timely manner so that it will be available to users before it loses its capacity to be of value in assessing accountability and making decisions.

Consistency   SEA information should be reported consistently from period to period to allow users to have a basis for comparing performance over time and to gain an understanding of the measures being used and their meaning. However, SEA measures also need to be reviewed regularly and modified or replaced as needed to reflect changing circumstances.

Reliability   For SEA information to be of value to users, it is essential that it be reliable. To be reliable, the information should be verifiable and free from bias and should faithfully represent what it purports to represent. Therefore, SEA information should be derived from systems that produce controlled and verifiable data. The value of a strong internal control structure has long been recognized when dealing with financial information. If SEA information is to be considered for inclusion as part of the information required for GPEFR, it is important that the systems and methods used to gather and verify the information be subjected to analysis similar to that used for financial information systems.

1. *Cost,* including the determination of the appropriate treatment for various classes of indirect costs, has yet to be defined for purposes of SEA reporting. However, SEA measurement will require cost information for programs, activities, and services. Development of cost information is a critical part of SEA reporting for governmental entities.
2. For many outcomes, a definite cause-and-effect relationship between the output and the outcome cannot be established because of their complex nature and factors beyond the control of the entity that affect the outcome being measured.
3. This applies to services the entity is responsible for providing regardless of whether the governmental entity provides the service itself or contracts for it.

For Further Reference

Ahnell, Leif; Linda Davidson; and Karen McKenzie. "Case Note: A First Experience with SEA Reporting." *International Journal of Public Administration* 18, nos. 2 and 3 (1995): 581–91.

Ammons, David N. "Overcoming the Inadequacies of Performance Measurement in Local Government: The Case of Libraries and Leisure Services." *Public Administration Review* 55 (January/February 1995): 37–47.

Bens, Charles K. *Measuring City Hall Performance: Finally, A How-To-Guide.* Denver: National Civic League Press, 1991.

Bens, Charles K. "Strategies for Implementing Performance Measurement." *Management Information Services Report* 18, no. 11 (November 1986).

Bruder, Kenneth A., Jr., and Edward M. Gray. "Public-Sector Benchmarking: A Practical Approach." *Public Management* 76 (September 1994): S9–S14.

Burnaby, Priscilla A., and Susan H. Herhold. *Water and Wastewater Treatment: Service Efforts and Accomplishments Report-ing—Its Time Has Come.* Norwalk, CT: GASB, 1990.

Carpenter, Vivian L.; Linda Ruchala; and John B. Waller, Jr. *Public Health: Service Efforts and Accomplishments Reporting—Its Time Has Come.* Norwalk, CT: GASB, 1991.

Chan, Amy. "Managing a Government Like a Business: The Sunnyvale System." *Government Finance Review* 10 (April 1994): 7–12.

City of Berkeley, California. "Performance Management System Manual." ICMA Clearinghouse Report. Washington, DC: ICMA, 1990.

City of Boston. *Enhanced Program Reporting: A Manual for Program Managers.* Boston: Office of Budget and Program Evaluation, December 1991.

Comptroller General of the United States. *Governmental Auditing Standards: Standards for Audit of Governmental Organizations, Programs, Activities, and Functions.* Rev. ed. Washington, DC: GPO, 1988.

Congressional Budget Office. *Using Performance Measures in the*

Federal Budget Process. Washington, DC: CBO, 1993.

Drebin, Allan, and Marguerite Brannon. *Police Department Programs: Service Efforts and Accomplishments Reporting— Its Time Has Come.* Norwalk, CT: GASB, 1992.

Epstein, Paul D. "Measuring the Performance of Public Services." In *Public Productivity Handbook,* edited by Marc Holzer. New York: Marcel Dekker, 1992.

Epstein, Paul D. *Using Performance Measurement in Local Government: A Guide to Improving Decisions, Performance, and Accountability.* New York: Van Nostrand Reinhold, 1984.

Fischer, Richard J. "An Overview of Performance Measurement." *Public Management* 76 (September 1994): S2–S8.

Fountain, James, Jr., and Mitchell Roob. "Service Efforts and Accomplishments Measures: Development and Use for Government Services." *Public Management* 76 (March 1994): 6–12.

Fowler, Pat. "The Establishment of Health Indicators in Municipal Health Departments." *Texas Town & City* (February 1992): 20–24.

Gay, William G. "Benchmarking: Achieving Superior Performance in Fire and Emergency Medical Services." *Management Information Services Report* 25, no. 2 (February 1993).

Glaser, Mark. "Tailoring Performance Measurement to Fit the Organization: From Generic to Germane." *Public Productivity and Management Review* 14 (spring 1991): 303–19.

Governmental Accounting Standards Board. *Concepts Statement No. 2 of the Governmental Accounting Standards Board on Concepts Related to Service Efforts and Accomplishments Reporting.* Norwalk, CT: GASB, April 1994.

Griesemer, James R. "The Power of Performance Measurement: A Computer Performance Model and Examples from Colorado Cities." *Government Finance Review* 9 (October 1993): 17–21.

Grifel, Stuart S. "Organizational Culture: Its Importance in Performance Measurement." *Public Management* 76 (September 1994): S19–S20.

Grifel, Stuart S. "Performance Measurement and Budgetary Decision Making." *Public Productivity and Management Review* 16 (summer 1993): 403–7.

Harris, Jean. "Bibliography: Service Efforts and Accomplishments Reporting." *International Journal of Public Administration* 18, nos. 2 and 3 (1995): 593–608.

Harris, Jean. "Service Efforts and Accomplishments: A Primer of Current Practice and an Agenda for Future Research." *International Journal of Public Administration* 18, nos. 2 and 3 (1995): 253–76.

Hatry, Harry P. "Determining the Effectiveness of Government Services." In *Handbook of Public Administration,* edited by James L. Perry. San Francisco: Jossey-Bass, 1989.

Hatry, Harry P.; Craig Gerhart; and Martha Marshall. "Eleven Ways to Make Performance Measurement More Useful to Public Managers." *Public Management* 76 (September 1994): S15–S18.

Hatry, Harry P.; Louis H. Blair; Donald M. Fisk; John M. Greiner; John R. Hall, Jr.; and

Philip S. Schaenman. *How Effective Are Your Community Services? Procedures for Measuring Their Quality,* 2d ed. Washington, DC: The Urban Institute and ICMA, 1992.

Hatry, Harry P., and Donald M. Fisk. "Measuring Productivity in the Public Sector." In *Public Productivity Handbook,* edited by Marc Holzer. New York: Marcel Dekker, 1992.

Hatry, Harry P.; John M. Greiner; and Maria Swanson. "Monitoring the Quality of Local Government Services." *Management Information Services Report* 19, no. 2 (February 1987).

Hatry, Harry P. "Performance Measurement Principles and Techniques: An Overview for Local Government." *Public Productivity Review* 4 (December 1980): 312–39.

Hatry, Harry P.; James R. Fountain, Jr.; Jonathan M. Sullivan; and Lorraine Kremer. *Service Efforts and Accomplishments Reporting—Its Time Has Come: An Overview.* Norwalk, CT: GASB, 1990.

Hyman, William A.; Roemer M. Alfelor; and Joan A. Allen. *Road Maintenance: Service Efforts and Accomplishments Reporting—Its Time Has Come.* Norwalk, CT: GASB, 1993.

Jreisat, Jamil E. "Productivity Measurement: Trial and Error in St. Petersburg." *Public Productivity Review* 11 (winter 1987): 3–18.

Kamensky, John M. "Program Performance Measures: Designing a System to Manage for Results." *Public Productivity and Management Review* 16 (summer 1993): 395–402.

Kline, James J. "Quality Tools Are Applicable to Local Government." *Government Finance Review* 9 (August 1993): 15–19.

Lauria, Jolene Ann. "Performance Auditing for Local Government." *Management Information Services Report* 21, no. 1 (January 1989).

Malan, Roland M.; James R. Fountain, Jr.; Donald S. Arrowsmith; and Robert L. Lockridge II. *Performance Auditing in Local Government.* Chicago: Government Finance Officers Association, 1984.

Managing for Results: Performance Measures in Government. 1993 Conference Proceedings. Austin: The University of Texas, 1994.

Miller, Thomas I., and Michelle A. Miller. "Standards of Excellence: U.S. Residents' Evaluations of Local Government Services." *Public Administration Review* 51 (November/December 1991): 503–14.

Morley, Elaine. "Establishing and Using a Productivity Measurement System." In *A Practitioner's Guide to Public Sector Productivity Improvement.* New York: Van Nostrand Reinhold, 1986.

Mundt, Barry M.; Raymond T. Olsen; and Harold I. Steinberg. *Managing Public Resources.* Peat Marwick International, 1982.

National Local Government Productivity Council. *Measuring Productivity in Local Government: A Guide.* Malvern (Victoria), Australia: NLGPC, May 1993.

Neves, Carol M. P.; James F. Wolf; and Bill B. Benton. "The Use of Management Indicators in Monitoring the Performance of Human Service Agencies." In *Performance and Credibility: Developing Excellence in Public and Nonprofit Organizations,* edited by Joseph S. Wholey, Mark A. Abramson, and Christopher Bellavita. Lexington, MA: Lexington Books/D.C. Heath and Co., 1986.

O'Connell, Gary B. "Rate Your City—Here's How!" *Public Management* 71 (June 1989): 7–10.

Parry, Robert W., Jr.; Florence Cowan Sharp; Jannet Vreeland; and Wanda A. Wallace. *Fire Department Programs: Service Efforts and Accomplishments Reporting—Its Time Has Come.* Norwalk, CT: GASB, 1991.

Performance Measurement: The Link to Effective Government. GFOA Research Bulletin. Chicago: Government Finance Officers Association, April 1994.

Poister, Theodore H. *Performance Monitoring.* Lexington, MA: Lexington Books, 1983.

Price Waterhouse. *Performance Measurement: The Key to Accelerating Organizational Improvement.* Price Waterhouse, 1993.

Price Waterhouse. *Who Will Bell the Cat? A Fable for Our Time: A Guide to Performance Measurement in Government.* Washington, DC: Price Waterhouse, 1993.

Ridley, Clarence E., and Herbert A. Simon. *Measuring Municipal Activities: A Survey of Suggested Criteria for Appraising Administration.* Chicago: International City Managers' Association, 1943.

Rosen, Ellen Doree. *Improving Public Sector Productivity: Concepts and Practice.* Newbury Park, CA: Sage Publications, 1993.

Rouse, John. "Resource and Performance Management in Public Service Organizations." In *Management in the Public Sector: Challenge and Change,* edited by Kester Isaac-Henry, Chris Painter, and Chris Barnes. London: Chapman and Hall, 1993.

Rubin, Marc A. *Sanitation Collection and Disposal: Service Efforts and Accomplishments Reporting—Its Time Has Come.* Norwalk, CT: GASB, 1991.

Smith, Peter. "On the Unintended Consequences of Publishing Performance Data in the Public Sector." *International Journal of Public Administration* 18, nos. 2 and 3 (1995): 277–310.

Streib, Gregory. "Dusting Off a Forgotten Management Tool: The Citizen Survey." *Public Management* 72 (August 1990): 17–19.

Swiss, James E. *Public Management Systems: Monitoring and Managing Government Performance.* Englewood Cliffs, NJ: Prentice-Hall, 1991.

The Use of Performance Measures in City and County Budgets. GFOA Research Report. Chicago: Government Finance Officers Association, October 1994.

Tracy, Richard. "The City of Portland, Oregon: Reporting Service Efforts and Accomplishments." In *Managing for Results: Performance Measures in Government.* 1993 Conference Proceedings. Austin: University of Texas, 1994.

Ukeles, Jacob B. *Doing More with Less: Turning Public Management Around.* New York: AMACOM, 1982.

U.S. General Accounting Office. *Increased Use of Productivity Management Can Help Control Government Costs.* GAO/AFMD-84-11. 10 November 1983.

Van Houten, Therese, and Harry P. Hatry. *How to Conduct a Citizen Survey.* Planning Advisory Service Report Number 404. Chicago: American Planning Association, 1987.

Wallace, Wanda A. *Mass Transit: Service Efforts and Accomplishments Reporting—Its Time Has Come.* Norwalk, CT: GASB, 1991.

Washnis, George J., ed. *Productivity Improvement Handbook for State and Local Government.* New York: John Wiley and Sons, 1980.

Webb, Kenneth, and Harry P. Hatry. *Obtaining Citizen Feedback: The Application of Citizen Surveys to Local Governments.* Washington, DC: The Urban Institute, 1973.

Wholey, Joseph S. *Evaluation and Effective Public Management.* Boston: Little, Brown and Company, 1983.

Wholey, Joseph S., and Harry P. Hatry. "The Case for Performance Monitoring." *Public Administration Review* 52 (November/December 1992): 604–10.

Practical Management Series

**Accountability for Performance:
Measurement and Monitoring in
Local Government**

Text type
New Century Schoolbook

Composition
Graphic Sciences Corporation
Cedar Rapids, Iowa

Printing and binding
R. R. Donnelley & Sons Company
Harrisonburg, Virginia

Cover design
Becky Geanaros